W0081580

THE SCORE

ALSO BY C. THI NGUYEN

Games:
Agency As Art

THE
SCORE

HOW TO STOP
PLAYING SOMEBODY
ELSE'S GAME

C. Thi Nguyen

PENGUIN PRESS   NEW YORK   2026

PENGUIN PRESS
An imprint of Penguin Random House LLC
1745 Broadway, New York, NY 10019
penguinrandomhouse.com

Copyright © 2026 by Christopher Thi Nguyen

Penguin Random House values and supports copyright. Copyright fuels creativity, encourages diverse voices, promotes free speech, and creates a vibrant culture. Thank you for buying an authorized edition of this book and for complying with copyright laws by not reproducing, scanning, or distributing any part of it in any form without permission. You are supporting writers and allowing Penguin Random House to continue to publish books for every reader. Please note that no part of this book may be used or reproduced in any manner for the purpose of training artificial intelligence technologies or systems.

PP colophon is a registered trademark of Penguin Random House LLC.

Book design by Daniel Lagin

ISBN 9780593655658 (hardcover)
ISBN 9780593655665 (ebook)

Printed in the United States of America
1st Printing

The authorized representative in the EU for product safety and compliance is Penguin Random House Ireland, Morrison Chambers, 32 Nassau Street, Dublin D02 YH68, Ireland, https://eu-contact.penguin.ie.

For Mel

CONTENTS

PART 4

STANDARDIZED VALUES

PART 5

WHAT DO WE DO?

PART 1

OPENING MOVES

CHAPTER 1

Is This the Game You Really Want to Be Playing?

R ock climbing saved me.

I was in a miserable season of my life — staying up late every night, trying to dredge more work out of myself. I was anxious, consumed with self-loathing. I needed something to change.

A friend suggested that I try rock climbing, that it was a "technical balance sport" for people who loved solving puzzles. This seemed utterly ridiculous to me. Rock climbing was for thrill-seeking adventure bros. Rock climbing was muscling your way up a wall while you rage-screamed. And I was a clumsy nerd.

It took me about half an hour in my university's ratty little climbing gym to see that I'd been completely wrong.

I'd been failing, over and over again, on one specific move. I was supposed to reach over to a hold way up left; every time I'd go for it, I'd lose my balance and fall. I was ready to give up; I was just too weak. But then another climber explained the proper technique: I could kick out my leg all the way to the right, as a counterbalance, and then the rest of my body would just float up to the left, to the next hold. It felt amazing; my whole body was suddenly a fluid, coordinated thing. I felt, maybe for the first time in my life, like I was moving elegantly.

My friend was right, it turns out. Climbing isn't just about adrenaline and brawn. It's problem-solving. It's staring down a set of impossibly tiny holds and inventing intricate sequences of careful movements to make it through. Climbing is solving physics puzzles with your body, in the alphabet of yoga.

I've played games my whole life. Games offer me the joy of complete absorption in performing one clear task in a precise, well-defined world. They banish the nauseating complexity of ordinary life. They give me the refuge of clear rules and clear goals. In their restrictions, there is freedom.

Up until that point, I'd only played mental games: chess, poker, computer strategy games. I hated my body, which was a sludgy and uncooperative thing. But climbing asked me to devote the whole of my attention to the precise relationship between my body and the rock. Sometimes a climb would demand that I carefully balance myself on my tippy-toes on a tiny dime's edge of rock, and then carefully ease my center of gravity over. Sometimes a climb asked me to drive myself up with an explosive twist of my hips. Climbing demanded a deep understanding of how the parts of my body connected, of how a movement flowed through me.

I met Sherwood at that ratty university climbing gym. He was a beautifully perverse climber. He loved nothing more than to get stuck in some awful, contorted position on the rock—one leg over his shoulder, the other leg trapped under an elbow. He'd groan and curse, rocking back and forth in a tangle—and then suddenly find a way through in an ecstatic burst of motion. He had cultivated a climbing style that gave him precisely his desired ratio of joy to masochism.

We were climbing in Joshua Tree National Park one weekend—

climbing real rock, working on tricky, delicate problems. I'd been climbing for a couple of years by then, and I was trying to break through to the next level.

Every established rock climb has a difficulty grade attached—a rating derived from community consensus. For the dominant rock-climbing culture, this difficulty rating basically serves as a scoring system. Your primary score is the difficulty rating of the hardest climbs you can do. The climb I was trying was the next level up of difficulty from anything I'd climbed before. I wanted that next number so badly; I wanted that level-up. And the more desperately I wanted it, the grosser my climbing got. Sherwood saw my desperate flailing, shook his head, and said, "Man, you gotta just *savor* the movement."

We were climbing for different reasons. I wanted to get to the top any way I could—anything that would count as a victory, that would give me that next number. Sherwood would climb a route, get to the top, frown, and mutter, "Well, OK, but that was pretty ugly," and then keep climbing it over and over again until the movement felt beautiful to him. His comment—that I had to savor the movement—got stuck in my head over the next few months. It changed my whole relationship to climbing. I started to pay more attention to the sweet joy of the movement—to lavish loving attention on the microscopic adjustments, the explosive hip twists. At night, I would dream about how it *felt*.

A lot of the time, we don't know the real reason we're doing something. I had been telling myself that climbing was making me fitter, and that I was learning some skills. But in retrospect, what I actually loved was how it felt to be climbing. It was an experience of my own grace, a rare taste of loveliness flowing through my bones and fingers. And it was the fact that my life suddenly had rowdy road trips and drunk bonfires in it. I came back from climbing weekends cheerful, refreshed. Climbing made me feel complete.

And here's the strangest thing: What I truly loved was a feeling, a loving involvement with the difficulty of the physical world, that went far beyond the simple goals of climbing. But I also couldn't have found that feeling without that scoring system. The game of climbing has a very specific definition of success: You have succeeded if you get to the top. And the scoring system also tells you, over the course of a climbing life, that you should be trying to climb evermore difficult climbs. This gave me a focus. It shaped a very specific kind of activity; without that goal, I would never have paid enough attention to my body, never would have refined my movement enough, to discover a pure joy in movement.

Given just a rock wall, there's no particular reason for a modern, tool-using human to try to move up a particular line of tiny holds using nothing but their hands and feet. But climbing is a game that tells you what to do; it forces you to take one hard pathway up the rock, and it tells you that it will count as a success only if you follow the rules—if you climb the rock using only your hands and feet on the rock itself. And it tells you to keep trying harder and harder climbs.

This structure forced me to tune in to how I was moving. It keyed me into a new form of beauty. It gave me a richer form of freedom than I had anywhere else in my life. It showed me the way to a new kind of agency.

I'M A PHILOSOPHY PROFESSOR NOW. THERE IS, IN MY PROFESsion, a single list of all the major philosophy departments, ranked by prestige. There is another list of all the philosophy journals you could publish in, also ranked by prestige. These are the scoring systems of philosophy.

Nobody is forcing people to use these systems. They're just a pair of websites, each compiled by a small group of professionals, based on some annual surveys. In the end, they're just a summary of a few people's subjective impressions of status. We could have just as well decided to ignore them; they have no official authority. But that's not what happened. Most professional philosophers pay intense, close, and regular attention to these lists. Most of us know exactly how we're doing on the rankings.

I didn't care about those rankings when I first fell in love with philosophy. I didn't even know about them. I got into the field because I was obsessed with some big, weird old questions. I wanted to understand the meaning of life, and where it came from. I wanted to know if there was any kind of objective morality. I wanted to know if beauty was real, if art actually mattered, or if it was all just a con. And I wanted to know why we trusted ourselves—our ability to reason, our moral instincts.

I loved the conversations I was having with other people, trying to figure these things out: late nights out with other philosophy majors, gleefully shouting at each other and scribbling logic diagrams on napkins. My parents wanted me to be a doctor or a lawyer or a programmer, something real. But I couldn't give up on these huge questions. My parents thought I was throwing away my chance at a safe and productive career.

I went to graduate school in philosophy precisely because I loved those wild, unmanageable questions. Then the stupidest thing happened. I met those rankings and they got under my skin. But the questions I loved weren't what got you into those highly ranked journals and departments. If you wanted to do well on the rankings, you had to write small, precise articles on fairly arcane technical questions. So, over the years, I stopped chasing the questions I cared about. I spent all my energy trying to climb those rankings. And all my joy in philosophy started draining away.

I don't think I would have cared nearly so much about status without the brutal clarity of the rankings. Before the rankings, I certainly wanted some respect, but only from very specific people: the particular philosophers I thought were cool. Before the rankings, my desires were grounded in my own sense of what mattered. But that wasn't what was in the rankings. The rankings represent the summarized views of other people—people who had been designated as supposed authorities by some other supposed authorities. I didn't actually trust anybody involved with the ranking process. But the fact that all their opinions had been aggregated into a single, clear ranking—a ranking that everybody knew about—made them powerful. The rankings compressed a mess of human opinions into a single neat score. That clarity sucked me into caring about something I'd never cared about before: the average respect of the whole profession.

The political philosopher Thomas Hobbes thought what ultimately mattered in politics was power. The rightful ruler is whoever has the power to control other people's actions. But for Hobbes, the true source of power wasn't strength or military might. He believed that ultimate power comes from the ability to *control language* and *define terms*—especially the terms of success. The power over definitions is stronger than military or economic power. Because if you can define what good and evil mean for people, if you can control what success and failure mean for them, then you can control them from the inside.

GAMES WAKE US UP TO A LIFE OF PLAY; METRICS DRIVE US DOWN into grueling optimization. And sometimes, we let some external, institutional systems—rankings, metrics, and measures—set our desires and goals. Let's give this phenomenon a name. Call it *value capture*. Value capture happens when:

1. Your values are rich and subtle — or developing that way.

2. You enter some social (typically institutional) setting that offers you simplified, often quantified renditions of your values.

3. The simplified versions take over.

If you want a portable version, try this: *Value capture occurs when you get your values from some external source and let them rule you without adapting them.*

Value capture happens when a restaurant stops caring about making good food and starts caring about maximizing its Yelp ratings. It happens when students stop caring about education and start caring about their GPA. It happens when scientists stop caring about finding truth and start caring about getting the biggest grants. It even happens in religion. A pastor recently told me that his church had become completely obsessed with baptism rates. The higher-ups had established an internal leaderboard in which the pastors competed on monthly baptism rates, and it was starting to dominate everybody's attention. He'd found himself caring less about the long-term spiritual development of his flock and focusing more on trying to deliver popular sermons that would up his baptism rates and move him up that leaderboard.

In value capture, you're *outsourcing your values* to an institution. Instead of setting your values in the light of your own particular experiences, instead of adjusting them to your particular personality, you're letting distant bureaucratic forces set them for you.

Maybe this wouldn't matter if the institutional metrics got it exactly right — if they truly captured what is valuable in the world. But that almost never happens. Metrics are shaped by institutional forces. They are subject to demands for fast, efficient data collection at scale, to demands of fitting into spreadsheets and action reports. Institutional metrics are part of a system that abstracts away from personal difference and local detail and identifies some thin, measurable detail. And what's easily measurable is rarely the same as what's *really valuable*.

AFTER A FEW YEARS OF SOUL-SEARCHING, I FINALLY MANAGED to shake off the grip of the philosophy rankings and remember my love for those weird old questions. But a couple of years later, it happened to me all over again. I went on Twitter.

I got on originally to talk to people, and to learn from them. There was a brief moment, years ago, when Twitter seemed genuinely magical. You could make friends you would never have found in any other place, find ideas and conversations that would have been impossible otherwise. Twitter was, for a little while, a bonanza of surprising but meaningful connection.

But then I went minorly viral a few times and caught that delicious, feverish high of seeing my numbers soar. And every time, I'd be gripped with the need for more. I started ransacking my thoughts, imagining how each one would look on Twitter. It started to matter less for me whether the thing was true or deep or wise. I just wanted thoughts that were peppy and sharp and quick enough to blow up.

It's particularly easy, with Twitter, to see the exact contours of the value shift. The platform's scoring system—its Likes and Retweets and Follows—doesn't register empathy, or understanding, or finding out something that really transforms you down the line. It measures quick-fire popularity. Twitter's metrics don't capture the difference between somebody who chuckled for a second at your tweet and somebody who was shaken to their core. If they both just click Like, then Twitter counts them the same.

Twitter captures a binary information state. It does not record the difference between loving something, being mildly amused by it, or having it change your life. It flattens complex information into a single binary bit of data. And it captures that data at one narrow moment: the moment of first reading. You encounter a deep tweet. At first you don't like it; you disagree with it. But it sticks in your craw; it gnaws at you. Slowly, it changes your mind—but that takes a week. The value of that tweet comes in a slow burn. But it's pretty unlikely that you'll go back and find that tweet to Like it. The interface of social media tends to capture positive reactions in the first moment of exposure. One of the central reasons we communicate with each other is to learn, to be challenged, to have our understanding transformed, which takes time. But that kind of communication isn't valued by Twitter's scoring system.

Call this *the Gap*. The Gap is the distance between what's being measured and what actually matters.

REINER KNIZIA IS SOMETIMES CALLED THE MOZART OF GERMAN game design—the bizarre prodigy who effortlessly churns out these elegant, profoundly original game designs. As the German and larger European board-game scene was heating up in the 1980s and '90s, Knizia was sitting on top of it all, spewing forth hundreds of new games.

In a lecture on his game design process, Knizia said that the most important tool in his game design toolbox was the scoring system, because it *sets the player's motivations* in the game. Scores tell the players what they'll want during the game. And this is the heart of how game designers shape our actions—and how those actions will feel—in the game. A scoring system specifies motivations for the player to adopt.

You can make a game out of the simplest things: a few rules and a goal. One of the more elegant modern game designs is *The Mind*. The game is comically simple. There's a deck with a hundred cards in it, numbered from 1 to 100. For level one, you shuffle the deck and deal each player one random card. The goal is for all players to work together as a team to play the cards in order, from lowest to highest. But there is one single, glorious catch: You're not allowed to communicate. You can't talk, signal, grunt, or gesture to each other. You have to coordinate wordlessly to play those cards in order. If you can do it for level one, you go up to level two: Reshuffle the deck, and deal two random cards to each person. For a four-player game, you win the game if you can beat level eight—that's eight random cards dealt to each person, to be played out in perfect order, in total silence.

The game asks you to do the seemingly impossible: to be telepathic. And then it teaches you how that's actually possible. You play the game by developing a shared sense of timing for how long you should wait to play a given card. And you can get very good at it together. Your group can play these wild, precise sequences in lockstep tempo. It will start to feel like you can touch the inside of each other's brains and hear a collective clock ticking.

How does *The Mind* accomplish this little miracle? What's it made out of? There are two basic parts to the game. First it gives you *restrictions*: The game strips away all your normal avenues for communication. Then it gives you a *goal*. It tells you to play these cards in sequential order. Out of these simplest of pieces, the game shapes a very specific set of actions and challenges—and through those, it shapes a mental state.

This is the peculiarity at the heart of games: They tell you what to desire. And we players are fluid enough that we can let those scoring systems shape our desires. We can slip into alternate motivational states like a new set of clothes. We have the ability to start a game, find out what will get us points, and then—for a period of time—care intensely, exactly as we're told to.

It's not just that a game tells you what counts as winning for this game. It sets the deeper meaning of winning. A game can tell you whether you're selfish or part of a larger collective. Start up *The Mind*. The game tells you you're all on a team together, and you win or lose as one. Now your desires are unified; you are a perfect coordinated unit. Start up another game, like the classic first-person shooter *Quake III Arena*. This video game throws you into an online arena, where you score points by killing other players. Now you are an unapologetic psychopath, a being of pure selfishness, dodging, whirling, bouncing grenades down the hall, head-shotting people as they come down the corner.

Start up another game: Go outside and play a game of pickup basketball. Now you're divided into teams, and the basic shape of your cares shifts to match. It doesn't matter that Tessa is your best friend; she's on the opposite team now, and your job is to steal her passes and block her shots. It doesn't matter that in ordinary life you hate Sam. He's on your team now, and if he's open, you pass him the damn ball. Because for a period, your goals and Sam's goals are aligned.

Games play around with who you are, what you care about, and the basic shape of your relationships to other people. Games reach into you and give you a new form of agency, and you can, for a while, become completely absorbed in that new agency. And what enables that, in crucial part, is the clarity, the simplicity, and the unambiguity of the scoring system. Games let somebody else design a new self for you, for you to slip into.

———

PERHAPS THIS SEEMS UNNERVING, LETTING ANOTHER HUMAN being inside our heads to tinker with our goals. But this goal manipulation can be relatively safe in games. Because often in games, the goal isn't what really matters. We adopt the goal in order to *experience the process*. The beauty is in the struggle.

This is a very specific kind of orientation. Let's give it a name: *striving play*. In striving play, you try to win not because winning is important, but because the act of trying to win gives you a delicious struggle. In striving play, you don't really care about winning in a lasting way. You temporarily induce in yourself a desire to win, so you can enjoy the process of trying.

Striving play involves a motivational inversion of ordinary, practical life. In normal life, we struggle in order to attain some goal that we really want. In striving play, we adopt a goal in order to have the struggle that we really want.

This may seem bizarre, but striving play is perfectly ordinary. Your friends come over, and you decide to play a silly party game, like charades. There is a paradox at the heart of charades. Most people play the game, not to win, but to break the ice and get goofy. But when you play charades, you have to actually try to win to have fun. A game like charades is fun only when you're moderately invested—when you're genuinely trying to communicate some silly little phrase through gestures, when you're truly frustrated that people aren't getting it. Getting emotionally invested in winning charges the whole experience, and gives it spice.

But most of us don't actually care about winning charades. If you lost but everybody had lots of fun, you probably wouldn't feel disappointed. Because deep in your heart, you already know that winning isn't the point. Having fun is.

———

THE STANDARD SCORING SYSTEM OF CLIMBING WAS GOOD FOR
me, for the first few years. It made me stronger and more graceful than
I'd ever been. But over time, it stopped working. I'm not naturally
very athletic, and I didn't have the time to train hard. The standard
scoring system said there was one goal: Climb more difficult climbs.
After a while, I got stuck. The difficulty game just had me throwing
myself against gruelingly difficult climbs, and mostly failing. The
whole thing turned tedious. It took me a while to remember that I
had never really cared about being a great rock climber. I loved rock
climbing because it showed me the beauty in my own moving body.
I loved it when it changed my experience of the natural world—when
it sensitized me to microscopic details in the rock and the landscape.

I eventually found a way to love rock climbing again by tweaking
the goals. I stopped being laser-focused on pure difficulty. I looked for
middlingly hard but interesting climbs, which pushed me into new
kinds of movement. And I didn't declare myself finished with a particular climb after the first time I climbed it. I took the Sherwood path.
I aimed for smoothness, flow, and total mastery of the climb. What I
most wanted was the feeling of complete organized attunement—
and I got that from seeking elegant mastery over moderate climbs,
and not from the perpetual quest for more difficult climbs.

In other words, I was turning into a game designer, by creating my
own personal version of the game. I was starting to play around with
what counted as winning. I was starting to tune the game to my own
purposes, to give me that specific mental state of ecstatic organization and flow.

Games tell you what to desire, through the scoring system. But
you can also take charge of which games you play, and choose which
scoring systems you adopt. You can tweak your games, shift to new

ones, jump from ordinary *Super Mario Odyssey* to speedrunning it. Or you can quit Mario entirely and learn archery, or start a Dungeons & Dragons campaign.

You can use games to explore different ways of thinking and caring. You can become a planning, optimizing, resource-maximizing being. You can become a goofy gesticulating charades being. You can become a twitchy being of reflexes, dodging and whirling and sniping with angelic grace. You can merge yourself into a telepathic group mind.

In a game, you can plunge into an alternate self. And scoring systems are at the center. They make it easier for us to change what we target and what we care about. Scoring systems are an instruction manual for new values.

ONCE, A FEW YEARS BEFORE THE RISE OF CHATGPT, I WAS IN A room with a bunch of computer scientists who were working on building a creative artificial intelligence—an AI that could make good art. I asked, "So what target data are you using? What counts as success when training the AI?"

One team explained that they were using the Netflix database about engagement hours. Their AI was "successful" when its output most resembled the Netflix shows that got viewers to watch the most hours of TV. The problem is that engagement hours are not the same as good art. Art can be good in so many ways. It can move us; it can make us more sensitive and empathic; it can enrich our understanding of one another. But none of those qualities are necessarily measured by engagement hours.

I said all this. I said that they were training their AI not to make good art, but to make addictive shows. They were optimizing for total engagement hours, and not for the quality of those hours. The

AI wranglers responded, "Well, that's the dataset we have. Show us a better dataset for good art and we'll optimize for that instead."

And that's the core problem: We don't have a massive dataset for good art, but we do have a massive dataset for engagement hours. And this is no accident. Some kinds of things are *systematically harder to measure* because they are more variable, more personal, or more delicate. This is what a lot of this book will be about: why so many of the important things in life seem to consistently defy measurement. They vanish from sight when we insist on using the measurement tools of large-scale institutions and bureaucracy. What's meaningful is intimate and unpredictable; it eludes easy classification. If we let institutional metrics set our values and drive our lives, we end up chasing what's easy to count, and not what's really important.

When we play games—when we are in charge of them—we are touring a whole ecosystem of deeply different rules and scoring systems, choosing and tweaking them to fit our own purposes. But our relationship to metrics is different. Our institutional lives are usually ruled by very small number of pervasive metrics. We have very little power over which ones dominate our lives, and what they measure. And these metrics have been engineered not to give us a meaningful life but for the convenience of vast bureaucratic information systems.

WHY ARE WE SO DRAWN TO SIMPLE SCORING SYSTEMS? SCORING systems offer us relief from the painful complexity of life. When we leave ourselves fully exposed to the value density of real life, it's hard to know what to do. My own life is full of a hundred conflicting claims and hopes. I want to be a loving parent, a good teacher, and a thoughtful scholar. I want to write beautiful things, to help advance the dream of a kinder and more just world. I want to be a good partner to my spouse. I want to keep my body healthy, and to get better at climbing. I want to keep in touch with the world of new music and new comics. And I want to indulge my weird obsessions, like my current overwhelming desire to perfect my chile verde. All of those things clamor for my attention.

Suppose we focus down on just one part of life—say, my desire to be a good parent. Even then, it's still hard to know how well you're doing. It's late; my kid has been sad all day because he's frustrated about learning math, but finally he's happy because we found a great new anime to watch together. Now it's two hours past his bedtime; he's bouncing off the walls, shouting about what special powers he wants. He's inventing his own spin-off versions of the story, throwing around his stuffed animals into a massive mess on the floor, and pretending to be Luffy the rubber pirate hero. Am I being a good parent? An indulgent parent? A parent fostering creativity? How the hell am I supposed to know?

Our actual values are often unclear; it isn't obvious how each value applies to a particular situation. On top of that, real life is full of a nauseating tangle of different unclear values, which I constantly have to weigh and decide between. How do I compare the value of spending an hour reading to my toddler with the value of spending an hour lifting weights? How do I calculate the relative value of spending this Saturday morning reading an exciting new sci-fi novel versus hacking away at my email pile? Life is a jumble of different values, all shouting at each other, with no clear centralized method for making sense of it all.

But games are different.

Games grant us a precious experience of clarity. It is a clarity of purpose—a clarity of value. In a game, for once in our lives, we know exactly what we're supposed to be doing, and afterward, we know exactly how well we have done. There are no larger questions about the meaning of our lives, no existential angst about our goals, no ambiguity. We know what we are pursuing in explicit, immaculate, unquestionable detail. Games offer *value clarity*. They are an existential balm for the confusion of ordinary life.

And games also tell us exactly what everybody else wants. They coordinate our values and make it easy for us to make sense to each other. They create a quick, artificial community.

I spend half my life hiding what I really I love. I am a goddamn weirdo who has spent vats of time chasing bizarre obsessions, all mostly incomprehensible to the larger world. Our cares are so different; they speak in different languages of meaning. Climbing speaks to me in the language of getting stronger, mastering movement, finding solutions. Jazz speaks to me in the language of thrilling improvisation, of group creativity at speed, of the beauty of mathematics made sonic. Philosophy speaks to me in the language of curiosity, connection, and gorgeous ideas. To many other people, these languages of meaning are completely opaque. And other people care about different things, with different languages of meaning, which are unfamiliar and uninterpretable to me.

But games define all that difference away. In most games, there are no difficult questions about other people's motives. There are no vast gulfs between our very different loves. The rules set precisely the same goals for all of us. They create a shared language of success. Explaining ourselves becomes effortless. Scoring systems make us entirely comprehensible to one another. There are now only the simple, practical questions: What are the most efficient means to achieve that shared, clear goal?

Games offer us *social value clarity*.

In most games, that clarity is happily artificial. The points are made up. In most games, the goals are things we invented for the sake of fun or satisfaction—to shape some delicious form of action. Game goals can be adopted and then thrown away again. Game cares are temporary and disposable.

But metrics offer us a different bargain. They promise the same delicious clarity: that if we adopt some simple scoring system, our values will become clear and easy to communicate. University rankings, social media follower counts, page views—each of these promises to simplify the meaning of success in the world. But the cost is different. Because metrics are designed to measure something in the world, something real. Maybe it's health, education, or well-being. Maybe it's popularity or status. It's when mechanical scoring systems try to capture some real truths that we have to start worrying about the possibility of error—about the possibility of a mismatch between the clarity of the score and the density of the real world. That's when we are in danger of being seduced away from what's really important, by an artificially clarified rendition of value.

I SPENT YEARS CHASING THE PHILOSOPHY RANKINGS, UNTIL IT almost destroyed my soul. I became a miserable, clenched person—hating what I was reading, hating what I was writing. And everybody else hated it, too. But in my quiet hours, I'd started a tiny little side project, on a question that almost nobody in my profession took seriously: Why do we play games? The question fascinated me. But it didn't count as a real question in the world of official academic philosophy, so I mostly hid it from serious company, and worked on it in stolen moments.

A few years later, the rankings quest had gotten me to such a point of misery that I was starting to consider quitting philosophy, giving up my professor gig, and finding something else to do with my life. Instead, I took one last shot. I let myself indulge in what seemed, from the standards of my profession, like the most ludicrous possible quest: to figure out the value of games. I ended up spending years obsessed with it—trying to articulate the peculiar beauty of games, the value of play, and how game designers are a unique kind of artist who use scoring systems to shape our desires and our actions into something beautiful.

I cared about it because I cared about games. I've spent my entire life playing games of every kind. I played my first computer game at about the age of ten. My dad went from being a Vietnamese refugee to being a programmer at Intel in the 1980s. He'd bought us a cast-off Intel computer at a sale for employees. It was a primitive thing, the size of a refrigerator. The only place for it was in our garage. I used it to play one of the earliest computer games: *Colossal Cave Adventure*, a fully text-based adventure in which the game gave you written descriptions of what was happening, and you had to struggle with its primitive text parser to tell it what you wanted to do. "Go west." "Get lamp." "Get water." "Pour water."

I grew up as computer games grew up. I played tons of text adventure games, and then the first adventure games with graphics. I played some of the first computer role-playing games, where you wandered through endless dungeons killing monsters and getting experience points. I played other games, too. I learned chess; I learned poker. I fell in love with go—possibly the most beautiful of all games, a game of depth and profundity. I also lost months of my life to the gruelingly addictive strategy computer game *Civilization*—possibly the only game I truly regret playing. And later on, I'd discover the exploding world of European board games. I played fascinating subtle auction games and resource-management games. I'd stay up late at night playing board games with my friends, and then afterward talk for hours analyzing the experience—trying to figure out what made one game so boringly mechanical and another game so explosively delicious. I started posting on online forums, reviewing board games, trying to figure out exactly what made certain games just so vibratingly alive. And then this somehow merged with my academic career, and I ended up writing an entire philosophy book about the peculiar magic of games.

But at the same time, I was dealing with metrics. At my first professor job, I was the "learning outcomes liaison" for my philosophy department. This meant that I had to gather quantitative data about how our department was doing in promoting student success, to show that we weren't all just bullshitters wasting taxpayer money. And I had to do it in an environment where student success had become defined by administrators, in a particularly narrow way. "Student success" had been officially defined as a weighted average of graduation rate and graduation speed.

This definition captured almost nothing about what I or my fellow philosophy professors cared about in teaching. But it ruled our lives; it was the language we had to speak in whenever we wanted to justify a new hire or a budgetary line item. So I started writing about the philosophy of that, too: about why metrics are usually formulated in terms that squash whatever is really important to us; about why metrics so often drain the life out of what really matters.

And I realized at some point that I had an entire theory about games, in which clear and simple scoring systems were the magic ingredient that opened up the door to a whole world of delightful play. And I had an entire theory about metrics, in which clear and simple scoring systems killed what really mattered.

I became obsessed with a new question, which seemed for a while to matter only to me: Why is it that mechanical scoring systems are, in games, the site of so much joy and fluidity and play? And why, in the realm of public measures and institutional metrics, do they drain the life out of everything?

That is the question that led to the book you're reading now. And the answer is going to come in two stages, roughly divided into the halves of this book.

In the first half, we're going to discover that we can each approach scoring systems with two very different attitudes. We can approach them *playfully*—bending ourselves in and out of them, dancing between them, changing them, modifying them. Or we can be *captured* by them—we can let scoring systems dictate our goals and targets to us, even when those goals fit poorly with our lives. So at first, it's going to look a lot like the difference is a matter of individual attitude. Maybe, you think, the solution is simple: We should, as individuals, try to have the right attitude, and just be more playful about everything.

But in the second half, we're going to discover why the solution isn't so easy. Because the world often makes it extremely hard to be playful. The basic nature of games and their social environment—their quickness, their disconnection, their disposability—encourages in us the playful attitude and makes it easy to find and sustain. The nature of metrics discourages playfulness. They encourage, instead, value capture: a rigid attachment to an external system of values. We will discover value capture everywhere—in journalism, education, and business, but also in our food, our hobbies, and the way we measure our own health and happiness.

Sometimes, metrics pull on us because they are tied to simple incentives: money, opportunity, status, power. But incentives don't explain everything. Often, metrics do give us status and power—but only because everybody else has gotten sucked in already. Again, philosophers could have ignored the philosophy rankings; they had no official authority. But we gave them power, by believing in them.

And most fascinating of all is that so many of us get sucked into public metrics even when they don't give us status—even when it hurts us. Pursuing weight loss into declining health and sorrow; obsessively chasing more Likes and Follows even when it doesn't matter for our job. The very clarity and universal comprehensibility of metrics seduce us into value capture, even when it makes us miserable.

Metrics are understandable, interconnected, and perfectly transparent. And in this clarity is a certain kind of trap. We become beholden to what everybody can understand. Games are isolated, disconnected, and unimportant. The joy we take in them is often private and opaque to others. And that opacity gives us the space to be free.

I'M WRITING THIS BOOK BECAUSE OF AN EMAIL FROM A STUdent. She'd seen one of my lectures, where I'd talked about the mystery of why games and metrics hit so differently. I had talked about the two main threads at the center of the mystery: striving play and value capture. When I gave the lecture, I didn't have a good answer yet; I was just fumbling around, chasing a chaos of connections. But the student wrote me, and said the talk had pulled her out of a five-year depressive spiral.

She turned out to be a lot like me: an Asian American kid, the child of immigrants, pushed by her parents to keep a perfect 4.0 GPA and get into the most highly ranked college. She was also an athlete, a competitive golfer. And, she said, she'd been struggling with anorexia, obsessed with her BMI.

She said my talk had made her realize that she'd been trapped in all kinds of bad games. Life had given her some scoring systems and she'd just been trying to get as high a score as she could, without wondering if she should have accepted them into her heart in the first place. Thinking about these things as games, she said, had helped her get some distance from the rankings and metrics. She could step back and ask herself if she actually wanted to accept these systems, if they really mattered to her.

She sent me a picture of her phone. She'd changed the default background so it gave her a message, a reminder, every time she looked at it.

Her phone says, "Is this the game you really want to be playing?"

CHAPTER 2

Striving Play

I t was the pandemic. I was in Utah, and I was learning to fly-fish to keep myself from falling down a despair hole. Fly-fishing was exactly what I needed in my life at that moment—in my forties, overloaded with parenting and admin. And it was exactly what I needed during lockdown. I was spending most of my days stuck in an improvised home office in my basement, trying to Zoom-teach to a screen full of blank boxes. But when you're out there, standing in a river, staring intently into the details of moving water—it cleans out your brain and soul.

Fly-fishing is full of dudes who have this intense, addictive relationship to the sport. My own private theory is that what a lot of these guys need is meditation, but they can't admit it. Fly-fishing gives them a sufficiently masculine cover story, so they can get the spiritual cleansing they really need.

For me, the peak of fly-fishing is dry fly-fishing. This is when you're fishing with a tiny imitation insect, which floats, and you're trying to get a fish to eat your fly off the surface of the water. Fly-fishing is an act of perpetual attention to the natural world. You're stalking along the river, looking for signs of fish. Maybe you spot a subtly slow patch of water behind an underwater boulder—classic trout holding water. Or maybe, if you're lucky enough and watchful enough, you'll actually see a trout daintily feeding on the surface. Your goal now is to sneak up behind it and carefully cast your artificial fly to land, ever so softly, right in front of that trout. And if you actually manage to pull all this off, then sometimes the trout will swim up, inspect your floating fly, and slurp it down right there in front of you.

You net the fish, admire it briefly—and then you let it go. Because most fly-fishers don't fish for food; they catch and release. Taking fish was never the point. In fact, Nicole, one of the people who taught me to fly-fish, had even transcended the catching part. She told me that she'd started feeling bad enough about bothering fish, especially during the spawning season, that she'd sometimes cut the hook off her fly, and just try to get the trout to eat the fly. Fooling the trout was enough; actually hooking and netting the fish had become unnecessary for her version of the game.

For me, the central experience of fly-fishing is a sensual act of information management. You're looking at tiny details of the river, watching for the telltale signs of good trout holding water. There's the slow water that shelters the fish; the crisp current edges that bring them food. You're searching for little shadowy movement in the water—the subtle sway of camouflaged trout. And then you have to show them the right bug. When trout see a lot of fishing pressure, they get picky. So you have to study the insects, notice their color and size, and change your fly to match. In fly-fishing, you become a nexus point in this gorgeously overwhelming flow of information. You have to dance through it all, sorting the signal from the noise.

But this isn't only a superficial cover for meditation. If I just stood in a river and tried to clear my mind, I'd get pretty bored, fast. I can't simply will myself to focus on the surface of water. The pursuit of fish creates an attentional focal point. It structures the way I look at the river—it gives me a goal, tells me what to look for, what to see. This intense, diffuse attention produces in me a state of profoundly calm soft focus. Weirdly, taking on the goal of *catching fish* has the result of *meditation* through attention to the river.

The fly-fishing writer John Gierach often talks about the real point of fly-fishing. You do have to be trying to catch fish—and hoping for a big one. That goal organizes and energizes the whole activity. But catching fish isn't actually the point of the whole thing. This is particularly obvious for the catch-and-release fly-fisher, who mostly lets their fish go. It doesn't actually matter how many fish you catch, or how big they are. You might hit the river on a good day, monster fish jumping your fly on every cast. You might hike up a quiet river, casting in little pool after little pool, and only catch a few fish—but beautiful, wild ones. Or you might end up stuck all day casting to one tricky fish, spooking them over and over with imperfect casts, and finally fool the fish into hitting your fly once, only to miss the strike. But all of these are good days. They are time beautifully spent absorbed in the natural world—in careful movement, in fluid casting. The fish are the focus, but not the value of the activity. The real point is something larger, stranger, more mystical. You spend time on a river trying to catch fish, and you start noticing the slow cycle of different bugs throughout the day. You start noticing that the first hatch of mayflies tends to match the appearance of the hummingbirds, that wild asparagus will show up for a week in early spring. You start getting a feel for the rhythm and cycle of a river's ecosystem. The natural world is suddenly higher resolution. Catching fish is the *goal*—but not the *purpose*—of fly-fishing.

Gierach is a striving player.

———

THERE ARE TWO VERY DIFFERENT MOTIVATIONAL STATES IN which we can play a game. There's striving play, and then there's also *achievement play*. The achievement player is trying to win because they actually value winning. The striving player, on the other hand, doesn't actually care about the win, deep down. They are only trying to win because they value the struggle. The achievement player cares about the *win itself*; the striving player cares about the *process of trying to win*.

The achievement player, we might say, *genuinely* wants to win. They have a lasting interest in winning; their desire to win exists before, during, and after the game. It is the reason they play; playing games is valuable for them only if they win.

The striving player is different. They don't truly care about winning—not cosmically. They care about something else: fun, relaxation, a challenge, the experience of beautiful movement. But to get those cherished experiences, they need to get themselves into the mental state of wanting to win. Their interest in winning, however, is only temporary. They may get themselves to want to win pretty intensely during the game, but they throw away their interest in winning once they finish the game. Their real, lasting purpose lies in the struggle. For striving players, winning is a *disposable end*.

Striving play might sound weird described this abstractly, but you've probably already been doing it instinctively already. Say we're having a dinner party and decide to play a party game. Let's play *Spyfall*, a truly delightful game of hidden identities that reliably puts people into joyful hysterics. One person is the spy, trying to beat everybody else. Everybody else is on a team together, trying to figure out who the spy is. But, of course, since the spy's identity is hidden, none of the team players can be sure who, exactly, they can trust.

There is, for each round, a single specified location, which you're all supposed to be in together. Maybe you're all in a post office, or an opera house, or a submarine. You start the game by dealing out a card to each player, which assigns them a role: team player or spy. The team players each get similar cards, telling them all the same key fact: the location. But the spy's card does not reveal that location; it only says "SPY." The team players know the location, but they can't be sure who their real team members are, and who the spy is. The spy player knows everybody's true role, but not the location. Now the dance begins. If the spy figures out the specified location, then the spy wins. But if the team players figure out who the spy is, then the team wins. And now you all just talk—asking each other probing questions. ("When'd you get here? Hey, how long have you been working here? What's that in your hand?") The team players need to signal to each other that they're on the team, by hinting at their knowledge of the location. But they can't be too obvious about it, or the spy will figure out the location. (If the location is the opera house, a team player shouldn't just ask, "What'd you think of that last aria?" That gives away too much information to the spy.)

The whole game is a ludicrous dance in ambiguity, bullshit, and bullshit detection. Team players have to be hyper-attentive. They're trying to invent clever little litmus tests to figure out who's in the know, and who's only pretending. They have to signal to each other their true knowledge, but hide those signals under strategic vagueness. The spy has the reverse task. They have to speak ambiguously. They have to pretend that they're being strategically vague about the secret location, when they actually just don't know what it is. They have to issue fake litmus tests to the team players, to probe for the information they need.

The fun of the game—the thrills, the cleverly pointed questions, the glorious escapes—depends on the players caring about winning.

Otherwise, you don't get pulled into the intricate dance of the game; you won't have a reason to put every one of your fellow players' questions and answers under the microscope. You need to care about winning so you'll feel the tension, and the thrill when it all comes together and you finally figure it out.

But then one side loses and the other wins. The winner has a moment of glee, the losers hang their head for a second. But that moment passes as we leave the mindset of the game. Because in the long run, it doesn't really matter who won. From outside the game, most of us don't actually care if we won or lost—unless we're hypercompetitive assholes. Our interest in winning evaporates quickly. If you lost, you don't think you wasted your evening. What actually matters is that people had fun. Most of us naturally engage in striving play, with party games like *Spyfall*.

The achievement player is more psychologically straightforward. They care about winning, and then they try hard to get it. They have normal linear desires. But the striving player has a much odder motivational structure. There is an angle in their desires; their desires turn a corner. A striving player wants the experience of struggling to overcome obstacles. They want the absorption, the intensity, or the drama. They don't actually care about winning, but they do care about experiences that come from *trying hard to win*. But to get those experiences, they have to temporarily get themselves to want to win. But their interest in winning isn't permanent. It's just something they induce in themselves for the moment—a little mental trick that they play on themselves, in order to get that delightful struggle.

Striving play involves a motivational inversion. In ordinary, practical life, you take the means for the sake of the end. You struggle in order to get the reward; all your effort and strain is justified by the outcome. But in striving play, you take the end for the sake of the means. You chase the goal in order to have the struggle. If you want to understand the achievement player's motivation, you have to look at the value of winning for them. But to understand the striving player, you have to look at the joy of the struggle itself.

Maybe you're a striving player, or maybe you're more of an achievement player. Many of us fall somewhere in between. And we often shift in different contexts. Here's a litmus test: If you're in the striving play mindset, you can get what you want out of a game even if you lose. And you can fail to get what you really want even if you win. I can lose *Spyfall* and be utterly satisfied by how fun the whole thing was. Or I can win—but have been so viciously competitive that I'd ruined the fun for everybody. I may have achieved the in-game goal, but I failed at my real purpose for playing.

And notice that striving players don't just have to be in it for the sheer joy of the game. You can also be a striving player if you're using the game as a tool to get something else. You can play games for health or relaxation or to break the ice at a party. But a striving player gets those benefits from the struggle, not the victory. If you run marathons to improve your cardiovascular fitness, you're also a striving player—because you can get a fitness benefit even if you place last.

Maybe you doubt that striving play is real. But a lot of ordinary, everyday game-playing behavior only makes sense as striving play. For example, when I'm playing serious board games with my friends, I will pursue the win intensely during the game. But in the long term, I make choices that actually decrease my chances of winning.

I play a lot of board games with my spouse. We love exploring weird new games together. We have very different gaming skills, though. She's a chemist, and incredibly good at precision work, especially involving spatial manipulation. Anything that requires, say, *Tetris*-like mental geometry, she will destroy me at. And I am, to be perfectly honest, very good at games of deception and social manipulation. In most games, one of us is usually way better than the other.

But once in a while, we'll find a game that balances our different skill sets—a game that involves both precision geometry and deception. Now we're even; now we can have genuinely tense, fascinating matches. But then, late at night, I'll be wandering the internet, reading about the game, and I'll stumble across a strategy guide. My spouse would never read a strategy guide; that's not the kind of person she is. So if I read the strategy guide, my skill at the game will jump way ahead of hers and I'll start winning—but our games will lose their delicious balance and be much less exciting.

If there were no such thing as striving play—if we were all only achievement players—then there would be only one rational thing to do: Read the strategy guide and win. But in this case, I don't read the strategy guide—and I think that's a perfectly reasonable thing for me to do. What I truly care about is not the win, but the quality of the struggle. And that makes sense only if I'm a striving player.

Consider, too, a *stupid game*. A stupid game is one in which:

1. The fun part is failing.

2. It's only fun if you're trying to win.

Twister is a stupid game. So are many drinking games. My favorite stupid game is called Bag on Your Head. Bag on Your Head is a gloriously idiotic party game in which everybody puts a brown paper grocery bag over their head. The goal is to take the bags off of other people's heads. Once somebody takes the bag off your head, you're out. The game involves stumbling around, unable to see, bumping into furniture and people, and then getting into awkward flailing matches trying to rip the bag off each other's' heads. When you lose, you go stand by the side of the room and watch the rest of this ridiculous game play out. And the best part: At some point, there will be only one person left in the middle of the room, stumbling around by themselves, flailing about, groping for their nonexistent competitors. This is the winner. And the very best part of the game is for the losers, who get to watch how long it takes for the winner to figure out that they have, in fact, won.

Trying for a hard reach in *Twister* and then falling over into a heap—that's funny. But it wouldn't be as funny if we fell on purpose. That's because what's funny here is failure, and it's only a failure if you were actually trying to succeed. So the perverse logic of a stupid game is: You have to get yourself invested in something that you don't actually, from a cosmic perspective, care about. You have to genuinely try to win in order to get what you really want, which is hilarious failure.

In stupid games, the goal and purpose are entirely different. Stupid games prove that striving play is real.

MOST CASUAL VIDEO GAME PLAYERS ARE, I THINK, STRIVING players. I'm not talking about professional esports players, whose careers depend on success. I'm talking about the average person, like me, who picks a computer game because they think it'll be fun or interesting.

I've been obsessed lately with the kinds of action video games that put you at the edge of your reflexes, that overload you with too many enemies, forcing you to defocus. The most beautiful of these games is *Hyper Light Drifter*, a moody and brutally hard game of reflexes and rhythm. *Hyper Light Drifter* is set in the ruins of a postapocalyptic world. It is a quiet game, entirely free of dialogue. You play an enigmatic drifter, who appears on the scene sick—clutching his heart, coughing up blood. You wander mostly empty, quiet landscapes— until, in sudden rushes, the screen fills with swarms of enemies. You have to dash, dodge, parry bullets with your light-sword, shooting and slashing your way through the enemy swarms. The enemies move in patterns, each in their own rhythm, flitting and dashing around and then lunging for you. The game will feed you a few ene- mies in small numbers, giving you a moment to internalize the pat- tern. And then it will send them at you in droves, more than you can track with your conscious mind. You have to learn to dance through them instinctively, to find little emerging gaps and holes in the enemy patterns to weave through, as you dodge and slash.

And it all happens to music—the heartbeat rhythm of lushly bit- tersweet, pulsating electronic music. And the game works better if you tune in to its music. Because the secret of the game is that the en- emies and the music are subtly synchronized to that heartbeat pulse, and if you let yourself get carried away by the music, you can sud- denly find yourself dodging and dancing in gorgeous, electrifying synchronicity. (Alx Preston, the creator of *Hyper Light Drifter*, has spent a lifetime struggling with heart disease, under the constant threat of death. And he made a profoundly sad game about loss and isolation, all built around a heartbeat rhythm.)

I have not finished *Hyper Light Drifter*. I suspect I will never come close to beating this game. I am, in fact, terrible at games like this. If I actually want to win, I should play a different game—something I'm actually good at, like some slow, calculating turn-based game of optimizing economic systems. I certainly shouldn't play *Hyper Light Drifter*. But I do play it, because I don't really care about winning. I love the way the game makes me stretch my consciousness, how it forces me to give up on my rational brain and just become this react- ing thing, tuning in to the particular hidden pulse of each scene and letting my fingers dance to it. I care about the very specific kind of attention, the kind of mental acuity, the absorption in the flow, that trying to win pulls out of me. But I have to try to win—to actually get myself invested in the win—to experience that luscious flow.

A FRIEND OF MINE TOLD ME ABOUT A GAME OF MONOPOLY HE once played with his ten-year-old son. The son was winning for the first time in his life. The dad had been on the brink of defeat for hours, but he never quite lost and he didn't understand exactly why. And then the dad discovered that whenever he was about to run out of cash, his son would distract him and *reverse-cheat and sneak some extra money into the dad's pile*, so the game could keep going. The son was trying to stay there forever, perched in that glorious moment of total domination over his helpless dad.

It's funny because what the son was doing makes a certain amount of sense. The son actually got the basic spirit of striving play. He knew that he was playing *Monopoly* for the joy of the struggle. But he misunderstood the subtler logic of striving play.

The son's mistake was that he was acting too straightforwardly. He was taking action directly to elongate the game. He was openly pursuing his larger purpose of having an extended struggle, rather than just narrowly devoting himself to the local goal of in-game victory. What striving players actually need to do is much weirder and more complicated. We have a larger purpose (having a cool struggle) and then we mostly forget about it. We focus on a narrower local goal (winning). We internally *seal ourselves off from our larger purpose*. The seal isn't perfect, of course—if my opponent starts crying, or just looks miserably bored, we break the seal. But for the most part, we narrow our motivations during the game.

I love a long, challenging game of chess. My larger purpose is to experience a fascinating extended, fraught battle. I'd be disappointed if I achieved a quick, easy victory. But during the game itself, I can't let that larger purpose directly guide my in-game actions. I can't openly pursue a longer struggle, because then I'd have a reason to avoid making game-winning moves. That would actually destroy the game experience for me. It would lead to an awkward double consciousness, in which I'd somehow have to be trying to win and trying to avoid winning at the same time.

This is a paradox at the heart of striving play. In a game like chess, striving players want a prolonged, delicious fight. But the only way we can get the feeling we want is by playing to shorten the fight—by constantly trying to end the game as quickly and decisively as possible. To achieve our true purpose, we need to ignore it and just focus on the narrower in-game goal. We have to submerge ourselves in a simpler, alternate consciousness: one that just wants to win.

We often use striving play to sneak up sideways on these delicate mental states. A lot of the time, my true purpose in climbing is to relax. But if I aim at relaxation directly—if I consciously try to relax—I'll absolutely fail. The worst way to do it is to sit in a chair and try to will yourself to relax. To actually relax, I have to forget that I'm trying to relax. I have to put my true purpose out of my head and focus on a very simple, very narrow goal: to get to the top of the cliff.

Philosophers have a term for this kind of thing: a *self-effacing end*, which is an end that cannot be pursued directly. Games help us achieve self-effacing ends—relaxation, meditation, absorption—by providing us with smaller goals to focus on. This is why people often use goofy games as icebreakers. If you take a party full of awkward strangers and just tell them to relax and get to know each other, they'll probably fail. Social chill is a self-effacing end. But if you give them some stupid game, like charades or *Twister*, they actually might have some fun together.

—

A LOT OF PEOPLE THINK GAMES ARE A WASTE OF TIME—ALL THAT effort spent on pursuing some silly, arbitrary points. But games look empty only if you're looking in the wrong place. In isolation, the goal of a game can seem utterly absurd. A marathon runner goes in an enormous, exhausting circle to get to the marathon's finish line—which is one block over from where they started. A board game player spends the whole night trying to collect more wooden sheep than anybody else. And after hours of torturous effort, they count up their respective piles of sheep, declare a victor, and then just toss all those sheep back into the baggie. What the hell was it all for, anyway?

To understand why so many of us play games, you have to remember the distinction between goal and purpose. For achievement players, the goal and purpose are one: They want to win. But for striving players, goal and purpose are very far apart. The in-game goal is just a disposable tool that they use to approach their real purpose: the experience of that delicious struggle.

And this difference between goal and purpose is everywhere, far beyond games. For a lot of folks, the goal of knitting is to make scarves, but the purpose is to be buried in this pleasurable zen dance of delicate finger motions. And we can tell that scarves aren't the true purpose, because a lot of knitters end up with way more scarves than they could possibly need, having to give them away to anybody who will take them.

Striving play is at one end of the spectrum of the possible relationships we can have to scoring systems. In striving play, we adopt scoring systems for our own reasons. We dally with them for as long as it takes to get what we want. And then, when it's done, we throw those cares away. In striving play, we don't let the scoring system dominate us. We use it to give us focus, and to align our cares for a little while, so that we can abandon ourselves to a gorgeously ordered, intense, purified world. We care about points because they give us a particular thrill. The scoring system is just a means to an end.

And if we don't like a scoring system and what it's doing to us, we can just stop playing.

CHAPTER 3

Value Capture

I spent the beginning of my life completely in my head. I was always playing computer games or curled around a book. By the time I was twenty-two, my back hurt and my knees creaked when I walked. My doc looked at me one day, shook her head, and said, "Look, buddy, honestly, if you don't start doing something about it, your joints are only going to get worse."

So I flailed around trying to find some kind of exercise routine that I didn't totally hate. I started running on the treadmill; I went for hikes; I did some yoga. I started trying to eat less crap, too, cutting down on sodas and doughnuts and the huge bags of chips I used to binge on. For a while, it worked wonders. My back stopped hurting. I started feeling good, feeling healthy. I started paying attention to how my body and mind responded to food. I noticed how a massive meal of cheesy pasta made me weirdly sleepy and aimless, but a diet with plenty of protein and vegetables and rich, fatty stews made me feel amazing. I started going to the farmers market. I fell in love with fresh asparagus—with getting that perfect sear on them, so they ended up balanced just right between crisp and melting-soft, with that concentrated vegetal sweetness.

And then I started getting obsessed with some very specific numbers. I had dropped a few pounds naturally and easily with the diet shift, but that stalled out after a year. But I wanted more. I wanted to see the number on the scale keep ticking down. It felt like progress. So I started measuring my caloric intake. I bought an app that tracked my weight. Every morning I'd wake up and look at the line graph of my weight loss. The angle of that line mattered so much to me. Tracking my weight made me drop a bit more, but that stalled out after a while, too. That was no good; I was addicted to the feeling of progress. So I bought another app that tracked my macronutrients and started entering into it every single thing I ate—how many calories, how much protein. I started cutting out things I deeply loved, because they didn't have the optimum balance of macronutrients.

But figuring out the exact nutrient balance in each meal took a lot of work. To make things easier, I developed some standard meals. I knew their nutrition data better, which made it easier to enter my daily stats into the app. This made my eating life more boring, but the stats were more consistent and easier to log. That meant I could keep losing weight.

At some point, I stopped making those lovely stews. They had a ton of ingredients—lots of different meats and beans and vegetables. But because they were so complicated, the nutritional data was much harder to enter into the app. So I started eating more prepackaged meals—frozen meals and boxed pasta—because it was easier to enter the nutrient content right off the package. My body felt kind of hollow. I was spending more time on the treadmill, trying to burn more calories each day. My joints started hurting again.

Something had happened. I had gone into this whole thing for health, to make my joints hurt less, to make my body feel better. But then something shifted in me, and I stopped caring about how my back and joints felt. I started caring about a number on a scale— my weight—and continuing to make it go down. My original goals had changed. I was focused on achievement based on an external measure—and the form of the new goals was set, in part, by the demand for external clarity.

Here we run headlong into the Gap again—the distance between what's easy to measure and what matters. But there should have also been an easy solution to the Gap. I should have been able to think to myself: "I started this whole dieting thing to feel healthier. I adopted this simplified scoring system of dropping weight in order to feel healthier. But if those simple scoring systems aren't helping, I should just stop using them. They aren't getting me what I actually care about." Once I became aware that I had fallen into the Gap, I should have been able to course-correct and adjust my scoring system to achieve what was really important. But I didn't. I had slowly forgotten what I had originally cared about. I was letting the sharp, clear metric dominate my inner vision. I had been value captured. I wasn't using a scoring system to achieve my own values; I was letting the scoring system set my values for me.

In value capture, you adopt some simplified value *as given* and use it as is. If you start the road to exercise with a Fitbit and eventually start modulating the goals, hacking them to suit you, then that's not value capture. Value capture is when you ingest it wholesale.

Value capture doesn't only occur around metrics. You can be value-captured by a slogan or a simplified belief system. But some of the most obvious, most common, and most powerful versions of value capture happen when we are exposed to a simple public scoring system—a ranking, a metric, a numerical score—and it takes over our decision-making. Those simple quantifications invite value capture. They cut through the noise; they make decisions so much easier. Scoring systems are a particularly seductive format for simplified values.

And value capture isn't just for individuals. Groups can be value-captured by metrics and measures that come from external sources. A newspaper can be value-captured by clicks and page views; a whole police precinct can be value-captured by the case-closure rate. In fact, large-scale institutions will turn out to be among the most vulnerable to value capture, because metrics speak directly in the language of bureaucracy.

I named value capture after *regulatory capture*—a problem in which government regulators go astray. These regulators are supposed to serve the public interest. Regulatory capture occurs when they end up, instead, serving the interests of the very companies they're supposed to be regulating. For example, the Food and Drug Administration is supposed to regulate the pharmaceutical industry. But sometimes some government regulators become friends with folks in the pharmaceutical industry—and the cushiest job for retired government regulators is often on the other side. So they start identifying with the pharmaceutical companies and caring about those corporations' interests. Those regulators have been captured by the industries they were supposed to regulate.

So, too, with value capture: Your values might get captured by some external metric, so that they no longer serve your own interests, but the interests of some external institution or process.

Value capture is real. Empirical researchers—sociologists, anthropologists, and historians—have provided exhaustive documentation. Rankings tend to seize an outsize chunk of institutional and personal attention, even when they're clearly oversimplified.

But is value capture always harmful? Maybe you think I've cherrypicked particularly rotten metrics. Obviously we lose out when a corporation changes from caring about making beautiful and meaningful movies to caring about profits. It's a shift from beneficent motives toward selfish ones. But can't we find better metrics? It wouldn't be so wrong to adopt, as your own personal values, a well-designed, good-hearted metric. After all, these are measurements created by experts. Maybe the doctors understand health better than ordinary folks; maybe the psychologists understand happiness better. Perhaps we should just trust the experts.

A lot of us instinctively believe this won't work—that when it comes to measuring things like happiness, education, beauty, and well-being, even the best-designed metric will miss the mark. But why?

Let's start with a real-world case. One of the richest empirical studies of value capture is *Engines of Anxiety*, by sociologists Wendy Nelson Espeland and Michael Sauder. The authors studied the impact of the *U.S. News & World Report* law school rankings.

Before *U.S. News*, there was no ranking of American law schools. There was only *Barron's*, a guide to law schools that gave qualitative descriptions of each. *Barron's* had a blurb about each university's unique mission and potential—and different schools often had very different missions. Some were there to get their students into corporate law jobs, while others cared a ton about legal theory and research. Some were oriented toward helping train activists who'd fight for social justice; others aimed to help students in traditionally underserved populations.

The problem was that these blurbs were clearly PR written by the universities—and therefore untrustworthy. To get the real scoop, you had to know the right people. But if you weren't part of the in-crowd—if you were, say, like me, a first-generation immigrants' kid with zero connections in the world of fancy American education— you had no reliable source for that information. So, to help people like me, *U.S. News & World Report* started ranking universities, to take that insider knowledge and make it public. And it partly succeeded at that task: Its ranking system makes law school stats fully accessible.

But that publicity has a cost. In condensing all the complex information into a single ranking system, *U.S. News* changed how people thought about and valued law schools. The rankings heavily weight a small handful of stats, including the incoming class's average GPA and LSAT scores, and they measure the employment rate of students at the nine-month postgraduation mark.

Obviously, these are thin measures that leave out important information. But law schools have come to devote themselves to moving up in those rankings, which means they have put those thin measures at their very core. Huge shares of university resources have been diverted away from genuine pedagogical activity and toward efforts designed only to game the rankings. For example, the rankings care about the school's rejection rate for applicants, because a higher rejection rate is presumably an indicator of elite status. So many law schools have started spending a lot of resources on encouraging unlikely applicants to apply, simply so they'll have more people to reject.

Espeland and Sauder point to another, subtler effect. Law schools used to have genuinely different missions, but the rankings have mostly gotten rid of that value plurality. They impose a single, monolithic value system over the whole culture. A law school that, say, cared about serving a historically underrepresented community faced a bind. Students from such communities typically had lower GPA and LSAT scores, which meant that continuing to aim for an outreach mission would plunge a law school down the rankings. And the rankings are so powerful—they influence so much funding and student choice—that most law schools have been forced to give up on their original missions and devote themselves to the rankings.

But we do not yet have a clear case of value capture. These effects might simply be the result of bad incentives. An incentive is just an offer of some desirable resource—like money or attention—that can be used to get what you really want. Incentives can provide some motivation, but they don't change your core values. They just change which crap you have to slog through to get the resources that let you do what you really want. But you still have a choice. Let's say you really value your family. Your job incentivizes you to work more hours with bonus pay. Sometimes you'll choose to work those extra hours to get money to support your family. But you can also choose sometimes to ignore those incentives and take more time at home with your family.

Value capture is the next step. It happens when you internalize a metric—when you let it set your core values. And if you do that, you'll stop making trade-offs between the metric and what you really value—because the metric will have redefined your core sense of what's important.

Espeland and Sauder give us a perfect example of value capture. They studied archived online conversations between prospective law students discussing which law school to go to. And the rankings, the authors say, completely changed how law students thought and what they valued.

Espeland and Sauder report that before the rankings, the decision about which law school to go to often triggered some real soul-searching. Students had to decide between institutions that embodied deeply different values. This pushed them to ask big questions about their own values—about what they wanted out of their own legal education and future career. Did they care about money? A shot at a prestigious clerkship with the Supreme Court? Or did they care more about become an activist, using their legal skills to help defend the downtrodden? The choice of law schools was a value crossroads, which triggered a process of deep deliberation—about what kind of life looked meaningful to them.

U.S. News & World Report changed all that. The moment those rankings came out, students stopped trying to figure out what mattered to them personally. The rankings offered what looked like a single, objective answer to what counts as "best." Most students just took it on board, and assumed that their goal was to get into the highest-ranked law school they could. The rankings suppressed the richness of various values and offered, instead, a singular, monolithic value system. Instead of going through the difficult process of developing their own values for themselves, the students now had an easier route: they could adopt a prefabricated value system.

In value capture, you're *outsourcing* your values. You're letting an external metric or ranking set what's important for you. You're outsourcing the process of figuring out your own sense of meaning.

But is outsourcing your values bad? We outsource bits of our mind all the time. I outsource my memory to my Google Docs file and my phone's calendar app. I outsource my purchasing decisions about appliances to online reviewers. I even outsource my attention and exploration to Google, which searches the world for me and tells me what to look at first. But it matters what I'm outsourcing—whether I'm outsourcing something minor, or a central pillar of my identity. It seems particularly dangerous to outsource the big, life-driving decisions about our education, our hobbies, our career, our health. Value capture seems most threatening when it intrudes into our core values. And notice: Whatever's wrong with value capture, it can't just be a problem with consent. Often, we knowingly and willingly submit to value capture. We decide to wear that Fitbit precisely because it will amp up our motivation and drive our decisions. We decide to stay on social media, knowing it's capturing our attention and values.

This is why the "outsourcing" metaphor seems so right to me. The problem with outsourcing is not that it's involuntary. We can choose to outsource. And sometimes outsourcing makes good sense. It's quick and efficient. It lets us engage the power of external specialists and the efficiencies of scale. The whole point of looking at other people's reviews of, say, emergency flashlights is that the issue is complicated and technical and I really don't care all that much. So I can let some hardcore tech geek who actually loves flashlights do all the research for me and tell me what's best.

The problem with outsourcing is also not just that your values are coming from the outside. We learn most of our values from external sources: our upbringing, our culture, art, and religion. But when you pick up your values from your family or your community, you're free to modify them and adjust them on the fly as you live your life. You can start with an external value and then tailor it to fit. But something very different happens when you're value-captured by an institutional metric: You're binding yourself to an inflexible external standard.

And there are whole realms of human life that institutional metrics cannot penetrate. Metrics are formulated to meet the demands of large-scale institutions: They are made to be usable by anybody, comprehensible by anybody, and consistently applicable by anybody. There are limitations on every institutional metric, bound up with their basic function. They tend to track what's *easy to measure* — simple externalities and obvious outcomes. And they tend to be *rigid*. The very nature of institutional metrics resists adjustment and tailoring. Institutional metrics are made to fit the needs of fast and efficient organization at scale, and not to fit your particular individual needs or the needs of your small-scale community.

Much of our sense of meaning and worth is peculiar, personal, and local. And metrics will always be deeply insensitive to such intimate, small-scale senses of meaning. Metrics are tuned to the needs of massive institutions. They are blunt and insensitive tools for sensing the meaningfulness of life. This is what we'll spend much of the rest of this book exploring: how metrics aim at large-scale comprehensibility—and how the price for that is intimacy, sensitivity, and context. Outsourcing always involves a trade-off. What we gain in efficiency, we lose in personalization.

With value capture, you're buying your values off the rack. They won't be tailored to you; they won't be made for your specific life and personality.

Let me be clear: I'm not saying that metrics are useless, or that they're always made for malicious purposes. Many metrics are created by good people, for perfectly sensible reasons. Metrics can make our progress clearer and more transparent; they can introduce accountability into formerly opaque systems. They can make us more objective and help us get rid of biases. Their simple clarity can help push us toward the big but easy-to-measure social goods: reducing poverty, decreasing CO_2 emissions, increasing vaccination rates. The weakness of metrics lies in pursuing subtler goods. The clarity that helps them do their job—coordinating very different people—is precisely what makes them insensitive to more delicate forms of meaning.

But this leads us back to our big question: What makes metrics and games hit so differently? Because playing games—and fluidly picking up new desires from the victory conditions—looks an awful lot like outsourcing. And if what we really want is well-fitting metrics, maybe we can just turn institutional metrics into a kind of game. Why not tweak them until they fit and give us the life we want?

I want to say: It's not that easy.

I'm not saying that games are always good and metrics are always bad. You can be value-captured by a game. Plenty of high school ath-

letes get value-captured by the sports they play. I spent years obsessed with grinding my way up for more poker wins, until I realized
the whole thing just made me miserable. And it's possible to be playful with institutional metrics, to find the ones that make your life
fun. But it's unlikely. The basic nature of games encourages—but
does not mandate—playful freedom. And the nature of bureaucracies and institutions resists—but does not make impossible—that
kind of playful control.

To understand why, we need to look much more carefully at what
scoring systems are, and what they do for us—and to us. Scoring systems lie at the heart of many games and bureaucracies. All these
scoring systems perform a very similar task. They offer points,
which get turned into a ranking. They say who did better and who
did worse. But they can have profoundly different effects: deep and
joyful play in some circumstances, and misery in others. To see why,
we need to understand the basic function of scoring systems, and
how that function gets put to different uses in different contexts.

CHAPTER 4

Scoring Systems
Create Convergence

Scoring systems feel so natural to us now, but you don't always need them. You can have games—and even competition—without scores. Think about a bunch of skaters at a skate park, all competing to do the best trick. "Do the best trick" is a goal, but a flexible and vaguely specified one. Different people can have different opinions about which trick was the best. And there are different ways a trick can be good: One trick can be more daring, another more athletically stunning. A trick can have steeze—the skate-culture term for stylish ease.

It's pretty hard to compare the beauty of somebody skating a chilled-out, elegant line to somebody doing an explosive, high-flying flip. But with casual, everyday skating, you don't need to compare them and produce a single verdict. We don't all have to agree. And I don't even need to settle on a single winner in my own head. I can think that Shannon did the most athletically impressive trick, but Liang had this beautiful chilled-out flow, and I don't have to try to decide which one was the best. The very idea that there is a single "best trick" is already importing a hidden set of assumptions: that there is a single value by which to judge all tricks, and a single correct way to apply that one value.

But I don't need any of that to have a good time at the skate park. I can just admire all the different forms of loveliness without having to force them into a single ranking. And even if I did happen to think there was one best trick, there's no reason why anybody else has to share my judgment. We can all go skateboarding and come away with different views. That's fine. It might even be better that way.

We're so used to modern competitions, which usually deliver an official list of winners. But the joy of competition doesn't always demand that we reach a settled agreement about who won.

I used to do a drunk improv cooking competition with my friends. A dozen guests would come over and bring random ingredients, and a couple of us would get modestly drunk and then compete to see who could make the best dishes out of the chaos. The whole process was a ludicrous, sloppy, cheerful mess. It was fun to improvise weird dishes while your friends mocked your culinary choices. It was fun being in the audience, tormenting drunk cooks as they made questionable decisions. We had out-of-nowhere creative hits, like a sauce of mustard powder and poppy seeds fried in coconut oil, poured over popcorn. We had gut-wrenching failures, like my horror of a baked white bean casserole with coconut milk, dotted, in a moment of extreme hubris, with jelly beans. (Somehow, as I was making it, I was sure that I was achieving the height of culinary genius. I was so wrong.) But the unexpected hits and spectacular failures were all part of the delight.

And the disagreement over them was part of the joy. Some dishes were so bizarre that people could barely parse them. Once, I tried to make sweet baked beans with chocolate chips added. Not only did people radically disagree on whether it was good, they radically dis-

agreed on what the hell it was. ("Wait, is this *dinner* . . . or *dessert?*")
One person thought it was an abomination; another said it was their
new favorite comfort food. We loved the process, we loved the products, and we loved the arguing. And none of that depended on our
arriving at some singular, settled verdict.

But sometimes, we need to settle the winner publicly and decisively. Maybe only one person can go on to the skateboarding national competition from our region, or only one person can get the
jazz scholarship. Maybe there's a hundred-thousand-dollar cash prize
for the winner of the cooking competition, and fifteen thousand for
second place. In that case, we need an official verdict.

This is what a scoring system does. When we agree to use a scoring system, we are all agreeing to adopt the same clear process for
evaluation. That scoring system will deliver a single judgment, which
we have agreed to abide by. Scoring systems create agreement about
who won.

Let me offer a definition:

> A **scoring system** is a social process that delivers a *quantified*
> *evaluation*, and so enters a *singular verdict* into some *official*
> *record*.

A score is a quantified evaluation. It presents numbers to us not
as a report of neutral data, but as a sign of progress toward a goal.
And a scoring system makes it official. Not everybody needs to personally agree with the scoring system's verdict, but everybody usually agrees with the fact that it is, in fact, the official verdict. Think
about when you have judges who score some kind of artistic performance, like the artistry scores in Olympic figure skating. Competitors and audience members might easily disagree whether the judges
actually picked the most beautiful performance. But if we followed

the procedure properly, everybody will agree about who the official judges are, what points they gave, and what the official final scores were. With a scoring system, we may not agree about who deserved to win, but we will agree about who, in fact, won.

If you need it, here's a portable version: *Scoring systems engineer a convergence of judgments.*

But, you might ask, what's the big deal? A score is just what you get when you add up the points and find out who wins, right? But this hides the real action. Adding up the points is the easy part. By then, all the real work has already happened in the background. The hard part, the interesting part, is how we got the points in the first place— how we translate our achievements into clear numbers that can be easily added up.

Convergence doesn't appear magically. It requires that we seriously muck around with what we're evaluating. When skateboarding went professional—when it got sucked into the ESPN X Games and got connected up to big tournaments and big prizes—it started to change focus. Skateboarding in the tournament environment became less about flow, grace, and steeze, and emphasized the kind of achievements that are more obvious and countable: how high you can get and how many midair spins you can do. Importantly, competent judges may disagree deeply about which trick was the loveliest or most original. But judges with basic competence will all agree about how many flips you did. Height and number of flips are easier to *count publicly and together.* This is why we can all agree that Tony Hawk was the first person to land a 900—a two-and-a-half revolution midair spin—but there is no record holder for the cleanest kickflip.

I can count all kinds of things if I'm doing it on my own. I can count the number of truly great American poets in the twentieth century. I can count the number of good, authentic Chinese restaurants there are in Salt Lake City. I can count how many dependable people there are in my workplace. But not everybody will agree with my counts.

Public counting is a completely different beast. What we're counting has to be sufficiently obvious, so that very different people can follow the same procedure and come to the same result. This is objectivity, for a very specific sense of *objective*. Judging the originality or grace of a skateboard trick requires some skill, and not all judges will agree. But the height of a jump is different. There is no need for sensitivity or special insight to count height; it's a judgment that everybody can make. It's a *mechanical* score.

But notice what happened. We didn't keep to the same goal—cool, awesome tricks—and invent some incredibly profound better way of measuring coolness and awesomeness objectively. We changed the topic. We focused our judgments on something that was easier for us all to evaluate in the same way.

Mechanical scoring systems offer us a trade-off. We get automatic agreement by using a mechanical evaluation procedure, but there is a price to be paid for that automatic convergence. Mechanical scoring systems will tend to ignore things that are hard and subtle to count. They will tend to change what we score—and what we care about—to what is easy to count mechanically.

It's pretty hard for me to communicate my feelings of what makes a graceful skateboard trick, but it's easy to communicate a method for measuring the height of a skateboard jump. Scoring systems are, then, a way of clearly *writing down* goals and values, and specifying a *procedure* for evaluating our attempts at those goals.

Scoring systems are recipes for evaluation.

THE FOOD WRITER JOHN THORNE ONCE SAID THAT THE DIFFER-
ence between a *recipe* and a *dish* is that a dish is a live thing, an idea

of balance that's in a creative cook's head. A dish has to be remade anew each time, in response to changing ingredients and changing circumstances. But a recipe, he said, is a dead thing, a writing down of how a creative cook made something once.

This can encourage, in some people, a particular mindset: of just following the recipe exactly as written. The problem with strict and unyielding obedience to the recipe is that you're stuck on a dead thing. You don't explore. You won't respond and adapt to the particular details of the now—how this particular tomato tastes today, how this batch of garlic smells as it sizzles. You're stuck repeating how somebody made something once. You don't make the transition from the strict rules to the live idea of balance.

And it's easy, once you're an experienced cook, to disdain these crisp, standardized recipes as training wheels—which can limit your growth into a fully creative, fully free cook. But clear rules are also incredibly useful. The value of *mechanical recipes* lies precisely in their accessibility. They offer guidance for inexperienced people who don't have ready access to some wise and willing teacher.

Let's think about modern recipes—the kind that tell you exactly how many cups of flour to add, how long to bake it, and at what temperature. These are mechanical recipes. You can follow them unthinkingly. They tell you exactly what to do; you don't need to make any difficult judgment calls.

There are two mistakes you can make with mechanical recipes. The first is never using recipes at all. Recipes will help you expand into new cuisines, find your way to new dishes. There is a dish I love with all my heart: Georgian chicken, grilled with tarragon and then topped with this absurdly delicious sauce of raw garlic, walnuts, cilantro, and chilies all blended together. I had never tasted this dish before I made it. I could never have imagined, on my own, the way the sharp garlic and the smooth walnuts and the spike of the chilies would blend into this rich, warm sharpness beneath the toasty chicken. All I had was a recipe in a book. But I could make a delicious version of it, because somebody had written it down precisely enough that a Vietnamese American kid from California could make it.

The second mistake is total obedience to the recipe. Some people get stuck on a recipe. They will cook it for the hundredth time and still measure each ingredient precisely as instructed. A recipe is only *one* way to cook something; if you cook it the same way every time, you won't see what the variables are, and what happens when you make different choices. You won't *understand* the dish.

One of the first dishes I ever really understood was fried eggs over spaghetti, from Naples. It's quite an elegant recipe. In your pot, you boil some spaghetti. Meanwhile, in your pan, you heat up some olive oil with a couple of crushed cloves of garlic until the garlic infuses the oil. Then you fry the eggs in the olive oil for a bit, aiming to just barely set the whites while leaving the yolks still runny. Then you quickly break up the eggs in the pan and toss them with the spaghetti.

If you follow the recipe exactly, you get this lovely result. The runny yolks coat the spaghetti and form a soft, velvety sauce, and the egg whites turn into a bouncy, fluffy coating. It's gorgeous. And for a few years, I made it exactly by the recipe, and it came out delicious every time—but always in the same way.

The first time I changed things was an accident. I was lazy and hungry and couldn't be bothered to open the cookbook, and so I did it from memory, and I messed up some of the details. What I discovered was that there isn't just one right way to do it. There's a space I could explore, a set of choices I could make, that would let me push the dish in different directions. There were limits, which I discovered. Tripling the amount of garlic obliterates the balance of the dish. But I also discovered how much flex there was, how much freedom I had to tweak that balance. I could cook the eggs faster, which makes them crispier. I could cook them longer and get, instead of a silky sauce, a more crumbly, delightfully nubbly coating. I could double up the garlic and then get this aggressive, head-clearing wallop. Or I could put in almost no garlic, undercook the eggs a tad, and get this soft, soothing, warm custardy version.

If you cook it in enough different ways, you'll start to understand the dish—not as an exact procedure, but as a whole fluid decision space. But if you follow the recipe precisely every time, you won't explore; you won't come to see how much freedom you have. You won't learn how to adapt the recipe to different ingredients or to adjust it to fit your particular cravings for the day.

John Thorne knows these two problems well. This is why, in his food writing, he rails against obsession with precise recipes and praises the flexible, open-ended dish. But he also includes plenty of recipes in his books—because he knows that the dish is what really matters, but also that you can't write it down. So he gives you a recipe and simultaneously reminds you that it's only a starting point.

Thorne's writing reminds me of that old Zen saying: When you see a finger pointing at the moon, look at the moon—not the finger. Recipes are the finger, pointing the way to the moon. You shouldn't obsess over the finger. But you also need that finger, or you'll never find the moon—or that grilled Georgian chicken with garlic-walnut-cilantro sauce.

Scoring systems are recipes for values. They make the process of evaluation accessible. A game designer can write down how you score in a game, and somebody can read the rules and get it. Scoring systems also make the process of evaluation more rigid and less responsive to the weird particularities of the situation. When you're locked into a preset, mechanical scoring system, you won't adapt how you evaluate things in response to what's in front of you.

This is the central puzzle of this book. We have these clear, mechanical scoring systems—but they can do such different things for us. In games, these scoring systems often give us joy. They let us play, they encourage us to be fluid—to fool around with alternate selves and newfound joys. In games, scoring systems help us to find striving play in whichever form we prefer. But in bureaucracies and large-scale institutions, scoring systems seem to mostly just suck the life out of everything. They seduce us into accepting clarified, simplified values—and forgetting what we actually care about.

Why do scoring systems hit so differently?

From here, the road diverges. One path will go through play. We will need to understand how scoring systems support true play, and how they can help us to be more free. The puzzle here is why games need scoring systems at all. Why do we use explicit rules and strictly specified goals in order to play?

The other road will go through bureaucracy, metrics, and public life. We will need to understand the vital role that metrics perform in helping us coordinate—and the price we have to pay for that coordination. Scoring systems need to be rigid, inflexible, and authoritative in order to perform their bureaucratic function. Because from another angle, it is the painfulness of public metrics that can seem strange. After all, we use scoring systems all the time to have fun in games. Why can't we simply jigger our inner vision and treat the scoring systems in our schools, workplaces, and governments as games? Why not just gamify our work, our education, and everything else, and make them just as flexible and playful? What is it about metrics that seems to resist true play?

PART 2

WHAT SCORES DO

CHAPTER 5

The Art of Agency

W hat functions do scoring systems serve in games?
Say we've just gotten a new board game for Christmas.
We know nothing about it yet. We open it up and dump
all the pieces in a jumble—some are yellow, some are green, some are
red, some are shaped like little barnyard animals. Then we read
the rules, and the game tells us that the yellow pieces are worth one
point each, the little wooden cows are worth twenty points, and the
red pieces are worth minus-five points.

Freeze-frame on this exact moment. It is a moment so familiar
that we can miss its utter weirdness. Because when we read the rules
of the game, we discover what we are going to *desire* in the game. The
scoring system sets our in-game motivations with precision. It tells
us exactly what we need to do—what will count as success. One game
tells us to collect little wooden sheep; another game tells us to make
more money; another tells us to take over the world. And many of us
can just throw ourselves into the game, to acquire an intense desire
for whatever we're told to desire. I can get so into it that my armpits

sweat and my heart races at the prospect of getting a couple more wooden cows. And then the game ends; we throw all those pieces into a pile and scoop it back into the box, because they don't matter anymore.

Games set our desires. But why would we ever want to let them? Why do we let external systems, designed by other people, muck around with our psychologies? To answer that question, we need to get a better grip on the essential nature of games. And I mean "game" really broadly here. Fly-fishing, rock climbing, *Portal*, *The Mind*, basketball, *The Legend of Zelda*, *Starcraft II*, chess—these are all games to me. We need to understand the crucial role of designed, artificial goals in creating the structured play of games.

The best philosophical account of games I know of is in Bernard Suits's book *The Grasshopper: Games, Life and Utopia*—a hidden treasure of philosophy about what games are and why we play them. In it, Suits gives us a definition of games. Here is what he calls the "portable version" of the definition:

> To play a game is to voluntarily take on unnecessary obstacles to make possible the activity of struggling to overcome them.

In games, you're always trying to succeed in some way—to hit some specified goal. You're trying to cross the finish line, collect sheep, kill more zombies, catch more fish, or last longer at *Tetris*. But here's Suits's key insight: When you're playing a game, you're not trying to achieve that goal in the most efficient way possible. Recreational anglers don't just care about catching fish. If all they wanted was to have some fish, they'd use the most efficient method: a net, or maybe dynamite. Commercial fishermen use nets because that's the most efficient method to quickly extract fish. But it's not particularly fun. So recreational anglers use a very inefficient but enjoyable method: They try to catch a fish specifically by tricking it into biting a hook. You can't just net it; you have to *fool* it.

A game sets two artificialities. It declares a goal for you to pursue. And then it sets extra, unnecessary constraints in your path to that goal. So why would we possibly want to do that? The answer, says Suits, is that together these goals and constraints shape a new kind of activity. So what we care about in games is not the outcome by itself. We care about achieving that outcome by a certain inefficient path. In games, he says, we care about *going the long way*. We care about getting to the goal in a particular way, using a particular method.

If we cared only about the goal by itself—plain and disconnected from constraints—we'd just take the most efficient path. If all we cared about was getting the ball through the basketball hoop, we'd use a stepladder. But we don't, because the goal of making baskets has no value separate from the constraints. Making baskets is valuable only if we're doing it under certain restrictions—no ropes, no ladders, no trampolines. These restrictions force us to use a particular method: dribbling and jumping and throwing the ball. So the method—jumping and throwing—must be an essential part of the value of making baskets.

Another way to put it, for Suits, is that the goal in the game is *partially constituted by the constraints*. It doesn't even count as achieving the goal if you don't do it following the rules. Let's say you're running a marathon. The goal is to cross the finish line. Technically, the finish line is at the entrance to Central Park. But crossing it isn't just getting to that point in space. Otherwise you'd use a bike or call an Uber. But if you used a bike or an Uber, you wouldn't be running a marathon, and you wouldn't have crossed the finish line. To cross the finish line is to get to that spot while obeying a particular set of constraints. Game goals are social constructs; following the rules is an essential part of their being.

In games, *the value of the outcome is inseparable from the value of the process.*

SUITS GIVES A DEFINITION OF GAMES, BUT HE ALSO GIVES US A whole vision of what games are for—and why we would ever choose to submit ourselves to unnecessary constraints and external goals. Games create new kinds of action for you to savor.

Games sculpt action with incredible precision. Human beings are tool users, but the rules of rock climbing force us out of our technological heads. These rules drive you into your body, tell you to forget about using ladders and ropes. Instead, you discover how much you can accomplish just by becoming ever more precise with your foot placements, by being subtler with your balance and core tension.

Non-climbers will often find these rules arbitrary. Why not just pull yourself up with the rope? It'll make it so much easier! The answer is that you could haul yourself up with a rope, but then you'd be playing a different game. In fact, there's an older style of climbing that lets you do exactly that. It's called aid climbing, and it has very different rules. You're allowed to stick gear into the walls and cracks and then dangle various platforms and rope ladders from it, and you climb your way up on all that gear. The most common form of climbing in the modern era is free climbing, in which you don't touch the rope to go up, using only your hands and feet on the rock. (Free climbing is commonly confused with free solo climbing, which is the much more dangerous business of using no safety ropes at all. In free climbing, you have a rope, but it's only for safety, to catch you in case you fall.)

Free climbing mostly displaced aid climbing because the increased limitations create, for most climbers, a much more interesting form of activity. Aid climbing involves fairly repetitive movement. Because you're allowed to use rope ladders, you end up mostly ignoring the rock face and just climbing the ladder. The game of aid climbing is mostly about studying the rock to find places to insert the gear. Once you've stuck your rope ladder in the wall, going up is relatively straightforward.

Free climbing, on the other hand, orders you not to use the rope to ascend. This forces you to study and use the tiny features of the rock itself, which makes every different piece of rock its own special challenge. The climb might force you to invent some new technique for jamming your toe in, to find some new way of shimmying your hips and delicately balancing over to get that next hold. Free climbing forces you to tune into subtle variations in the rock and then come up with a new set of moves, carefully adapted to the particular and specific features of the rock in front of you.

This is what the activity of rock climbing is made of. We set a *goal* of ascending rock, combined with a *limitation* on using gear to do so. We forbid, in fact, the tools that would let you ignore the details of the rock, that would reduce different rock faces to more similar problems. The rules force you to confront the differences in rock. Together, that goal and those limitations create an activity of subtle attention and creative movement in response to the infinite varieties of rock.

To outsiders, the rules of climbing might seem pretty arbitrary. The rules of free climbing forbid the use of ropes and spikes to advance, but they do permit the use of modern climbing shoes. High-end climbing shoes are like ballet-slipper corsets for your feet. They force-squeeze your feet into an arched, downturn shape, turning them into sharpened claws. And they're covered in sticky rubber, optimized to cling to little bits of rock. This can seem, to a skeptical outsider, incoherent. Why allow some kinds of technology, like high-tech climbing shoes, but not others, like rope ladders that you can stick into the rock? If you're allowed fancy climbing shoes, which make climbing easier, why not rope ladders or grappling hooks? Where's the logical consistency?

With striving play, we pick the goals and restrictions of games in order to engineer a particular quality of action. If you're allowed to use a grappling hook, it decreases the variety of motion you need to use to climb. But fancy climbing shoes, coated with sticky rubber, actually increase the variety of possible movements. They let you hook more tightly into tiny dimples of rock. This makes some climbs easier, but it also opens up whole new kinds of climbs, on terrain that was formerly impossible—steeper climbs, on heavily overhung cliffs and even cave roofs. And this introduces a whole new realm of cool-ass movement in overhanging terrain, where you cling like a bat to a roof, doing all kinds of clever foot jams and gymnastic twists and flips.

The thing about modern climbing shoes is they don't just make the activity of climbing easier and therefore less interesting. They are a technological improvement that expand the possibility space, letting you climb new kinds of terrain. Modern, high-tech climbing shoes, though they make any particular climb easier, also open up whole new vistas of interesting climbing.

So why do we permit high-tech climbing shoes but not grappling hooks? The answer is that game design is not a matter of pure logic, but an art. It is about experimenting with the medium, trying out different things and seeing the result. Painters use brushstrokes, color, and shading; poets use words, rhythm, and images. And the game designer, as part of their art, uses rules, scorings systems, and constraints, adding and subtracting and tweaking until they get the feel they want out of the game.

Some people praise games that tell stories, that have good graphics or good dialogue. They praise games that are like movies—I think because movies are a more established and familiar form of art. But that's selling games short. The game designer isn't just telling stories or creating worlds. They can certainly do those things, but they're also doing something more, something unique. The game designer creates *new selves* for us to inhabit. They create an *action skeleton*—with a specified set of motivations and abilities—and then turn that engineered self loose in an engineered world. Game designers shape a new self for us, and when we play their games, we slip into that designed alternate self, and we experience new kinds of action.

Games are an art form that work in the medium of *agency itself*. Games are the art of agency. And scoring systems are the engines that drive that alternate, designed agency.

CHAPTER 6

Transparency Is Surveillance

What functions do scoring systems serve in public life? The full answer will turn out to be incredibly complicated. So let's start with a simpler case study in one particular kind of scoring system: *public transparency metrics*. Public transparency metrics are designed to reduce corruption and bias and increase accountability, by making the secretive workings of experts visible to the wider public. Transparency metrics will show us the costs and benefits of measurement processes designed for extreme accessibility.

Some kinds of transparency aren't so public. Some are designed so that experts can monitor other experts—as in scientific transparency, which involves one set of scientists making their data and calculations available for other experts to check. Public transparency metrics, on the other hand, are designed to be comprehensible to nonexperts—the larger public, or their legislative representatives.

Public transparency usually works by evaluating some group of experts and measuring their success in easily comprehensible terms.

In other words, these metrics are scoring systems, designed to render a public verdict about some experts' efforts. Most important, transparency metrics report some quality that we, the general public, can easily understand. When my state legislature demands that my philosophy department justify its existence in terms of a transparent metric, we can't just explain how we help students become more curious and reflective. Those judgments are complex and opaque; it takes expertise to make them and to check each other's work. If we justified ourselves in terms like that, we would be asking the world to trust our judgment. Transparency metrics work to avoid that opacity. They offer justification in publicly accessible terms, like graduation rates, graduation speed, or student satisfaction surveys.

Transparency metrics do genuinely good work. They are powerful tools for exposing corruption and fighting some kinds of social bias, like racial or gender bias. They block nepotism and subconscious favoritism. But they also have a cost, which arises directly from their core function of accessibility. Transparency undermines expertise.

FOR YEARS, WHENEVER I DID ANY CHARITABLE GIVING, I USED Charity Navigator, a watchdog organization that checks up on nonprofit organizations. Charity Navigator promised to give us a look inside the big charitable organizations, to rate them on their efficiency—to expose lazy, wasteful charities and reward efficient ones. Its primary output, for the public, was a single ranked list of charities, scored by efficiency and effectiveness. This is a public transparency metric, and a scoring system.

Charity Navigator's efficiency rating initially depended primarily on one metric: the "overhead ratio" for a charity. The overhead ratio is determined by looking at how much a nonprofit spends externally, doing good for the world, versus how much is lost to internal costs. This is supposed to sort efficient charities from wasteful ones. It looks good, it sounds good, and I myself used it for years to direct my charitable giving. I even used it in my introductory ethics classes. I had my students read arguments about whether there was some obligation to give money to charity. As a grand finale for the unit, I'd take donations from the class, I'd match their donations, and then we would discuss the most effective use for that money. I always had us look at Charity Navigator's efficiency ratings, and then we'd vote. The students inevitably picked a charity from near the top of the rankings. And then I'd give all our money away, right there in class. It was a satisfyingly dramatic moment.

But it turns out that the overhead ratio is a terrible metric. It targets internal costs—the amount a nonprofit spends on administrative costs, like paying its employees. It presumes that nonprofits do more good when they spend money externally, on things like digging wells, building houses, or buying food for tsunami victims. It presumes that internal costs are a form of waste. The metric paints a picture for us: Nonprofits are a pipeline for money. Good nonprofits pass money through as efficiently as possible; anything that gets stuck in the pipeline is a waste. The metric paints this picture by taking a neutral, simple, mechanical fact—the overhead ratio—and then using it as the *measure of success.*

This picture makes quick sense to outsiders, but it is vastly oversimplified. Imagine you run a nonprofit devoted to building shelters for unhoused people. Spending money on building shelters boosts your efficiency rating. According to the metric, this is good; this counts as success. But spending more money on paying your employees counts as overhead and drops your efficiency rating. According to the metric, this is failure. Now you have a problem. Suppose you want to hire a structural engineer or a materials expert to research which shelter materials will last the longest. This counts as internal costs, and the metric views them as wasteful. So how can you compete for skilled and expert employees to research better shelters if your rating plunges whenever you spend money on hiring them?

To people in the nonprofit sector, the overhead ratio metric is obviously broken. If you want to run a genuinely effective nonprofit, you actually have to spend money on things like office space and competitive salaries. The metric looks good to outsiders, but only because outsiders know very little about the space. Here is the Gap again, between the complexity of genuine effectiveness and the easier-to-measure quality of pipeline efficiency.

The problem is that nonprofits are trying to do good in complicated ways, like protecting ecosystems, building sustainable housing, or improving health care. Whether they have succeeded is actually a difficult matter. To evaluate it properly, you need to be buried in the particular domain of the nonprofit. Proper evaluation requires trusting other actual experts in the relevant field—housing, sanitation, education—along with experts in the particular geographical area.

Charity Navigator oversees charities in all kinds of different expert domains. The company itself doesn't have the expertise to assess whether a particular nonprofit succeeded in building better shelters for people. So they use a simple, easy-to-apply proxy: the overhead ratio. You don't have to know anything about the complexities of housing to apply the overhead ratio. It's appealing because all you need to do is look at a nonprofit's accounting—and accounting works similarly across all charities. We can mechanically measure pipeline throughput, which permits us to compare charities that are working in very different terrains. But it works by ignoring their differences.

The overhead ratio is exciting because it takes aim at an accessible juncture point— exactly the place where radically different charities end up using the most similar plumbing, which makes it easy to produce an objective-looking comparison. But it doesn't capture what the nonprofits are actually doing. What the overhead ratio has going for it is not accuracy, but extractability.

Maybe we should give up on the overhead ratio and try something better, like the number of houses built. Once again, that's a simple, easily counted number, but it doesn't capture any of the nuances. Were they good houses? Will they last long? Were they houses that actually served the needs of the people involved and fit the local environmental demands? Were they delivered to the people who needed them? Were they built where they would make the most impact— or just where it was easiest to build a lot of cheap houses and make your "houses built" stat look bigger?

You may be familiar with the Dunning-Kruger effect, which states that people with limited skill and expertise in a domain tend to overestimate their abilities. If you're stupid about a domain, it's easy to miss how stupid you are, because you don't know how much you don't know. Transparency metrics expose us to the Dunning-Kruger effect in fancy institutional dress. Many transparency metrics look good to us outsiders, but only because we have a shallow understanding of the terrain.

This particular story ends on a possibly upbeat note. Several major donor organizations eventually saw the problem with the overhead ratio. After significant study, they concluded that the pervasive use of this metric was forcing nonprofits to cut costs so dramatically that they couldn't function effectively. Charity Navigator has listened to pushback from experts in the nonprofit sector and moved to decrease the centrality of the overhead metric in its rating systems, though it's still controversial whether the company has done enough.

Here's another case study, from Sally Engle Merry. Merry was an anthropologist who specialized in human rights. She studied the US Department of State's attempts to rate how well different countries were doing in reducing sex trafficking in its annual *Trafficking in Persons Report*. During the time of Merry's study, the *TIP Report*'s rating was based on the conviction rate of sex traffickers. To most of the world, this is an extremely convincing metric, and world governments have been highly motivated to improve their *TIP* ratings.

But, says Merry, if you actually understand the complexities of sex trafficking, you'll see that this is a vastly oversimplified metric. The problem, she says, is that actual sex trafficking is incredibly hard for governments to track. It occurs in the shadows, far away from government surveillance. And what counts as sex trafficking turns out to be incredibly slippery. For example, says Merry, how do you define "sex trafficker"? Consider a woman facing starvation, who crosses an international border to work in a brothel in order to survive. She does well enough and makes enough money to bring back a little for her family. The next year, she brings a starving friend across that border to work with her at the brothel. Is the first woman now an international sex trafficker?

Faced with such invisibility and vagueness, the *TIP Report* focused on something far easier for governments to track: convictions of sex traffickers. Convictions are binary instead of vague, and they happen right in the government's sight. The problem with this metric, says Merry, is that it suggests an extremely narrow approach to sex trafficking. It focuses on policing as the only viable method.

But conviction rates are a very poor indicator of sex trafficking, according to Merry. Sex trafficking is highly correlated with overall poverty. If you decrease poverty, then sex trafficking tends to vanish on its own. But then there won't be any sex traffickers to catch and convict—they'll evaporate without coercion as the economic incentives shift. So if a country reduced its ambient poverty and as a result reduced sex trafficking, the *TIP Report*'s metrics would report that it had *failed*—because the conviction numbers had dropped.

The metric doesn't actually encourage countries to find a long-term solution to sex trafficking. Instead, it incentivizes countries to *keep sex trafficking around* so that there will be plenty of traffickers to convict. Here is the Gap again: Convictions are exactly the kind of clear, crisp objects that are easy to count publicly. They just don't correspond to what really matters.

You might think this was just because the overhead metric and the conviction rate metric are particularly crappy, and we can just make better ones. But the problem is much deeper than that. It's baked into the core logic of public transparency. The goal of public transparency is for the public to judge the success of some group of experts. To serve that function, *the metric has to be comprehensible by the public*. But the public, as a whole, can't understand expert reasoning. The whole point of experts is that they understand things the rest of us cannot.

We need experts precisely because we need to go beyond the average, minimal, baseline understanding. But the whole point of transparency is to bring experts within the reach of our average minimal, baseline understanding.

THE PHILOSOPHER ONORA O'NEILL STUDIED TRUST IN INSTITUTIONS— especially in medical experts. People, she said, think that trust and transparency go together. But in fact, they're deeply in tension. Transparency, she said, demands that experts explain themselves to nonexperts. But they can't actually do it, because an expert's real reasons are often opaque or incomprehensible to nonexperts. The whole reason you go to a doctor is that they understand things you don't.

Nobody has enough mental power to understand everything by themselves. The world is so vast and complicated that we have to divide it up—each of us devoting ourselves to understanding one particular patch of the world. So experts can't explain themselves fully to the public, because expert reasoning is, by its very nature, specialized.

O'Neill thought transparency forced experts to make up fake reasons for public consumption. This meant that transparency would force experts to deceive the public about what they did and why, and so undermine trust. I agree, but I'm also worried about an even worse effect: Transparency can also force experts to actually change what they do—to confine their actions to what they can justify in public. Transparency can significantly undermine expert action.

Of course, there are transparency measures that are based on expert understanding. The difficulty scale in rock climbing, for example, is built on the consensus of experienced rock climbers. But there's no way for outsiders to check on whether rock climbers are doing it right. In fact, when non-climbers assess the difficulty of climbs, they tend to get it completely wrong. Non-climbers are very impressed with fast climbing and big leaping movements between large holds, which are often relatively easy for experienced climbers. Non-climbers tend to radically underestimate the difficulty of painstakingly slow climbing on microscopic holds.

This doesn't matter much for climbing, but it matters massively for things like medicine, education, and government. Much of the time, we use transparency metrics because we are trying to figure out whether to trust a *whole community*. When I'm doing educational outcomes assessment for my philosophy department, I am reporting evidence of our success for a set of suspicious overseers. I have to do this because the public at large—as embodied, in this case, by the Utah state legislature—doesn't know whether to trust philosophers. A lot of people seem to think the whole enterprise of philosophy is just pure bullshit. So they want evidence that we philosophers are doing something useful. And they are unwilling to trust our opaque judgment. This is why educational outcomes metrics tend to focus on easy countables, like graduation rate, graduation speed, and employment rate. These measures require no trust because counting them requires no expertise, so it's easy for outsiders to check the work.

We can see the same de-experting logic at work in the history of arts funding. According to sociologist Jennifer Lena, American art funding institutions, like the National Endowment for the Arts, initially used specialists to decide which artists got the grants. They trusted artists, art critics, and people from the relevant art community to make the choice. But when the NEA was put under congressional oversight, congresspeople accused the organization of making bad, corrupt, and biased choices about where to send funds. Their evidence of corruption was that the NEA had funded performances that ended up with bad box office returns and ticket sales—proof, in the congresspeople's eyes, that the supposed experts didn't know what they were talking about.

The problem is that what makes art good isn't box office returns and ticket sales. Great art can bring incredible experiences of profound beauty, can move people to see the world in different ways. It can expand their emotional horizons and shake up their understanding of the world—all of which often translates to poor ticket sales. Box office returns only look like a good measure of art if you don't know much about art. But box office returns had more political power precisely because they are a metric that could be understood by nonexperts.

We're exposed here again to the Gap. And the Gap arises because of the profound distance between what is publicly accessible and what requires expert sensitivity and trained judgment to discern. And when experts are bound by public metrics, they are cut off from a crucial part of their expertise. The demand for public transparency intrudes on the process of goal setting. It forces experts to use goals that are comprehensible to the public. This prevents them from using their experience and expertise to set goals and targets. Their actions and choices will ultimately be driven instead by what the rushed, hurried public thinks is important.

The Gap can intrude through external pressure on experts, or incentives. If experts in an institution know they will be rewarded for doing well on the metric and punished for doing badly, then they'll be forced to take actions that advance that metric. Instead of using their own understanding of what's important, they'll be pushed to act on the public's understanding of what's important—at least when their actions are visible. But it will be even worse if the experts are value-captured by the transparency metric—if they start wholly substituting the metric's simple target for their own richer understanding of what's important. In that case, the expert will internalize the public's limited understanding in the core of all their decision-making.

To be absolutely clear: My claim isn't that there's some magical group of "real" experts who should rule everything, and then the dumb masses. The point is that the world is vast and complex, and there's too much to know about for any individual to handle. Each of us is an expert in our own patch, but a nonexpert in everything else. And I don't just mean formal expertise, like having a medical degree or a scientific PhD. We are all experts in the particular terrain of our lives: our jobs, our family, our local community, our weird hobbies. I'm an expert in a few parts of philosophy, the European board games of the 1980s and '90s, the politics of my university, and the history and culture of Vietnamese immigrants who grew up in San Jose. And about almost everything else, I'm a novice.

Collectively, as a public, we're inexpert about everything. And public transparency metrics puts us—the collective inexpert public—in charge.

MANY OF US HAVE BEEN TRAINED TO THINK TRANSPARENCY IS all good, and the more the better. But we are also intimately familiar with the downsides of transparency. It's easy to see the insensitivity and inexpertise of metrics when you're under the gun. When you're the expert and it's the rest of the world looking in—watching you, demanding that you justify yourself in clear, accessible, concrete terms—then you can see how much the metrics miss.

Crucially, public metrics get rid of intuition or gut instinct—the wordless certainty about the right thing to do. They force us to justify ourselves in the cold light of general comprehensibility. They kill opacity. This is often a very good thing; intuition is highly imperfect. Decades of empirical research have shown how our intuition can display enormous subconscious bias. Evaluations in hiring professional competence, for example, are highly subject to irrelevant influences from factors like race, gender, class, and regional accents. Transparency metrics are intended to remove such bias—and often succeed—by forcing us not to use our gut instinct.

But our opaque intuitions aren't always bad. Decades of empirical research have also shown that genuine expertise often works through fast, accurate intuition. Experienced pediatricians can walk into a waiting room and see, with extremely high accuracy, which kids are seriously ailing—which kids need emergency help, fast. Becoming an expert involves acquiring a huge store of experience and then having your subconscious produce a quick synthesis: a wordless intuition about the right thing to do, an immediate perception, in the case of pediatricians, of who's sick and who's healthy.

The problem is that our intuition isn't all good or all bad. Opaque intuition is where bias lives, but also where expertise and sensitivity thrive. By forcing experts to justify themselves in the harsh light of public scrutiny, metrics cut out both. They prevent corruption and bias—and they also prevent experts from using their sensitivity and trained instincts. Metrics cleanse our judgment process intrusively and indiscriminately. They are moral bleach.

Transparency is effective but costly. And that cost is essentially entangled with its effect. We need experts to act beyond what we can understand. But we cannot trust them perfectly, so we ask them to explain themselves to us. And that places a restriction on experts—to bind themselves to the actions and reasons that can be understood by the general public.

Transparency is surveillance. It puts people under the watchful eye of a suspicious public. And surveillance is a profoundly mixed blessing. It's costly, because it forces experts to be constantly worrying about how their actions will be interpreted—and misinterpreted—by outsiders who don't share their expertise. So surveillance is useful when it's deployed against the corrupt, the biased, or the incompetent. But it's limiting when it's deployed against the expert, the highly competent, and the extremely sensitive. The problem is that we don't know which is which ahead of time—which is the whole reason we needed surveillance in the first place.

By tying everybody to the demand for public justification, we do two things. We limit the harm that bad and incompetent people can do, but we also limit what good and competent people can do. Transparency leashes both kinds of people, forcing them all to operate within the public's comprehension. These two effects are inextricable, because transparency works precisely by eliminating trust and replacing it with public oversight.

TRANSPARENCY IS PARTICULARLY PAINFUL WHEN IT UNDERMINES expert judgment about values. And transparency metrics are usually, at their core, about values. Metrics are supposed to be sitting in judgment over whether some group has succeeded. To do that, they specify success in terms everybody can understand.

We often assume that expertise is just technical—the little picky stuff about how you do what you're trying to do. Experts are just there to run the machinery—but the goals and values guiding it all are always obvious and accessible to everybody. But this is a mistake. Expertise also involves seeing more deeply into what our true goals should be—grasping the subtle values of the terrain. The beginner martial artist may think the purpose of learning martial arts is to become a fighting badass; most serious martial artists will tell you that the value is in generating self-discipline and cultivating bodily awareness. My spouse started gardening because she thought she could get us some delicious vegetables, but she slowly discovered that gardening could give so much more. It immersed her in the beauty of growth, the joy of seeing plants thrive. It gave her the profound satisfaction of seeing the throbbing, interacting, tangled ecosystem hiding in our own backyard.

The value of activities is often quite subtle. It takes time, devotion, experience, and energy to see. The philosopher Talbot Brewer puts it this way: When you start a new activity, you often have a very naive grasp of what's valuable about it. And then you start in on it, guided by your oversimplified sense of what's important—but in doing so, you come to a richer and deeper sense of the value of the activity. That richer sense of value changes and deepens how you do the thing, which in turns deepens your understanding of its value, which feeds back and enriches how you do the thing, on and on in an ever-deepening cycle.

When I started trying to exercise, I had only the barest conception of what it could do for me. I thought the goal was to burn some calories by pounding out miles on a treadmill. Maybe it would decrease my chance of heart disease or something. I didn't realize how much else I would find in it. I couldn't have imagined that I could come to find profound joy in feeling my own body moving—that I would find delicious clarity in developing greater physical control. Before I started rock climbing and yoga, I didn't have enough bodily awareness to even imagine the pleasure and joy it could bring.

The problem with public transparency metrics is that they impose a vision of value from the outside. For people who are long-soaked in an activity, transparency imposes a superficial vision of value—a conception from people who haven't been soaked in the activity, who haven't learned what's truly valuable about it.

This seems awfully unfair when you're on the inside and know the value of what you're doing. But when you're on the outside, the need for transparency makes perfect sense. Because the world truly is full of bullshit. It's full of communities that claim to be doing something important: yoga teachers, psychiatrists, anti-psychiatric Scientologists, philosophers, chiropractors, wine connoisseurs, audiophiles, hipster coffee snobs, fashionistas, board game fans, economists, and flashlight collectors. Some of these are full of scammers, poseurs, and snobs. But right next to them are other communities that are onto something subtle but really important. The problem is that from the outside, poseurs and visionaries can be awfully hard to distinguish.

The methodology of transparency is *accessibility*. But accessibility is a double-edged sword. The demand for accessible explanations limits us to the kinds of things anybody can understand. If the value of the activity is subtle, then transparency metrics will miss the mark. And they will force experts to change their goals, to pursue unsubtle, obvious targets.

Trust and transparency live in constant uneasy tension. The more we trust experts, the more we leverage the power of specialization. But this requires that we let experts off the leash—that we let them act in ways that pass beyond our understanding. But the more we trust, the more room we leave for corruption and bias to sneak into the system. So we demand transparency—we secure ourselves from corruption—but we lose out on the power of trusting experts.

So what's the solution to this tension?

The hard truth is there is no solution. There's only a painful trade-off. We get to choose, in each case, where the slider goes. Sometimes we probably want more transparency—like in political cases, in which the dangers of corruption are vast. Sometimes the dangers of corruption are lower and the goods of trust are higher—like in arts education. The mistake lies in denying that there is always trade-off, in automatically trying to maximize transparency, always. Public metrics let us peer into each other's lives; they make us comprehensible to each other, which makes it easy to judge one another. But the price is that we are bound to use only those values that everybody can instantly understand.

CHAPTER 7

The Beauty of the Process

G ames are designed systems that serve a purpose. But what purpose? To understand that, we need to understand what experiences game designers are trying to create, and what experiences game players are trying to have. We need to understand the unique delightfulness of games. And I suspect that we often misunderstand games, because we're looking for their value in the wrong place.

What's magical about games—what's different from so many other art forms—is that in games, you act. You analyze the information, you make decisions, you try to enact your will upon the game world. And well-designed games make beautiful action more likely. They call it forth. Good games don't tell you what to do, exactly. They don't puppet you into beauty. They leave space for your freedom, for you to choose and decide and act and react. But they create the background conditions that make it likely that your own actions will be elegant, fascinating, and thrilling. The beauty is in the process—in what it feels like to be doing the thing. And games help steer you toward finding beauty in your own actions—in finding the answer yourself, figuring out the right move yourself, instinctively reacting out of your own trained skill.

This is what makes games unique as an art. In traditional art, the beauty is outside the viewer, in the art object itself. It is external beauty. But with games, much of the beauty shows up in the players' own actions—in the feeling of their own bodies and minds in action. And games lead you there, help you to find your way into elegant action or comical failure. Games help us find internal beauty, in our own bodies and minds.

But sometimes game players get anxious about the cultural status of games. When faced with the game skeptics—the people who say that games are a waste of time, or that they can never be real art—game lovers sometimes retreat from what makes games truly unique. Gamers often end up trying to defend their games by talking about how much they're like other, more familiar forms of art. People will try to talk up video games by pointing out how much they're like movies—the beautiful graphics, the cinematic soundtrack, the emotional story, the well-written characters, the serious and philosophical themes. They try to find traditional, external beauty in the game object itself. This tends to put the focus on a very particular kind of game: single-player narrative video games, the kind with a lot of pre-written cutscenes and dialogue and scripted stories. And it tends to leave out the really, purely game-y games: poker and *The Mind* and *Super Mario Odyssey*. Most important, it leaves out the distinctive heart of games: the part where we actually make choices and do things. And this seems kind of weird—as if we're so anxious to assimilate games to Serious Art that we'll trample over what makes them truly special.

This kind of thing happens with every new art form. When new technologies birth new mediums for art, you often see these bids for respectability. People try to force the new medium away from what it's uniquely good at, to make it look more like older, more familiar art forms. Photography, for example, is good at things that painting is not: clarity, freezing a particular real moment, capturing lots of unexpected details. But when photography first showed up, it was too jarring and weird for a lot of people's artistic sensibilities. Most people couldn't see it as real art. So early "art photographers" tried to use every method they could to eliminate that clarity and quickness. Even as cameras got faster and faster, people were still photographing highly controlled, static images—like your classic bowls of fruit—in an effort to resemble high-art paintings. They smeared petroleum jelly on the lens to blur the photographs to look like impressionist paintings; they cut up the negatives with razor blades to give them that scribbly look of fine-art drawings. They resisted letting photography do what it was naturally good at: capturing moments in crisp detail.

It wasn't until decades later that a new generation of photographers, like Henri Cartier-Bresson, would embrace the unique powers of photography. Photography, said Cartier-Bresson, was special because it let you capture that fleeting moment. He embraced the fact that photography wasn't completely under the photographer's control. Photography can surprise you; you can discover weird details and energy in your shot well after you took it. To truly love photography is to embrace what is peculiar about the medium: the strange balance between control and surprise.

So what's unique about games? In the traditional arts, the beauty is in the art object itself. It's in the painting, the song. It's the sculpture that's radiantly gorgeous, that novel that's bittersweet and moving. But in games, so much of the time, the beauty shows up not in the game but in the player. Games help mold, shape, and heighten beauty in the player's own actions.

Because here is the fascinating thing about our relationship with games: When I make a precise series of jumps in *Super Mario Odyssey*, that's me doing it; it's my skill that is beautiful. It's my mind, my body, my choices that let me weave through the world. In a sense, that elegance is mine. But a game's design can make particular kinds of elegance much more likely. The designers of *Super Mario Odyssey* created the possibility for that kind of high-energy, glorious timing. They tweaked the physics engine to make those jumps just barely possible. They shoved collectible objects into an environment that asks me to improvise wild, creative jumping sequences. And then they gave me a scoring system that told me to collect those objects.

The game prepares the way for me to be beautiful, and it summons forth that beauty by shaping and channeling my actions. Who is responsible for that beauty? It's a complex muddle, some weird mixture of game designer and player. But if we are too fixated on the old paradigm of art—if we are only willing to find beauty in the stable object made by some faraway artist, if we refuse to respect beauty when it shows up in our own fleeting actions—then we'll miss the most important bit.

I PLAYED CLASSICAL PIANO IN MY YOUTH—NOT PARTICULARLY well or with any great fervor but with the kind of mediocre dutifulness of a kid forced by his parents to play piano to pad out his college résumé. I did discover, though, this profound difference in what composers cared about. Beethoven didn't give a damn about what it feels like for the pianist to play his pieces. You could tell that he had this grand sonic architecture in his head, and you just have to force your fingers to make those sounds for him. Chopin, on the other hand, clearly loved the physical act of playing the piano: the feel of it, the expressive agility of it. And he wrote music that gave the pianist that feeling. To play Chopin is to feel beauty radiating from your fingers into the music. When the music is soaring, your right hand will have to jump in graceful hops back and forth over your left hand. When the music is delicate, your hands glide quietly over the keyboard. When it's tense and dramatic, you end up pounding down on the piano with tangled fingers, the agony of the music echoed in the deliciously awkward twists that the notes force your hands into.

But people rarely talk about that part of Chopin. Pianists will sometimes mention it in offhand moments. But it's not the officially important part that we're supposed to study and appreciate and write books about. The art culture I grew up in—that of Western Europe and its American kin—mostly just ignores the beauty of process, the beauty of doing. It ignores how the performance *feels* to the performer, on the inside. You never see a review of a ballet that says "Well, it sure looked beautiful, but, man, it must have been pure torture for the dancers."

You can see this emphasis of outward appearance over inner elegance everywhere. Take cookbook reviews. I remember, back when I was learning to cook, desperately trying to pull together impressive recipes from the kinds of fancy cookbooks written by chefs at famous high-end restaurants—like *The French Laundry Cookbook*. And, I will admit, what I produced was quite delicious. But the act of cooking was miserable. The recipes hadn't originally been designed to be cooked by one person. They were made for a whole professional kitchen, one that had somebody on staff to come in in the morning and create a set of different sauces and stocks, so that the line chefs could grab a bit of this and a bit of that. The cookbook had awkwardly compressed all that for the home chef. One recipe forced you to get five different sauces simmering simultaneously—an exhausting and stressful exercise. The authors obviously didn't care about how the process felt to the cook who actually had to make the god-damn thing.

In his cookbook on braising, Michael Ruhlman explains why you're supposed to dust the meat in flour and brown it in butter before you do the long, low-and-slow braise. It deepens and enriches the flavor, for sure. But the most important reason you do it, he says, is because it smells amazing for the cook.

Yet cookbook reviews almost never talk about the joys of cooking—which is funny because I often spend way more time on the cooking part than the eating part. The official culture ignores the beauty of the process, trains us not to pay attention to how it feels to act, to believe that joyous action doesn't matter.

And that disinterest in the process seems to be on the rise. Take the modern trend toward "perfect" recipes that have been "tested in our food laboratory" and are usually presented in a very scientific mode. These recipes tell you precise times and temperatures. I tried a recipe for french fries that had you cut potatoes into exactly ¼" × ¼" × 2" fries, then bring 4 cups of oil up to 375 degrees, drop in exactly 1 pound of precut potatoes, which would drop the oil temperature below 350 degrees, and then you had to carefully bring the oil temperature up and monitor it. When the ingredients are sufficiently standardized, this script will, in fact, produce reliably perfect results. But it sucks much of the joy out of the process. We've taken a deeply aesthetic, deeply satisfying set of sensory interactions with food—smelling it, tasting it, hearing it sizzle, being sensually immersed in the smells and sounds of food, and then making decisions triggered to those smells and sounds—and replaced it with staring at a stopwatch and a thermometer, mechanically executing a precise procedure. There are no choices, no judgments, no improvisation, and no sensory intuition. There is only following the rules.

PART OF THE REASON WE MISS THE BEAUTY OF GAMES IS THAT we don't have great language to describe these kinds of experiences. Quiet, unnamed things slip through our fingers and mind so easily. So let's make up some names.

There are two kinds of beauty in the world, one dominant in the cultural imaginary, and the other just as common in the world but neglected in the eyes of official art culture. Let's call them *object beauty* and *process beauty*. Object beauty is the familiar kind—the beauty of paintings, movies, ballet, novels, and rap. It's what we usually think about when we think about art. It's the beauty that's in the art object itself. It's the movie that's bittersweet, the novel that's inventive and weird.

Process beauty is different. It is the beauty of your own actions and choices. There is no easy line between a beautiful thing and the observer of beauty, between object and audience.

Process beauty is everywhere. Sometimes it happens spontaneously and accidentally. When you open a cupboard and a glass falls out and somehow you sweep your hand under it and catch it with a graceful little motion—it is your body, your movement that is graceful. But other times, we design artifacts specifically to get us there, to encourage and sculpt beautiful action. This is *process art*. And games are often designed to encourage and shape our action into something more beautiful, more thrilling, more funny. Games help us find our way into actions worth savoring.

But it's not just games. Process art has been all around us, all along, but we've been mostly taught to ignore it. I am inordinately fond of certain social food rituals, like hot pots and fondues. I grew up in a Vietnamese household, and my favorite special dinner was

Vietnamese hot pot. You put a Bunsen burner on the table, put a little pot of deliciously sour broth on top, get it simmering, and then lay out platters of uncooked foods: thin slices of raw beef, shrimp, mushrooms, onions. And then everybody cooks together, at the table. Some of the happiest memories I have with my family are of us all clustered around the little hot pot, arguing about whose shrimp was whose, yelling at each other for overcooking the beef or eating all the mushrooms.

This is definitely not the best way to get the most delicious food. Having a gang of people cooking simultaneously at the dinner table is far too chaotic for optimal results. But there is a glory, still, in the process of the hot pot—a weird, comic, intimate social glory. The hot pot is too small. There's not enough space for all the people and implements jockeying around. I have started to suspect that this is by design—or, at least, that the ensuing joyful chaos is part of why we keep returning to these things.

The hot pot ritual is a close cousin to games. It is a work of process art. The weird too-smallness is actually a design feature, a clever bit of social engineering, which leads to elbows knocking, chopsticks crossing, and confusion about whose mushroom is whose. Making tasty food is the goal—and in this case, that's an outcome that's valuable in itself. But we have also engineered a particularly awkward, inconvenient way of making that food that leads to all kinds of joyful chaos and argument. It reminds me, weirdly, a little bit of *Twister*—a game designed to get people tangled up, confused, and falling over each other, all for the hilarity of the failure.

Traditional art culture, when faced with the weirdness of games, often searches for beauty in the game itself—in the graphics, the music, the script, the fixed story. But to truly understand why many of us play games, we need to look at the process sculpted by the game—at what it feels like for the player to be playing.

I TAKE A PARTICULAR INTENSE PLEASURE IN A CERTAIN KIND
of spatial manipulation. In college, my undergraduate dorm was set
up not along a normal horizontal hallway, but vertically, up a set of
winding narrow stairs. On moving day, people would sometimes get
stuck trying to get a couch or a bookcase up and down those stairs. I
lived for those moments. I would poke my head out and casually offer
to help, like this wasn't the literal best part of my day. I'd stare at the
couch, turning it around and around in my mind, until I could see
the exact weird rotation that would let it slip over and around that
annoying banister, underneath the lamp, and slide on up. Later in
life, I loved helping my friends move. I took intense pleasure in that
last moment, at the end of a miserable day, where we had to jam too
much crap inside a little moving van or a tiny hatchback car, and I
had to carefully imagine every rotational possibility.

These might have been rare pleasures for me—a few isolated moments in a lifetime. But now I don't have to wait around for those
rare moments of stuck couches and overstuffed moving vans. Because now there's *Tetris*. This is a game that takes the pleasure of ro-
tating objects to fit and concentrates it, perfects it, and gives it to you
as much as you could possibly want. *Tetris* takes the joy and pleasure,
the feeling of internal grace and brilliance, that arises haphazardly
in ordinary life, and distills it.

The philosopher John Dewey says that every piece of art takes
some aspect of ordinary life and crystallizes it. Fiction takes the ordinary act of telling what happened to you and sharpens it—finds
unified stories with coherence and meaning. Painting takes the ordinary act of looking and concentrates it. And games take ordinary,
day-to-day *practical action*—making decisions and doing stuff—and
refines it. Crystallized action, pure and uncut.

This is why many of us adopt scoring systems in games. The scoring system aims us at something simple and obvious: faster times, higher levels. That is the goal of the game. But the goal is not the purpose; it is not why we play. We choose to adopt the scoring system, and our local goals become mechanically clear for a while, because that gives us a gateway to lovely, gorgeous action. Rules and goals are part of the art of the game designer. Their mechanical clarity lets a game designer sculpt action with precision and place us, more preciscly, at the doorway to a beautiful process.

Striving players may adopt a mechanical scoring system temporarily, but our real purpose is often larger and stranger. What we want is an inner feeling: the elegance in our own body moving, poetry in our mind thinking. What we want is fun, interest, and beauty, emerging from within our own acting selves.

In games, we *use* a scoring system as part of an artistic medium — to precisely shape a kind of action. But the reasons we have for engaging in that action can be deeply gushy. Our real reasons for play lie beyond the score.

CHAPTER 8

The Limits of Data

Scoring systems shape action. In well-designed games, the scoring systems have been tuned to produce interesting, satisfying, delightful action. Things are different in the world of metrics and institutional measures. There, we find scoring systems that have been designed for very different purposes—and that often drive us to miserable, grinding action.

Why? To understand that, we need to understand the forces that shape institutional metrics. Transparency metrics were a gateway to a bigger picture. They are a relatively simple case study, because their core function—public oversight—is so singular and clear. This makes it easy to see their price: how they undermine expertise. The costs of transparency metrics are relatively easy to understand, because public transparency metrics are, in a sense, stupid by design. Inexpertise is baked into their basic function.

Transparency metrics offer us a trade-off between trust and transparency. When we zoom out and survey the larger class of public metrics and measures, we will find a much more complicated set of trade-offs—because metrics are playing many functions at once. What we need now is to understand the *general functions* of metrics, and what the *typical costs and trade-offs* are of using them.

A metric, in its modern form, usually has two key components:

1. Metrics function as *scoring systems*, rendering a singular value judgment and making it official.

2. Metrics use *data* to render that judgment.

Not all data is packaged as a value. Data can be a neutral presentation of information. But metrics are data transformed into targets. A metric presents some direction as better: longer lifespans, faster student graduation rates, more page views, higher customer satisfaction scores. In doing so, a metric inherits any limitations within the data. So when we internalize a metric, we put those limitations at the center of our being.

This would be fine if data were truly lossless—if data-based scoring systems could capture everything that was important in the world. But they don't. To understand why, we need to see why metrics are the way they are. We need to understand the *design process* by which we engineer metrics to do a specific job. And we need to go to the root—to grasp what data is and how it functions. We need to understand the inherent limitations of data.

Because data isn't neutral. It is a specific format for understanding the world, one that exhaustively documents quantitative information and ignores qualitative information. It is a tool built for a very specific purpose. We need to understand the purpose and design of that tool, to understand when data-based approaches are appropriate—and when they are not.

Data is engineered information, and metrics are engineered values.

LET'S GET BACK TO OUR CORE WORRY: THAT WITH METRICS, *easy countability* automatically wins out over *actual importance*. Imagine that we're in the public health sector, and we're considering a policy proposal that doctors should strongly urge patients to do everything they can to lower their saturated fat intake. Lowering saturated fats nationally would lead to better health outcomes: lowered heart attack numbers and better average longevity. These are targets that speak in the loud, clear, inarguable language of hard data.

We also lose something when we avoid saturated fats, but those losses are harder to measure. Suppose our country has a long and rich tradition of cooking based around saturated fats—butter, cheese, animal fat. If we focused on cutting saturated fats, we could lose touch with our culinary traditions, disconnect from our food heritage. We could lose out on some profound culinary joys. I'm not saying that we shouldn't care about lifespan and heart attack rates. Those things are absolutely important. I'm just saying that the other stuff is important, too—but they tend to be drowned out because they're harder to count.

Tradition, community, culinary joy—I think a lot of us are tempted to call such things "intangibles." But actually, what's more tangible than a good cheese or a heartwarming fondue party with your friends? They are, in fact, among the most tangible and concrete of joys. What we actually mean is that in our modern institutional environment, such joys are hard to quantify with the measuring tools that come readily to hand. The problem isn't that cheese and dinner parties are intangible. It's the precise opposite. The problem with them, from the perspective of the modern world, is that they're *hard to abstract*. The goods of a gorgeous cheese are so obvious, but also hard to put into some kind of metric that you can report up the chain, aggregate in a spreadsheet, and then turn into a number that fits nicely in a PowerPoint bullet. Cheese is glorious in the mouth, but hard to express in the language of bureaucracy.

There's a trade-off here. Data-based approaches are incredibly powerful, but they narrow our focus to the parts of the world that are easier to quantify. There is a cost—a loss of attention to the subtler parts of the world. Sometimes, we may want to counterbalance data-based approaches with other, more qualitative methods of judgment—or occasionally avoid data-based approaches altogether. But it is very tempting to skip out on the decision and let the data choose for us. It's easy to forget the weird subtle stuff, because we don't have an easy metric for it.

You may have heard of Goodhart's Law: "When a measure become a target, it ceases to be a good measure." Goodhart's Law captures something familiar. When people are given a thin, simplified metric, they will tend to optimize only for what's measured and ignore everything else. It's tempting, once we have this nicely official name for it, to stop there. But naming it is only the beginning. Goodhart's Law doesn't actually explain what's going on under the hood. It doesn't explain why thin metrics are so captivating, even when they aren't tied to incentives. (Remember how compelling I found reducing my weight and leveling up my yoga, even when I got nothing from it.) More important, Goodhart's Law doesn't explain why metrics seem to systematically fail to capture what's important. Is it because the metrics we know are just sloppily made? Could we get around the problem by building better metrics, or getting more of them? Or is it something deeper: Some core feature of how metrics are, and how they're made?

We need a deeper understanding of why metrics are the way they are. We need to see why institutions seem to prefer actively thin, simplified metrics. And we need a better picture of the other side, too. We need to see why our values are often so subtle and dynamic that they defy measurement by institutional methods. We need to understand the weirdness of what matters. Only then will we get a fuller picture of where metrics work well, and where they flounder.

METRICS ARE BASED ON DATA, AND DATA IS A VERY SPECIFIC way of understanding the world, better suited for some things than for others. Some things are easy to capture in data; other things seem to elude its grasp. I'm not saying that data is false. I'm saying it's *selective*. Data-based methods, as they occur in real-life institutions under real-life limitations, systematically highlight some chunks of human life and ignore others.

One of the most informative, and profound, inquiries into the limits of data comes from Theodore Porter, a historian who specializes in quantification culture. His 1995 book, *Trust in Numbers*, is a pioneering study of the social power of numbers. Porter is interested in why quantified justification has become so predominant in political and bureaucratic life. Institutional actors seem to prefer statistics of any kind—even obviously bad ones—to richer, more qualitative modes of reasoning. Why do politicians and bureaucrats compulsively reach for statistics to justify their actions?

There are, says Porter, two basic modes of reasoning and justification. *Qualitative reasoning* uses words and descriptions, and *quantitative reasoning* uses numbers. For Porter, neither mode is essentially superior. Each has its own distinctive strengths and weaknesses, and there's always a trade-off between them. But we have come to use the quantitative reasoning compulsively, even when it's not the best tool for the job.

Qualitative reasoning, says Porter, is nuanced and dynamic. If I give a qualitative evaluation of something, I can choose, in that moment, which terms I use, which dimensions I explore. I can add in new, unexpected directions of evaluation, I can fill in necessary backstory. I can put in anything I need that I think is relevant. Qualitative reasoning is open-ended and flexible. We don't fix ahead of time what we're going to pay attention to and record. We can improvise, on the spot, what we put in. Qualitative reasoning can be *contoured to the precise needs of the local context.*

But that variability and flexibility has its downside. Qualitative reasons travel poorly between contexts. They usually require a lot of shared background to understand. And qualitative reasoning also doesn't aggregate well. There's no easy, automatic way to add up a lot of different paragraphs from different people to produce a single, collective summary.

Quantitative reasoning, on the other hand, travels easily between contexts—because it's been designed to. This is Porter's central insight: Institutional quantifications are engineered tools, forged for a specific purpose. They are made to *cross contexts.* To be clear, Porter isn't talking about every kind of quantification. He's not worried about math in principle. He's talking about the kinds of quantification that we typically find in institutions—that have been formulated to fit the informational style of bureaucracy. He's talking about systems for counting and aggregation that are designed to work at scale.

When we create an institutional quantification, we begin by creating *a context-invariant kernel.* We want to identify the bit that makes sense across contexts and strip off everything else—all the nuance, all the subtle stuff that requires a lot of shared background to understand. Once we've isolated that context-invariant kernel— once we've designed an info chunk that everybody can understand, no matter their background—then we've created a powerful tool. Everybody, from different contexts, can collect into that same kernel.

Everybody can understand the bits other people have collected. And all our collection efforts will add up easily, because we're collecting into the same, fixed kernel. Quantified information can pass easily between different contexts, because it's been *built to travel*.

And it can aggregate easily, because we have stabilized a standard nugget—a stackable, same-size box of information—for everybody to use. Quantitative data is designed so that everybody collects the same kind of thing, so that we can add them up easily. We fix the kernels, fix the categories, in advance, to make that possible. But the cost is that we have to decide ahead of time exactly which categories we're going to collect into—and we need everybody to use the same preset categories, or the data won't aggregate.

I'm a university professor. I spend a lot of my life grading student work. For every student essay, I offer two evaluations: a qualitative evaluation in the form of extended written feedback and commentary, and a quantitative evaluation—a letter grade, in which every letter corresponds to a number, in a way that has been standardized across American educational institutions.

When I'm writing qualitative evaluations, I can be quite flexible and responsive. If one student is taking risks, pushing for a bold and original new synthesis, I can comment on their originality, focus on their attempts to create something new, and look at the big picture. If another student is trying to precisely explain a tiny bit of difficult text, with absolute care and attention to every detail, I can respond in kind, paying attention to how carefully they've worked with the details, looking for tiny bits of text they've missed. I can respond in multiple dimensions, praising their originality but warning them for being sloppy—or praising their thorough research but pushing them to be clearer about their overall argument. And I can tailor my comments to their needs. If one student really wants to be a journalist, we can focus on their writing quality. If another student cares about their ability to argue in the courtroom, I can focus on the clarity and crispness of their arguments.

And for all of this, I can use the language and the understanding we forged together in class. In my classes, we often spend the entire semester talking about what makes arguments strong or weak, what makes an analysis rich or shallow. So my evaluations can lean on that solid background. We can communicate richly because we've had time to develop a shared language—with shared examples and shared moments.

But these kinds of rich qualitative assessments travel poorly. I know that my written comments—steeped in the particular language and ideas of our class—wouldn't really be fully comprehensible to, say, a statistics professor, or the dean of the business school, or a future employer in Silicon Valley. (And the statistics professors' and business professors' qualitative comments on their students' work wouldn't be fully comprehensible to me.)

Qualitative assessments don't aggregate well, either. Imagine if a student comes out of school with just a stack of hundreds of long open-ended qualitative evaluations. Each one would discuss the student along a set of different dimensions of quality—and different evaluations might use totally different dimensions. My philosophy evaluations might discuss originality, writing clarity, argumentative rigor, and insight. But evaluations from, say, a computer science class might discuss a student's problem-solving ability, the precision of their coding, and their ability to work well in development teams. From this mess of lush detail, there's no easy way to generate an automatic summary. The stack is useless to external examiners who need a quick synopsis: law school admissions officers, future employers, all of whom need to look through hundreds of résumés in an hour.

But think about what we had to shed to get this context-crossing ability to aggregate. I have to leave out the little nuances that depend on our shared time together. I have to leave out all the multidimensional complexity: that this student was sloppy but original; that this other student is only all right at logic, but amazing as a community builder. This is all stripped out. A letter grade is a simple representation of a position on a single scale. And that is exactly the point. That radical de-nuancing is the core design feature of letter grades. Grades travel well across context because they have been cut down to a single simple context-invariant kernel, which anybody can understand. They are narrow by design.

QUALITATIVE REASONING DOESN'T ADD UP WELL, PRECISELY

because it's open-ended. Each of us is allowed to put in what we think is important, and we may not divide up the world in the same way. When we collect qualitative information, we end up with a grab bag of all kinds of different things. Qualitative reasoning can make use of subtle sensitivity. You can use your experience, your training, and your hard-fought knowledge to make sense of what's important, to say what's going on. But that kind of reasoning can't make its way into an institutional metric because it loses meaning as it crosses contexts.

Quantitative information is designed to be *portable*. It travels easily between contexts because it's been prepared to do so, by having context-sensitive bits stripped out. This is Porter's portability theory of quantification.

Porter is showing us the deep tension at the root of quantified information. The power of quantification depends on us gathering an enormous amount of information from various sources and aggregating it into a small set of manageable numbers—like condensing an entire student's lifetime of work into a single GPA or condensing an entire school district's worth of students' work into an aggregate GPA. That power gives you an immense summary view. But the price of the summary is the loss of context, the loss of nuance.

This is the thought that actually keeps me awake at night. Porter reveals a grim truth about the heart of data. At the center of institutional quantification is a single demand: that the evaluation procedure, and its product, be comprehensible across contexts. And that demand profoundly limits what the metric can measure.

Portability and the process of decontextualization are responsible for both the power of data and its weakness. Data is powerful because it has been designed to be universally comprehensible. It has more weight in any large-scale social or institutional conversation precisely because it has been engineered for easy use. But that engineering procedure involves, necessarily, cutting out high-context understanding and specialized sensitivity. The insensitive and decontextualized nature is also precisely why data speaks so loudly. The power of data is inextricable from its price.

SO HERE IS A FIRST PASS AT THE PROBLEM OF VALUE CAPTURE by metrics. You're pegging your values to some kind of institutional quantification. But we've learned that institutional quantifications have a particular character. They have two primary functions: They are built to cross contexts and to aggregate easily. To do that job, they have to be narrowed down to a context-invariant kernel that's easily deployed by anybody in the institution.

In value capture, you're taking that decontextualized nugget and internalizing it. You're letting it set your values. You're guiding your life using an evaluative technology that has been engineered to travel between contexts, by stripping it of nuance. You're centering a value that has been built to *ignore* anything particular about your context and personality, and anything that requires special sensitivity to deploy. You are making yourself more comprehensible, but less particular.

Health and well-being measures typically target things like weight, BMI, and lifespan. They generally don't target things like joy, being surrounded by richly beautiful things, or having a vivid social life. It's not that there is no way to describe the amount of joy in your life, and no difference between a life surrounded by aesthetic texture and a life devoid of it. We have plenty of ways to describe it—in words, in song, in poetry. But there's no institutional metric that tracks those things because understanding them requires exactly the kind of intimacy and sensitivity that are intentionally filtered out by metrics.

My deepest worry here is not that metrics are inevitably false. Rather, they can be quite true of what they are measuring. But they speak so clearly—so accessibly—that they can drown out our awareness of everything else. Metrics tend to draw our attention to the easily and mechanically countable, and away from subtler kinds of meaning.

PORTER'S THEORY IS A FIRST STEP TOWARD UNDERSTANDING the complex impact of metrics. Things will get even more complicated from here because, it will turn out, scoring systems and metrics serve a number of different functions. They are a nexus point in a complex, interwoven set of bureaucratic pressures.

It might be hard to keep track of all the moving parts, so let me offer a mnemonic aid. One device we cognitively limited human beings use, when faced with the astonishing complexity of the world, is to create myths—to personify, in some easy-to-remember figures, the forces of the world. In an earlier era, we had the Four Horsemen of the Apocalypse—War, Famine, Plague, and Death. These embodied the crucial forces that shaped an earlier era. We still need myths to understand the world, but the world has changed. So let me introduce a new set of myths, for our new age: the Four Horsemen of Bureaucracy.

We have just met our first Horseman: Scale. And like all the other Horsemen, Scale is no accident. He is no alien force. Scale's power arises from the basic workings of human life. Every Horseman places pressure on us, but only because we want a job to be done. Think of the Horsemen as a demanding kind of god: They will bring us a gift, but they will ask for a sacrifice.

The Horseman of Scale gives us a powerful gift: He makes things comprehensible across vast territories, across very different people. He connects us quickly and easily. The Horseman of Scale makes coordinated action possible across great numbers of people. This is useful for all sorts of things: government bureaucracies trying to manage its citizens, corporations seeking profit, scientists researching for the greater good. But Scale asks for a sacrifice. To gain his power, we can no longer make nuanced judgments and use our sensitive understanding that arises from our particular background.

Scale gives us the power of portability. He asks us to sacrifice context.

CHAPTER 9

The Score Shapes the Struggle

et's get back to our big question about games: Why do we adopt rigid scoring systems in order to play? Why give up creative freedom and force ourselves to desire what the game tells us to desire? We've made some progress already; we've learned that when we adopt a game's scoring system, we are letting the game shape our desires and how we'll act. This lets us plunge into the alternate self that the game has prepared for us. But why would we ever want to do that?

In games, scoring systems serve the function of *communicating goals*. But this allows another function: It lets the game shape and communicate new kinds of action. This is why we take on restrictions and goals in games—because we want to experience a specific kind of action that another person has carefully sculpted for us.

Games are an art form. And when we experience art, we aren't completely free. When we read a novel, we don't imagine whatever the hell comes into our heads; we let the novel direct our imagination. When I read a novel, there is plenty of room for me to freely

respond. I can have different emotional reactions, different inter-
pretations. I can fill in the blank spots of the world in my own way.
But that only happens when we follow lots of fairly strict rules: rules
about grammar, about what different words mean, about what order
to read the novel in. (If you read all the words of *Moby Dick* in scrambled, random order, you haven't actually read *Moby Dick*.)

Art uses shared rules to create a stable bridge between people.
This stability permits the precise transmission of experiences and
ideas. A novelist uses language, with all its rules and shared meanings, in order to tell us a story about specific people doing specific
things. A game designer is doing something analogous, but in a different medium. The game designer uses scores and rules to shape who
we will be and what we will face in the game. And they do that to give
us all kinds of new experiences of action—of fascinating struggles,
tense decisions, brilliant epiphanies, and delightful motion.

The game designer has incredibly fine-grained control over our
play. So much of what we do in a game—what actions we take and how
they feel—is set by the exact rules and scoring system of the game.

First, game designers set our abilities during the game. In sports,
they often do this by subtraction. You take a basic human being
and then you tell them what they're not allowed to do. These limitations can create a fascinatingly narrow focus, which can plunge us
into unexplored parts of our abilities. For those of us who don't play
soccer, we mostly just use our feet for basic foot-type stuff: standing
and walking. But soccer forbids us to use our hands, and so plunges
us into our feet—and pushes us to discover exactly how mobile, controlled, and precise they can be.

One of my favorite experimental role-playing games is *Sign*,
from Thorny Games. It's a live-action role-playing game, based on
the real-life story of the invention of Nicaraguan Sign Language.
In 1977, Nicaragua had no sign language of its own. The government

tried a project: They gathered together fifty deaf schoolchildren from around the country and tried to teach them to lip-read. Instead, the children spontaneously invented their own sign language—a rich, fully functional one, which eventually became the official sign language of Nicaragua. It's a minor human miracle that linguists still study to this day.

In *Sign*, your group plays as these schoolchildren. The game is played in complete silence. At the beginning of the game, you are assigned a goal: an inner secret that you are yearning to express. (In my first game, it was "I miss my cat more than I miss my parents.") But you have no means to express it. Over the course of a few hours, you will all have to invent a sign language together, in order to communicate. To make it playable in an evening, the game permits each player to clearly set the meaning of three signs. The first sign will be their own name. The other two signs can be connected to any concept they choose. In my game, I created a sign for *love*: tapping a fist to my heart.

Then you use these signs to improvise new ones. And you hope, desperately, that you're all understanding these new signs the same way. I needed a sign for *hate*, so I built it off *love*—I moved my fist toward my heart, then blocked it with my other hand and threw it away dramatically. I thought people knew what I meant, but there was no way to know for sure. I just had to use the sign, and feel out if other people seemed to be comprehending and signing it back to me in the same way. And then you use your new signs to build even more new signs, erecting a teetering staircase of uncertain language.

Our first game was so intense—so frustrating, and so deep, so connecting and isolating all at once—that my spouse burst into tears in the middle of it. At the end of the game, we blew out the candles, turned the lights back up, and started talking again. Immediately, people wanted to reveal their inner secrets, to see if we had successfully communicated and won. But I forbade it. I made people burn the little sheets of paper with their inner secrets and never discuss it again. This, I felt, was in the spirit of the game: that we are always just hoping, but could never be absolutely sure, that we have, in fact, connected.

THE GOAL IS THE HEART OF A GAME—THE THING THAT SETS THE whole contraption into clattering motion. In *Sign*, the restriction is no speech—but there is no game until we add the goal of communicating our inner secret.

By setting a goal, we bring the obstacles into being. And if you change the goals, you change the obstacles. Here is a rocky cliff, full of massive outcroppings and little cracks. Look at it with no goals in your head. Nothing is an obstacle yet. The cracks are just cracks, the blank spots are just blank spots. Nothing on the cliff is useful or challenging, because there's nothing we're trying to do. Now add a goal: climb to the top. Now the big outcroppings become major obstacles to our progress. The cracks and holes become useful aids— places to stick our hands and feet. And the blank, featureless spots are the most fearsome obstacles of all, because there's nothing to step on or grab.

Let's change games. We'll keep the same cliff but change the goal. Let's play a speed-painting game, in which we try to quickly paint an accurate watercolor of the cliff. The obstacles change completely. The blank patches of wall are now the easy parts; I can paint those with a couple of big loose wet brushstrokes. The cracks and holes are now the hard part, full of painstaking details to capture. Obstacles don't become obstacles until you're trying to get past them, so different goals create different obstacles.

This is one of Bernard Suits's core insights: There is a paradox of freedom at the heart of games. Game rules seem to restrict us, but they're actually creating more freedom and possibilities—because game rules bring new kinds of action into being. Before we created the rules of basketball, there was no such thing as dribbling, passing, or blocking a pass. Those goals and constraints summoned those actions into reality. Before the rules of chess, there was no such thing as checkmating your opponent, or starting with a Queen's Gambit, or playing a clever sacrifice. Before games, there was no such thing as a real-time-strategy grunt rush, or assembling a fast Magic deck, or rolling a critical hit in Dungeons & Dragons (D&D).

And by finely controlling the goals, abilities, and obstacles, we can precisely control the resulting action and how it makes us feel. Change the scoring system just a tiny bit—what counts as points, what counts toward victory—and you change the entire feel of the game.

Some of the most intricate and gorgeous scoring system designs I've found lately are from the world of indie tabletop role-playing. This is what happens when you take the basic framework of Dungeons & Dragons and give it to weirdo experimental artists. The community of indie role-players has spent years bending the basic framework of D&D to make it even more creative, more emotional, and more expressive of the weirder corners of the human soul.

Dungeons & Dragons is a narrative, storytelling game, in which you play through various adventures using rules, dice, and your imagination to conquer dungeons and complete quests. In D&D, players take on the role of a unique character whose abilities are specified numerically. These are your stats: Strength, Dexterity, Constitution, Intelligence, Wisdom, Charisma, and your various skills, each represented by a single number. You go through the world trying to overcome various challenges, and the game tests whether you can do them by asking you to roll against a certain stat. The higher your stat, the more likely your in-game character is to perform the task. The game is run by the Dungeon Master, who is in charge of the world. They set the world, play all the other incidental characters and the monsters, create the obstacles, and fill in all the external narrative.

The game rewards the players for their various successes with two kinds of points: gold and experience points, or XP. D&D, in its earliest versions, was very clear about the main source of XP and gold: killing monsters and looting their bodies. And D&D was clear about the main use of XP and gold: improving your gear and stats, which let you kill harder monsters. These mechanics pushed players toward a very specific vibe. As one of D&D's critics put it, when you just follow the basic rule set, it tends to generate one standard narrative: Go into a new room, kill some anonymous strangers, loot their bodies, and repeat, occasionally interspersed with shopping. That system fit some players' purposes nicely—especially those who wanted to play a game of optimizing their gear and stats for maximum speedy progression.

But it was a poor fit for many other players' interests. Lots of folks came to D&D to have epic adventures, to go on high fantasy quests, to make interesting moral choices, to be heroes and paragons of virtue. But the game system pushed them toward this endless kill-loot-shop cycle. You could, of course, ignore the point system and go do something else. But the basic mechanics of the game—the baked-in rules and scoring system—were largely oriented toward kill-loot-shop. And many players, including my friends and me, followed the scoring system into endless rooms of anonymous murder, and then wondered afterward why our stories weren't quite as epic as we'd hoped.

Some indie game designers decided that these problems arose from the basic rule system and incentive structure of old-school D&D.

Nothing, for example, in old-school D&D rules incentivizes you to act in character. Your character may have low Intelligence and do badly when you roll on that stat—but you have no incentive to make your character do dumb things. And the team has no incentive to bicker or create character conflict. When you kill something or complete a quest, the XP is, by default, shared equally among all players. These incentives push you to being a well-oiled, efficient kill squad—which may be good for a story about a military special-ops team. But it's less good for inspiring twisty narratives of character conflict and drama.

So the indie folks started playing around with the basic mechanics of role-playing, and came up with some truly astonishing game design innovations. Much of it involved hacking the scoring system—giving points for acting in character and driving the narrative into interesting places. John Harper's extraordinary design *Lady Blackbird* shows off many of these innovations. The primary rule set is only one page long, and it comes with a prepackaged set of characters and a scenario. Just like in D&D, the game rewards you with XP that you can use to improve your character. But unlike in D&D, there are no automatic XP for killing monsters, or even for completing quests. Instead, your character comes with a set of "Keys," which are their core motivations or character traits. And you get XP for hitting your Keys—for acting in character.

The game comes with ready-made characters, built with Keys that put them at constant odds with each other. The noblewoman Lady Blackbird's Keys are to escape the Empire and meet up with her space-pirate lover, Uriah Flint. The bodyguard Naomi Bishop's Keys are to protect Lady Blackbird, to crush the Empire, and to battle worthy foes. The airship captain Cyrus Vance has been paid to escort Lady Blackbird to Uriah Flint—but his Key is to act on his hidden longing for Lady Blackbird. And the goblin pilot Snargle just has the Key of doing stupid daredevil stuff to show off at every possible opportunity. The players fill in the details, but the basic mechanics push them relentlessly toward glorious, inventive conflict.

The rules also say you get XP for hitting your Keys, but you earn double points for doing so in a way that gets you and your teammates into trouble. This point system creates an entirely different set of motivations for the players. The players are constantly looking for opportunities to stir shit up in character. The scoring system orients them toward creating narrative tension by playing in character. And it works. *Lady Blackbird* reliably gets great stories out of the players. (Later editions of D&D have begun borrowing innovations from the indie scene and giving points for acting in character.)

Lady Blackbird has my single favorite rule in any role-playing game, involving a secondary point system. Characters start the game with a small pool of "energy points," which they use to add bonuses to their dice roll—making them more likely to pull off any daring stunts. But your energy points run out quickly. To get them back, you need to have a "refreshment scene," in which you and another character have a moment of intimacy—where you talk and reveal shared backstory. Instead of driving the players to endlessly kill and loot, this point system pushes the players to invent more and more character history and motivation. And the rule gives the whole game a deliciously cinematic rhythm. You have escapades, use up all your energy points, and barely survive. And then you hide out in a cave or a back room somewhere and have that quiet, intimate moment, and you emerge renewed and ready for more. The game mechanics push toward a delightfully cinematic rhythm of alternating action, exhaustion, and renewal through character connection.

All this narrative isn't preset by the game designer. It emerges spontaneously from a thousand player decisions. And the decisions and stories are the players' own—but they are deeply shaped by the game system. I've played this game a dozen times, and every time the story turned out completely different. But the game system reliably generated rich, dramatic narratives—and it was the mechanics and point system that helped push us there.

Game designers have a profound control over the general shape of the players' actions. But the curious thing about games is that this control isn't total. Game designers usually don't tell us exactly what to do. They aren't like novelists, who fix every action of every character. Game designers work a step back. They shape the general contours of our action, but not the precise details. They give us motivations and abilities, and an environment full of obstacles to face — but then set us free to act, to figure out how to achieve those goals. Our actions are still our own.

In *Lady Blackbird*, we once invented a backstory about how I, the captain, first met my goblin sky pilot when we were on opposite sides of a war. We'd shot each other out of the sky, landed on the same desert island, and became friends when we had to learn to dive into the coral reefs to harvest whale snot to eat. That story was ours. But it's the game designers who set up the rules that drove us relentlessly toward such delightfully weird-ass stories like that—by specifying the motivations, the abilities, and the obstacles of our in-game selves.

PART 3

WHY USE MECHANICAL SCORING?

CHAPTER 10

Scoring Systems
Change the Subject

Yoga was incredible, at first. The first couple of years of yoga changed my basic relationship to my body. Before that, I'd mostly ignored my physical self and lived through my mind: reading, playing games. Now I was learning to listen to the quiet signals from my body. Elise, my first yoga teacher, said that yoga was an act of attention. It was noticing what kinds of movement made your body comfortable, and which ones freaked your body out. Yoga tuned up my self-awareness.

The yoga teacher and author Donna Farhi says that in every pose you have an inner edge and an outer edge. Your outer edge is where you're maxed out, at the absolute limit of your flexibility. Your inner edge is much quieter. It is the place where you first feel any hint of strain. When doing a yoga pose, she says, most people just slam themselves up against their outer edge. But that's where your body tenses up, making it hard to stretch into new spaces. To find flexibility, she said, you want to go to your inner edge—to find the tiniest bit of stretch and hang out there until that sensation vanishes. Then you move a bit deeper into the pose and find the new place your inner edge has moved to—and then you wait again.

Surfing your inner edge takes a different kind of discipline: a discipline of delicacy. It's easy to go to your outer edge: You just bend over as hard as you can, until you can't move anymore. It takes more effort to notice and be guided by that faint internal sensation.

After a couple of years, I got more hardcore about yoga. I wanted more and faster progress. I changed to a particularly aggressive power yoga studio. And that studio had a hidden scoring system. There was a preset traditional sequence of yoga poses. The teacher assigned you your own short sequence, and you showed up to the studio every morning and did your sequence. If you did it well, the teacher would add another pose. This was progress. This was leveling up.

To get that next level, you needed to demonstrate "mastery" of all your poses. What this meant, in the context of my power yoga studio, was that you had to achieve some very clear external markers of success. You had to touch your forehead to your shins in a forward fold or clasp your hands together behind your back in a certain twist. If you made your marks, you'd get the next pose.

The whole procedure was very motivating. And those crisp demarcations changed my focus. I started caring where I was in the progression of my practice. I started pushing hard, trying to make certain poses work that my body wasn't ready for. I started throwing myself into poses, lunging hard to make my head touch my shins. And I started tweaking little spots in my back, hurling myself into twists.

A lot depends on what counts as getting it right. If you're motivated by a sense of success, then what you do depends on what, exactly, counts as success—on what's scored. In that yoga studio, what mattered was just achieving that clear, externally recognizable position. You had to touch the ground with your forehead in this forward bend or clasp your hands behind your back in that twist. Imagine a different yoga studio, where I could level up only if I'd done the pose with *good form and sensitivity*. My points-oriented soul would have followed those victory conditions instead and aimed for good form and sensitivity.

The problem is that subtle inner movement is hard to track for an outside observer. A really good yoga teacher can judge if you're doing your poses with good form and care—if they're paying a ton of attention. But in my new studio, there were usually thirty or forty students and one teacher, who ran the class continuously for four hours every morning. And there was only so much he could monitor, only so much attention he had to give. So he mostly looked for the clear, simple signals. This made scoring easier; everybody could tell when you made your pose. But this scoring system didn't care very much about you getting the delicate internal positions right—the ones that would protect your back and joints. So I started hurling myself at my limits, aiming at that outer mark—and I kept hurting myself. Sometimes my knees hurt so badly I couldn't get up the stairs.

I had been value-captured by the scoring system. And the problem here wasn't just that the scoring system came from outside me. Elise had given me an external set of goals and values, which helped me find my way into what yoga was really about. The problem was that in my new yoga studio, I'd been given a scoring system focused on easy-to-recognize signals, at the expense of care and sensitivity.

Scoring systems aren't the only way to evaluate ourselves. We can go by gut, by feel, by intuition, by vibes. But none of that stuff is a scoring system. Scoring systems are a specific kind of social technology. They are designed to get us all to agree on the score. They get us to reach the same judgment; they engineer convergence. And to do that, scoring systems need to transform the whole process of evaluation. Convergence isn't free. Scoring systems need to systematically change what we target, in order to make agreement easy.

Scoring systems are incredibly powerful precisely because they can align the judgments of vast numbers of different people. They aren't just for games. They are the engine at the heart of the modern world. They occupy a central role in bureaucracy, because bureaucracies need different people to accept each other's work—to coordinate around the same shared conclusions about success. Scoring systems enable messy people in a messy world to behave, for a little while, as a tightly coordinated unit. But there is a price.

To understand that price, we need to look at how scoring systems hook onto the world. How is it possible to get a mess of people, with their very different perspectives, intellectual styles, and cares, to automatically agree? The answer is that scoring systems usually work by *changing the subject*. There is a particular kind of thing that makes convergence easy for scoring systems: They like to score objects and events with *mechanical edges*: objects whose boundaries are easy to process with mechanical procedures.

We're on the track of the second Horseman now, who is a close partner to Scale. The second Horsman lives in the realm of mechanical rules, inflexible policies, and clear procedures. What is his offer? What powers does he promise us, and what sacrifice does he ask?

THE AMOUNT OF ENGINEERED CONVERGENCE VARIES. TAKE games. Some games have only partial convergence. Fishing has a couple of different ways to keep score: the number of fish you catch, the weight of the biggest fish, the length of the biggest fish. Within each scoring sub-method, there's a singular verdict, but there's no mechanical system that combines these separate scores into a single overall verdict. On a day of fishing, I might catch more fish, and you might catch the biggest fish—but there is no final, official decision about who did the best at fishing. There is no system that automatically computes the relative value of weight versus number. Everyday, informal fishing gives you some degrees of freedom about the terms by which you will ultimately evaluate yourself.

But in more formal settings, we eradicate that freedom of judgment. We lock everybody into the same judgment procedure. In a bass fishing tournament, there's an official rule about how we sum up the various measures into a single score. In some tournaments, your score is the combined weight of your three heaviest fish. And it's clear why we need such a convergence: Tournaments are designed to offer singular verdicts about who won, which are often connected to various cash prizes.

Here's the key: Scoring systems don't just *discover* a convergence that was already there. They *produce* convergence. Like courts of law, they take messy, complex situations and produce singular clear judgments—which we put into the official record, so that we can all move on with the matter publicly settled.

People naturally tend to diverge and disagree. So scoring systems need a procedure to create that single official verdict. Sometimes the procedure is that we agree on who the official judges will be and promise to accept their judgment. This is what happens at, say, a short-story competition. We pick a few expert judges and agree to abide by their judgments, even if we don't agree in our hearts. But often, we do something even more strict. We eliminate the space for fuzz. We set clear targets that leave no room for disagreement at any step. We find procedures that allow us to evaluate success *mechanically*.

Think about the scoring rule for the total weight of your three heaviest fish. This is mechanical at every step. There's no question about how to choose the fish, measure them, or combine them. Anybody could execute those steps, or inspect them, and come to the same conclusion. We don't need to trust a judge. The mechanicity of the steps eliminates disagreement about the procedure. Unlike with figure skating, there's no room left for your own private opinion. Mechanical scoring systems *foreclose the possibility of disagreement*.

Imagine a totally different kind of fishing competition: a beautiful-fish competition, where the goal is to catch the three most beautiful fish. To figure out who won, just take the three most beautiful fish you caught and add up their beauty. Put that way, it sounds ridiculous. Beauty doesn't work that way. Not everything in the world naturally comes in a form that you can automatically sum up.

But perhaps we could translate beauty into a form that we *could* add up. Let's say we kill our fish, have them mounted, and then put them up for sale on eBay. Now we have transformed their beauty into numbers, which we can add up easily to produce a beauty score. But what we've proposed, in fact, is adding a scoring system. We've offered a procedure in which we do some additional work, which takes something fuzzy and non-computable—fish beauty—and turns it into hard numbers that are easy to add up.

But this is a transformation, and it isn't perfect. The price you can get for something on eBay isn't a full indicator of its value. We've managed to quantify the beauty of the fish by introducing a particular assessment method: seeing what a stranger would pay for them in an online shop. But the quick estimate of online shoppers doesn't see everything there is to see about the value of a thing, especially when that value is subtle.

My spouse's grandparents spent three decades carefully building the strangest, most wonderful house in the suburbs of San Diego. Her grandfather was a retired naval engineer; he made a lot of the furniture himself, building bookcases and cabinets into the walls.

Her grandparents were these gorgeously weird people, with their own peculiar and rambling sense of humor. And they built their sense of humor into their house. There were secret doors, hidden rooms. I remember, after we'd spent a full day camped out in their guest room, my spouse opened up one of the closet doors to reveal a secret entrance to a tunnel, which led to a hidden craft room.

Her grandparents had also carefully and lovingly built, in their modest suburban backyard, this extraordinarily dense garden. They'd spent years tuning the mix of trees and shrubs and vegetable beds into ecological harmony, where all the plants worked together. Tall trees would shade short bushes; short bushes would keep down erosion; one plant would take nitrogen from the soil and another would put nitrogen back in. Their garden yielded a shocking amount of delicious food from that little space. The term for this kind of thing, among a certain sect of hardcore gardeners, is a "food forest"—a concentrated and interconnected web of highly diverse plants, supporting each other like a natural ecosystem.

When her grandparents died, I went with my spouse to clean that house and pack up a few mementos that she wanted to keep. And then, because nobody in the family still lived in San Diego, they decided to sell it to some house flippers.

The flippers took the house apart. They removed all the weird old stuff. They took out her grandfather's handmade bookcases and replaced them with Ikea furniture. They removed all the secret doors and hidden tunnels. And they leveled the food forest, cutting down all the trees and shrubs and networks of vegetables, and replaced it with concrete and an ordinary grass lawn.

It was a fucking tragedy, but a completely predictable one. Because the food forest and the hidden tunnels were *weird*. They had value to a very specific kind of person, with a distinct sensibility. And maintaining the food forest required a deep knowledge of gardening and a willingness to learn about the specific microclimate of the area. The value wasn't obvious; it wasn't readily transferrable. To the right person, that house would have been incredibly valuable. But that's not how the housing market works, and it's not something that house flippers can deal with. The flippers' business model involved moving the house quickly, which meant finding a buyer quickly, which meant removing any odd or subtly valuable features and changing them out for the kind of features that anybody could value.

You might think there's an easy, neutral way to compare the values of things: Just put them on the market and see what price they bring. But that method is not neutral. It tends to prefer things with highly accessible value. And when we use that method intensively, we'll start to see the world only in terms of those easy values.

This is the central idea of part three. We're going to focus on a common and deeply transformative type of scoring system: the mechanical scoring system. We're going to discover how scoring systems systematically change the subject. And we're going to ask: Why do we let it happen? What *use* do we get out of submitting to the strictness of mechanical scoring systems?

And we're going to try to get a fuller answer to our central question: Why do mechanical scoring systems have such different effects? And can we learn from games how to use scoring systems without being limited by them?

CHAPTER 11

Mechanical Values

We have a choice. We could leave our goals and values fuzzy. We can value things like wisdom, communication, friendship, community. These are recognizable and very human values, but without further sharpening, we will probably disagree viciously about how to apply them. Or we can make our values mechanical. The more explicit and mechanical we make our goals and values, the easier it will be to coordinate, and the easier it will be to figure out exactly how well we've done. Mechanical values give us a particular kind of objectivity. They give us a repeatable procedure for evaluation, which different people can follow consistently.

But it can also feel like mechanical values are systematically missing out on something else, something crucial—something hard to name but absolutely essential to human life. To get a clearer grip on what that something is, we need to understand what happens when we change between fuzzy values and mechanical values.

I've been using the term *mechanical* loosely, but now we need to dive in and figure out exactly what it means to have mechanical edges and values. To do that, we need to do about as dorkily philo-sophical a thing as I can imagine. We need to figure out *exactly what counting is* and *what happens when we count things*. And then we will see how we can make counting easier, by making the process mechanical—and how that changes what we're counting in the first place. Because how, exactly, we count things—and how we change the world to make it more countable—is one of the most important hidden drivers of the modern world.

COUNTING IS SORTING. WHEN WE COUNT THINGS, WHAT WE'RE actually doing is sorting them into categories. Suppose I need to count the adults and the children in a room. I need to be able to rec-ognize who the adults are and who the children are. I need a *sorting rule* to tell the difference. (And even if you tell me to count only one thing, I'm still sorting. If you tell me to count the kids, I'm still sort-ing kids from adults.)

There are lots of different sorting rules I can use. Here's one: Count as adults the people who seem mature to me, and count as children the people who seem immature. This rule is pretty fuzzy at the edges and requires a lot of judgment on my part. It tells me to lean on my own intuition, which is an unpredictable resource. When we use fuzzy rules like that, different people will often make very different judg-ment calls. Alternatively, I can use a mechanical sorting rule: age eighteen and over counts as adult; under eighteen counts as child. This rule requires no subtlety or discerning judgment; everybody should be able to apply it in the same way. It shuts out any room for intuition and subjectivity. It closes the door to bias. And in the vot-ing case, it's clear why the mechanical sorting rule is better. But in other cases, we may want to abandon the mechanical sorting rule and let people exercise less explainable forms of judgment. Because mechanical rules also shut out sensitivity and intuition honed by long experience.

So what, exactly, are mechanical rules? And what are the costs and benefits of using them over fuzzier kinds of rules? We can turn for help to the intellectual historian Lorraine Daston, who has given us a profound investigation into the nature of a rule.

Historically, says Daston, we've used three incredibly different ideas of a rule. The older conceptions are nonmechanical, but the newest one is highly mechanical.

The first kind of rule is a *principle*. This is a general abstract statement about what to do—but there are exceptions. A principle isn't meant to be applied unthinkingly and automatically. It's supposed to be applied with judgment and care—and the knowledge that the rule won't always work. But to recognize the exceptions, you have to understand the reason behind the rule, and that cannot be fully captured in the explicit language of the rule.

When I was taking creative writing classes, my teachers always told us the rule: "Show, don't tell." That means when you're writing fiction, don't give the big, general conclusions directly. Describe the action in its details and let the reader come to the conclusions themselves. Don't just say that a character is manipulative and evil; show them being two-faced, or being cruel when they think nobody is looking. For the most part, good fiction follows the "show, don't tell" rule. But if you search through great literature, you'll find plenty of exceptions. Tolstoy starts *Anna Karenina* with one of the finest opening lines in all of literature: "Happy families are all alike; every unhappy family is unhappy in its own way." This is one of the most beloved moments in Western literature, and Tolstoy is telling and not showing.

I was the kind of smart-ass who loved pointing out exceptions like this. But my creative writing teacher said that I was missing the point. "Show, don't tell" is a general guideline, not an absolute rule. It works most of the time, and beginners would do well to generally follow it. But if you really know what you're doing—if you understand the deep reason underneath the simple rule—you know when to break it. You have to understand how most fiction builds its absorptive reality out of concrete sensory details and the particulars of small-scale action. And then you will recognize those rare circumstances when you can boldly tell to great effect without destroying that absorptive reality.

In essence, principles are generalities meant to be applied with care, judgment, and discretion. A principle is useful as a rough guide, but you can't just apply it unthinkingly, because there are always exceptions. However, there's no complete list of all those exceptions, no explicit flowchart guaranteed to catch them all, so you need to apply the rule with an open mind, sensitive to the possibility that this case may be an exception.

The second kind of rule is what Daston calls a *model*. This is an ideal—a role model, an exemplar. Daston turns to an old religious manual, the *Rule of Saint Benedict*. And it turns out the rule here isn't some explicit statement in words. The rule is Saint Benedict himself, the actual historical person. To follow the rule of Saint Benedict isn't to follow some explicit procedure, but to model yourself on Saint Benedict, to do what he would have done. This is the kind of rule embodied in mottoes like What Would Jesus Do? And notice that when you apply a model, you aren't following some mechanical formula. You have a complex and open-ended process: activating your understanding of this model person, and imagining how they'd act in some new situation.

Principles and models both require careful judgment to apply. Whether such a rule applies to this particular case will always be open to interpretation and up for debate.

The third kind of rule is completely different. This is a rule as an *algorithm*, an explicit directive meant to be applied mechanically—without discretion or judgment, exactly as it is written, with no exceptions. And it is this algorithmic conception of a rule that has become dominant in the past century, says Daston. It is so dominant, in fact, that people can have a hard time wrapping their heads around these older conceptions of rules—to see what they're for and why we might ever prefer the fuzzier, more open-ended principles and models to the more precise, complete algorithms.

The algorithmic rule, says Daston, is a relatively modern invention. You might think algorithmic rules arose with the rise of computing machines. But they actually showed up about a hundred years earlier, she says, in a move to cheapen labor. Older mathematical methods often involved principles—that is, mathematical rules that had to be applied with care and discretion. For a given problem, you would have your choice of different mathematical tools and methods, each of which would yield a different result. You'd have to use your judgment to know which method was best for a particular problem, and how exactly to apply it.

A simplified example: There are many different methods to split a slice of pie in two. You can do it by weight. You can divide it according to an exact angle, which you have measured with a protractor. Or you can use the "I cut, you choose" method. Each yields a slightly different result, and different situations call for different methods. If the goal is to create two perfect-looking slices of pie for an advertising photo shoot, maybe you want a protractor. If you are a chemist trying to figure out the exact caloric count of a serving of pie, you should use weight. If the goal is to let two feuding siblings split a piece of pie without either of them feeling like they got screwed— then use the "I cut, you choose" method.

For complicated problems, choosing the right method took a considerable amount of expertise, so you had to hire people with lots of mathematical training and experience in the right field. Such trained mathematicians were rare and expensive. So corporations and governments spent a lot of resources creating an alternative to expensive, experienced experts: rule sets that anybody could mechanically follow.

This, says Daston, is an algorithmic rule: a procedure that anybody can follow.

Early examples of algorithmic rules include logarithm tables and various tables for performing navigational calculations. Such tables could be used by virtually anybody, and their work could be checked by virtually anybody else. There was no choice about which method to use: You just took some numbers and plugged them into the charts. So now you could hire cheaper workers—basically unskilled labor— to do the same job. And anybody could audit a worker's performance; you didn't need to pay another specialized expert to check over your first specialized expert's work.

To be an algorithm here doesn't mean that something is executed on a machine rather than by a human. To be an algorithm is to be a rule that has been written to be used *without significant skill, judgment, or discretion*. In fact, says Daston, the term *calculator* didn't originally mean a machine for doing math, but referred to teams of relatively unskilled laborers applying these algorithmic tables and charts. Mechanical is a state of mind.

Daston has given us an extremely clear account of what it means to be mechanical. A rule is mechanical precisely because anybody can apply it in the same way. Mechanical rules are accessible; they enable consistency across different people. They eliminate the uneven unpredictability of rules that require discretion, judgment, and interpretation.

So why transform our procedures from principles to algorithms? Why mechanize things? Because, says Daston, mechanical procedures are cheaper and more accessible. They are faster to learn and easier to use, by a broader range of people. But there is, once again, a massive trade-off. According to Daston, algorithmic rules work well when the context in which they're applied is similar to the context in which they were formulated. But they work badly once the context changes. They can't adapt to new details. Algorithmic rules are highly efficient in stable environments, but bad in dynamic environments.

This all might seem pretty abstract. So let's turn to thinking about a very familiar and concrete case of mechanical rules: recipes.

MY MOTHER WAS AN EXCELLENT COOK. SHE LEARNED TO COOK not from cookbooks and recipes, but from her family and friends in Vietnam. Like a lot of people from her generation, she cooked relatively few dishes, but she cooked them extraordinarily well. This is completely unlike lots of younger people, like me, who often cook something different every night, following some recipe we found in a cookbook or by googling.

I learned to cook a couple of years after I'd graduated from college. My mother never tried to teach me. She expressed a lot of regret over this later. She admitted that it hadn't even occurred to her to try to teach a boy to cook.

I taught myself to cook after college through recipes, using a few key classic cookbooks: Julia Child's French cookbooks and Marcella

Hazan's Italian cookbooks. And I got great results. So on one visit home, I asked my mom to teach me my very favorite Vietnamese dish: hot and sour catfish soup. So she did—or she tried to. What she gave me wasn't anything I could follow; it was nothing like a recipe at all. It seemed to me, at the time, like this vast and disorganized ramble, a weird organic messy flowchart of possibilities and decisions and judgment calls. I was supposed to add tomato and pineapple but I was supposed to taste the ingredients first. If one was sweet and the other sour, I was probably fine. But if they were both particularly sweet, I would need to balance them with some extra vinegar. Or if they were both sour, I might need to add a little brown sugar. My mom wouldn't ever tell me how much; it all depended on how things were tasting that day. And I had to smell the catfish—was it a particularly clean, farmed variety, or was it one of those funky-smelling wild ones?

I was horrified by the mess of what she was giving me. And what I said to her then, to my eternal shame, was: "Mom, what is this Third World bullshit? Give me a *real* recipe!"

What I didn't understand then was that my mom *was* giving me something real—something profoundly real. But it was completely different from the kinds of tidy recipes I was used to from my modern cookbooks. I was used to recipes where I didn't have to taste the food as I went, where I didn't have to make judgment calls—where I could just dump in the required ingredients in the exact specified amounts. These precise, modern recipes had, in a weird way, disrupted my sense of what cooking was and could be. I had come to assume that cooking—real cooking—had to proceed via an algorithm. I had refused to accept that real cooking might involve a messy and organic decision space, full of a thousand decision points and judgment calls.

Daston points out that there has been an enormous shift in the kinds of recipes we find in cookbooks over time. Old-school cookbooks often gave recipes that would look unrecognizably vague to the modern eye. A recipe for egg bread might look like this:

> Combine about ten handfuls of flour, four or five eggs, and a handful of warm water with a bit of yeast. Knead vigorously, adding more flour or water as needed, to maintain workable dough. Knead until the dough has a pleasantly stretchy texture. Bake in a medium-hot oven, adding some splashes of water to the oven to keep the air modestly moist, until the bread is golden brown and has a nice hollow ring when knocked.

Compare that to a typical modern recipe for bread:

> 3 cups flour
> 4 eggs
> ⅔ cup warm water (110 degrees F)
> 2 (0.25 oz) packets instant yeast
> 1 tsp salt
>
> Combine ingredients and knead until the dough can be stretched to sufficient transparency to read through. Bake at 350 degrees for 45 minutes. Let rest 10 minutes before slicing.

The old-school recipe is made up of principles, and the new-school recipe is made up of algorithms. The old-school recipe requires a bunch of judgment calls to apply, and those calls involve having a fair bit of experience with bread—with having a sense of how dough feels when kneaded appropriately, and how one might adjust to find that feeling by adding more flour and sugar. The new-school recipe mostly removes judgment calls, substituting various algorithmic rules that can be executed by almost anybody.

The advantages of the new-school, algorithmic recipe are obvious. First and foremost, it is highly accessible. Anybody, so long as they have access to the requisite measuring equipment, can execute the recipe, and the variation between different recipe users will be relatively low. I am not a particularly good baker, but I have used modern, algorithmic recipes to produce delicious bread on the first try.

Let me be clear here: I learned to cook from algorithmic recipes, and I never would have been able to get a start with cooking Japanese, Mexican, or Russian food without them. The old-school recipe might be a useful guide for an experienced baker. But for a total novice, it is miserably cryptic—full of tough decisions and subtle sensory cues. Algorithmic recipes are a useful means of finding your way into a new cuisine. They are a great starting point—but hopefully, you eventually move past them.

Algorithmic recipes are also great if you're a massive fast-food franchise and want to use low-skill, replaceable employees to produce food that tastes the same in every location. But in this case, algorithmic recipes aren't just the starting point. These fast-food companies want the food to taste the same no matter who's making it, so they demand workers stick to the algorithmic recipe. And to make this work, industrial-scale food companies also need to standardize the inputs. They need to make sure that the buns and the burger patties and the cheese they're shipping to each of their franchises are exactly the same. Standardized inputs plus algorithmic procedures equals consistent results, without any need for expert workers.

The relative disadvantages of the algorithmic recipe are rather subtler, but they are very real. The algorithmic recipe is profoundly nonadaptable if you follow it as written. And if you diverge from it, then you've lost much of the advantages of algorithms. Your divergence requires you to use your judgment, to lean on your experience. So what are the downsides of following an algorithmic recipe precisely, exactly as it's written? What is the cost of engineered accessibility?

Back in an earlier era of my life, when I was a food writer, I interviewed an incredible pizza chef in L.A. He ran a wild-yeast sourdough Neapolitan pizza shop called Mother Dough that made some of the most glorious, absurdly radiant pizzas I have ever had in my life. He wasn't from Naples; he was Lebanese. He told me that one day, eating a perfect Neapolitan pizza, he'd had a mystical insight about the unity of all the flatbread traditions, about the beautiful spectrum that encompassed both Lebanese flatbreads and Neapolitan pizza. So he moved to Naples and apprenticed himself to a pizza master for a decade, and then moved to L.A. and opened up his shop.

I asked him how he made pizza so good—God-pizza, pizza that sang with the most delicate balance of crispy to chewy, that gave me the most angelic hit of pure beauty, while smacking me with pure animal gut-joy. He pointed out the enormous wood-fired copper pizza oven at the back of the shop. "See that?" he said. "That's the temperature gauge. I painted it over, with black paint, so I couldn't look at it. It's a distraction. You have to put your hand here"—he placed his hand directly at the open mouth of the pizza oven—"and feel how it's breathing. It will tell you how the pizza wants to be cooked that day. You can't trust the temperature gauge to tell you the truth."

What he meant was that temperature wasn't all that mattered, but if you had the temperature gauge, you would be tempted to hyper-focus on it to the exclusion of all else. Baking is a complex act, where a live product—yeast and dough—reacts to a complex set of ever-changing environmental qualities. Temperature matters, but also humidity, air flow, air pressure. And all that atmospheric stuff is changing, every day. There is no single correct baking time and temperature. What you need to do changes each day, in response to those changing variables. And this pizza chef had learned to perform, by feel, a complex synthesis of all these factors. He had painted over his temperature gauge because it was a distraction. It tempted you to focus completely on one thing, to treat the single measurement it tracked—temperature—as the all-important one, instead of looking at the complex interaction of all the relevant qualities.

His shop was also incredibly consistent. It produced amazing wood-fired pizzas, and he nailed that exact texture of dough every single day. Other shops—those where people were following an algorithm, baking a pizza with an exact amount of time and temperature each day—were actually far more inconsistent in their *results*. They had crispy pizza dough one day and rubbery dough the next, even though their *procedure* was more consistent. Why? Because the rigidity of the algorithm, when followed mechanically, prevents the cooks from adapting to continually changing conditions. Air pressure changes, humidity changes, yeast changes, but the algorithm remains the same. The true master cook adapts their procedures to changing inputs.

And the demand for mechanicity pushes us toward avoiding the use of our trained sensitivities. Let's go back to the old-school bread recipe, where you're supposed to bake the bread until it rings in a certain way when knocked. Here, the recipe is asking you to look for a specific quality that is deeply tied to what really matters. The sound is an indicator of internal loft. In the new-school recipe, we've removed the sensory judgment and substituted a simple measurement of time. "Bake at 350 degrees for 45 minutes" is a mechanical rule. It is an explicit directive that refers to clear demarcations that anybody can find, with access to the standard tools.

But time isn't always a reliable indicator of doneness in bread. A lot depends on the temperature of the dough when it goes in the oven, on the ambient humidity, on all that stuff. The sound of the bread is actually a more reliable indicator of doneness, but it requires experience and trained sensory capacity to exercise. In the new-school recipe, we've substituted a mechanical standard—one that anybody can apply if they have access to the basic tools. The new-school recipe isn't actually more reliable. The old-school recipe sounds, to modern ears, weirdly primitive—but it's more accurate where it counts. It exercises your skill and trained sensitivity to track the most important quality, which is internal loft. But this old-school, principle-based recipe isn't usable by everybody.

The new-school recipe trades *accuracy* for *accessibility*. And it does so because real accuracy, in real-world situations, with a complex changing environment, requires flexibility and adaptation. When we substitute a simple mechanical rule, we're removing the demand for skilled adaptability. And, weirdly enough, what makes the modern recipe feel modern is precisely the fact that it excludes the use of trained judgment and developed sensitivity. It feels modern because it's mechanical. For people like me, raised on modern cookbooks, these recipes feel more real, because they've been written to be *usable without skill*.

You can make algorithmic recipes work better, though, by decreasing the variety of the world. My mom gave me complex directions in which I had to taste the tomatoes and the pineapple and then adjust everything in response, because these are particularly variable ingredients. Some days tomatoes and pineapples are more sweet, and other days they're more sour, and you have to compensate. One way out of the need for adaptation is to standardize your tomatoes and pineapples. Many of my Italian cookbooks call for a specific variety of canned tomatoes: San Marzanos, which are all grown in one region of Italy, in very similar volcanic soil. This is a very stable ingredient; every can tastes pretty much the same, year after year. If all the ingredients have been fixed to be the same, then we can, indeed, just follow an algorithmic recipe. Like Daston says, algorithms work well when the world doesn't change. But the sense that such recipes are perfectly reliable is partially an illusion. It depends on the vast amount of work spent making the world of ingredients consistent. But that reliability vanishes once you leave that space of artificial stability.

When I started shopping at farmers markets and buying these incredibly flavorful but highly variable heirloom tomatoes from different stands, I had a moment of pure confusion. The tomatoes I was tasting raw were incredible—these dense, explosively flavorful things—but when I started cooking with them, my recipes stopped working. It took me a while to realize why. I went from using highly invariant canned tomatoes to buying delicious but ever-changing fresh tomatoes. I'd left the world of carefully constructed standardization. But I was still cooking algorithmically, dumping in the exact amounts called for, without tasting or adjusting to my constantly variable tomatoes. So I had to learn to do exactly what I'd rejected in my mom's messy flowchart. I had to taste, I had to decide, and I had to make on-the-fly judgments based on my experience. I had to adapt.

A RECIPE IS A SIMPLE EXAMPLE OF A MECHANICAL PROCEDURE. A procedure is mechanical if it's consistently applicable, by different people, without the need for judgment. (Daston uses the words *algorithmic* and *mechanical* somewhat interchangeably, but I'm going to simplify the language from this point and just talk about mechanical rules.) And that consistency is often quite narrow. A mechanical recipe leads to consistency in procedure, but not necessarily in the final results.

By implementing mechanical procedures, we can rid ourselves of the need for skill or sensitivity, to varying degrees. Your typical recipe is built to be followed by anybody who can read and has access to some basic cup measures. There are also mechanical procedures for experts, like a standard procedure for running a test for chem lab techs. These are written assuming a greater level of background knowledge, but once you have that background knowledge, it'll be executed in the same way, by all users—without the need for judgment.

Here is the trade-off between fuzzy principles and mechanical procedures. Fuzzy principles, like those old-school recipes, require the trained judgment of a highly experienced person to apply, which means they can use all the experience, sensitivity, and attunement of that judge. They can use complex cues for action, like "Bake until it makes a hollow ringing sound," or "Add pineapple until it tastes balanced." That linguistic fuzziness opens a space for expertise and sensitivity. Fuzzy language is a cue for the person executing the rule to exercise their own judgment. But that procedure won't be as easy to execute by the public at large, nor can the public as easily inspect and oversee other people's applications of the procedure. And different experts might end up doing different things following that procedure.

A mechanical procedure, on the other hand, is highly repeatable and accessible. Mechanical procedures work best with the kinds of things that are naturally public and observable by everybody. This is when we truly get to harness the power of scale, and reap the rewards of massive collections of data. But other times, the situation may be subtler—something that requires discernment, sensitivity, and expertise to notice. And in those cases, mechanical procedures are far less accurate. They will miss the mark in subtle terrain, because they're bound by the demand that the steps be clear and explicit enough that they may be consistently applied by anybody.

Mechanical evaluation systems have a power. They grant us portability, and freedom from a certain kind of corruption and bias. They create easy convergence. But they also introduce a new kind of bias: a bias toward *paying attention to the kinds of things that we can count mechanically*, and especially toward what's easy to count mechanically.

WE HAVE NOW MET THE SECOND HORSEMAN OF BUREAUCRACY. His name is Rules (full name: Mechanical Rules). He gives us clear procedures that everybody can follow in the same way. By giving us this tool, Rules offers us an enormous power. Rules will make policies consistent and easy-to-follow for everybody. He offers *accessibility* and *consistency*, which are the bedrock for coordinating across vast scale. This is why Rules and Scale ride together. Rules makes the way easy for Scale. Scale wants to cross contexts, to have processes that work universally. Rules can give us that by making mechanical procedures that are designed for everybody to follow consistently. And at their best, Rules and Scale give us the power of data: vast collections of information that have been collected in a consistent manner, because the rules have been written so that everybody can collect them in the same way.

But Rules also charges a heavy price. Rules confines us to operating in the terrain where everybody can repeat a procedure consistently. When the terrain is more obvious, that's fine. But when it's more subtle, Rules will want to change what we target and count, to something that everyone can repeat with the same result. And in order to serve Scale—in order to get us working precisely together, in the same system, emitting the same results—we need to follow Rules without deviation. We need to be locked in. We can't make exceptions based on our judgment, or shift around how we apply the rule, or we lose out on much of that power. We can't use our discretion to adapt to changing circumstances.

Rules offers us the power of *accessibility*. What he asks us to sacrifice is *adaptability*.

CHAPTER 12

Flexibility Through Restriction

After the previous chapter, you might have started to think the true problem, at the root of things, is just using mechanical rules for evaluation—that any kind of mechanical rule set in a scoring system will suck the life out of everything, and that we should perpetually try to keep things soft, gushy, and ill-defined whenever we're evaluating anything. But that, I think, is an oversimplification. Because there's a clear upside to mechanical scoring systems. And the shining example has been staring us in the face the whole time.

Games often have incredibly clear and perfectly mechanical scoring systems. And when taken in the right spirit, they are the opposite of soul-deadening. In games, mechanical scoring systems can be the gateway to delight, fluidity, and flexibility. Games are a place where mechanical scoring systems can help us explore the space of values. The paradox of mechanical rules is: Sometimes they trap us, and sometimes they set us free.

So what's the difference?

—

GAMES SUGGEST THE OUTLINES OF AN ALTERNATE SELF, AND we flow into it, taking on alternate desires and alternate abilities. We pay attention to different reasons. What matters in ordinary life falls away; new things start mattering keenly. Our agency is fluid, and games provide a container that we can pour ourselves into. They provide a temporary shape for us to take on in our souls.

This fluidity of agency is not unique to games; it happens all over the place. Games just make it easier to see.

The notion of agency I'm using here is an old one. I'm talking about it in the sense that trading companies had agents, or that I have a literary agent. In that old sense of the word, an *agent* is somebody who represents some set of interests. If you have an agent, they represent you. When they are acting as your agent, they are supposed to make choices—not out of their own interests and values, but out of yours. As the philosopher Carol Rovane puts it: An agent is some entity that considers reasons, makes choices based on those reasons, and acts. And if you change the reasons that you act on, you change your agency.

It turns out that our cares and desires and rationality are more fluid than we might have thought. We can shift between different perspectives, change how we reason and what we care about. This isn't unique to games. We do this all the time. We shift roles, which involves changing how we reason and what drives us. I, for example, have a "teacher" mode. When I'm in teacher mode, I dampen down a lot of my normal self. It didn't always used to be that way. When I was a new teacher, I brought my full self into the classroom, and this actually caused all kinds of problems. For example, I could tell that certain students were from my tribe. They liked the same bands I liked, had the same sense of humor, the same politics. I vibed with them more; I was nicer and chiller and more relaxed talking to them. And this, it turned out, was a terrible way to teach. I had personal favorites, and the other students resented it. So, over the years, I learned to turn that part of myself off. My social side that loves certain personalities and detests others—I pretty much get rid of that in the classroom. Instead, I carve out a smaller self, a more impartial self. I become a person aimed at providing an equal educational opportunity to every student, helping everybody become better at reading and reflecting and analyzing.

Such role-shifting is incredibly common. I used to be a food critic, and I can still put on my critic hat. I can look at any piece of art—paintings, comics, TV shows, pop songs, a taco—and go merciless mode. From that mental angle, I will be deeply picky and deeply critical. I will be on a relentless hunt for real originality and subtlety. Then there's another role I play: parent. And in that role, every single drawing my kid makes is *absolutely goddamn amazing.*

We humans have an enormous capacity for agential fluidity. We can shift roles and reasons like changing hats. What it is to be an official, to act in an official capacity, is to ignore a lot of your personal reasons. A police officer, a tax commissioner—they're not supposed to make choices based on who they like, who is part of their tribe, who shares their musical tastes. They're only supposed pay attention to a narrow set of official reasons. Weirdly, what we want from our officials is to have our particular humanity be substantially ignored.

IN GAMES, I ALSO IGNORE A LOT OF MY USUAL SOCIAL RELATION-ships. I ignore the fact that this person is my spouse or my friend—

and I just go all out to defeat them. Or I temporarily cancel out my hatred for a person if they're on my team. But this time I do it not to be an impartial official, but because it's fun.

And games make our fluidity far easier and quicker to exercise. It took me about five years to learn to enter the "impartial teacher" role. But in games, we can do it in an instant. We can open up a rule book, read the rules, and plunge ourselves into a new form of agency. How is this possible?

Here is my proposal: *Games can support such quick agential fluidity precisely because the rules and scoring system of a game are mechanical.*

Mechanical rules are engineered to be clear, so that everybody knows how to apply them. Most game scoring systems are mechanical: They tell you exactly what you need to do to get a point. In Dungeons & Dragons, each monster is worth an explicit number of experience points, and you collect those points by killing the monster, which involves damaging it past its explicit number of hit points.

John Dewey suggested that every art form crystallized something that we did naturally—extracted it from normal life and made it more intense and perfect. Games take the natural agency-shifting that we already do—our ability to flit between different abilities and motivations—and heighten it. They play with our natural fluidity, sculpting it with precision.

WE'VE ARRIVED AT ANOTHER ONE OF THESE WEIRD PARADOXES of human life: how strict rules can sometimes make us more playful and more exploratory.

One of the curious things about tabletop role-playing games is that you're trying to engage in a creative act, one of storytelling and play, but then you saddle yourself with all these rules and point structures. Outsiders of the hobby will sometimes ask why. Why do all that, why confine yourself with those rules? Why restrict yourself when you're just playing? Why not just cut loose, throw away the rules, and tell stories out of the pure freedom of your mind?

Weirdly, pure freedom usually doesn't work out all that well. Role-playing designers have experimented with minimal rule sets, getting rid of scoring systems and character skill points, and just pointing you in the general direction of a story. It turns out minimal, rule-less role-playing systems don't work that well for most people. They often end up just telling the same tired stories over and over again. More rules and restrictions — more structure — strangely enough, often lead to more creativity.

It's an old idea that constraints spur creativity. Poets know it. Writing free verse can freeze you up, but when you make yourself stick to a specific poetic form, the intense restrictions can spur you to creative heights. Role-playing game players and designers know that very well, too. The structure of constraints in role-playing offers a spur to creativity.

Take, for instance, rolling the dice. Almost every successful role-playing game has dice rolls. Designers have tried to eliminate dice from role-playing games, but found that diceless games usually made for worse stories. Why? One theory is that without dice rolls, people are more free — and when they're free, they tend to tell predictable stories. Under pressure, players usually end up rehashing the standard tropes and clichés.

But everything changes when you're forced to roll some dice and see if you succeed. The mechanics of the system push you into unexpected events. You thought your master swordsman would have no trouble showing off and you try to do an acrobatic swing from the rafters — but you make an incredibly unlucky roll, and the dice say you fail. The system forces something unexpected on you, and now it's off the rails—and the story becomes new and alive.

The scoring system can also be tuned toward creativity. Recall *Lady Blackbird*, where you got points for acting in character, and double points for getting into trouble by acting in character. Once again, the clarity of the rules goads people into action. It's one thing to say, "Your character is a sad ex-orphan with parental authority issues and a need to prove themselves. Act in character." It's another thing to say, "Your character gets a point whenever they show off in front of their friends, and gets a point whenever they refuse an order." The latter system is far easier to be guided by in the heat of high-speed improvisational storytelling.

Of course, a trained improv actor could use the nonmechanical instruction set and do a great job. But they're also using a system—a subtler and more inchoate one that they learned through plenty of practice. My point is not that mechanical scoring systems are the only way to get good storytelling or good character work. It's that they make it easier and quicker to dive into an alternate character. They make new perspectives more accessible.

BUT HOW DO RIGID RULES ENABLE PLAYFULNESS AND EXPLOration? Some people think rules and play are deeply opposed in spirit. The games and play scholar Miguel Sicart believes games kill play. True play, he says, is about getting beyond the rules, transcending restrictions. Games with prespecified rules and goals are antithetical to the spirit of pure creativity and freedom.

I think this is a false dilemma. Games are a rigid structure that cultivates playfulness, a structured system that encourages lightness. They are *temporary rigid structures* that can actually help you be more free.

All communication requires a certain amount of rigidity. We can't communicate at all if every single person invents their own peculiar language. We need to share some rules in order to talk. We need a stable structure as a foundation, to enable the fast exchange of ideas, the easy flow of creativity between people.

Art is also at the nexus of rigidity and freedom. Literature, for example, is a powerful goad to the imagination. Literature lets us explore alternate social systems and emotional landscapes. But this all depends on an underlying rigid structure of language and narrative convention. Jane Austen couldn't exercise her brand of laser-focused psychological insight and cutting wit without access to an enormous body of stable meanings. Language involves rigid rules about exactly what each word means, and how we should interpret particular grammatical structures. Language connects us, but for that we need a pretty stiff bridge.

Games can do something similar. They communicate new kinds of life by using clear rules, such as absolutely mechanical conditions for victory. In fact, game designers often work by taking fuzzy activities and transforming them into something more precise and mechanical.

Imagine a version of basketball in which people are awarded points for displaying physical skill and athletic virtuosity, period. Those categories, as stated, are quite hard to judge. There aren't any mechanical criteria for skill and virtuosity. So we created one: the basketball hoop. This is a *mechanization device* that creates a clear, mechanical binary condition for victory. It's a system designed to transform some inchoate judgment of physical skill and athletic virtuosity into a quantized point system. (And the basketball net is actually an accessibility device, to amplify the visual clarity of the achievement. If you had the hoop alone, with no net, people might argue about whether the ball went through.)

Games with mechanical scoring conditions make it far easier to shift your agency around, by providing a *clear, explicit recipe for evaluation*. They tell you how to evaluate your success, in terms that anybody can pick up on. They orient you with precision. It's hard to know what exactly you're aiming for if somebody tells you, "Be physically virtuosic and skillful." But it's easy to know what to do when somebody tells you, "Put the ball through the hoop."

There is a board game called *Imperial*, which I love beyond measure. It is also, thematically, spectacularly evil. The game is set during World War I. All the great European powers are fighting it out on the board—the German Empire, Great Britain, France, Austria-Hungary. They are fighting it out in what looks like a perfectly ordinary board game of war. There are little army pieces and navy pieces that move around and fight each other, and little factory pieces that let countries build those armies and navies.

Except you don't play as the countries. Each of the players takes the role of a shadowy investor behind the scenes, investing in the various countries and manipulating the course of the war for their own profit. You control any country you have the most invested in, but control can shift. More important, the scoring system is about how much your investments are worth, not whether your countries win the war. This leads to some truly evil strategies, like starting a war between two countries you own to make a profit.

It captures a mindset not of total war, but of watching and manipulating shared incentives. The first time I felt I truly understood the game was when I realized how the players' interests and motivations were deeply separate from the countries' interests. On our first play, before we had really come to terms with how the game was asking us to play, we were all playing it like a regular war game, like *Risk*. Each of us invested mostly in one country and tried to win the war with that country. At one point, I was heavily invested in Great Britain, and another player, Sarah, was heavily invested in Austria-Hungary. I could see that Austria-Hungary was gearing up to attack Great Britain. And I thought a war was inevitable.

Until I realized that the right move was not for Sarah and me to fight it out. Instead, I let her have some cheap stock in Britain. This meant I had less control of Britain, and Britain's profits were now split between Sarah and me. But it also meant we were coinvested in Britain, and she no longer had much reason to direct Austria-Hungary to attack Britain—because she now, in fact, owned a third of Britain.

The game simulates a Machiavellian mindset, but one that is oriented toward watching and manipulating shared incentives. And it trained a part of my brain that I still use, every time I'm in some university meeting, fighting for the life of the philosophy department against the systematic defunding of humanities programs. *Imperial* trained me in this mode of getting people to do what you want by giving them a piece of the action. And it's not just training some technical skill. *Imperial* gave me a whole outlook, a whole attentional focus—zeroed in on studying and manipulating the structure of shared incentives.

This isn't, obviously, the only way to get those skills and perspectives—just as reading literature isn't the only way to gain empathy and sensitivity. You can do it by living life, learning hard lessons from grim experience, and talking to people. And recipes aren't the only way to learn to cook—you can do it by apprenticing yourself to a master, or through trial and error. But games, literature, and recipes are all very convenient communicative packages, which crystallize different parts of human life into highly accessible and portable forms. Games aren't the only way to expand your agency, but they're a particularly sharp and quick way of *encoding* agency—of writing it down, storing it, and passing it on to new people. And at the heart of many games is a mechanical scoring system, because a mechanical scoring system *makes radically different values accessible to anybody.*

Games are a way of writing down different practical perspectives. Games let us communicate new modes of agency. And mechanical scoring systems are at their center because they let us easily communicate goals and values. Scoring systems can be used to explore alternate selves. Games are a library of agency.

I LEARNED THE BEST WAY OF UNDERSTANDING THE WEIRD RE-lationship between rigid rules and deep flexibility from a yoga teacher. She would rattle off these incredibly precise movement cues, telling us to lift our chest like a line was pulling it straight toward the ceiling, to arch our back like a cat and send a wave up our spine, rolling up one vertebra at a time. Sometimes I'd rebel or my mind would wander, and I'd just vaguely make some random movement instead of doing exactly what she said. And she'd scold me. She said the whole problem was that so many of us were trapped in old habits, in unthinking movement patterns. We tended to stand the same way, to hunch in the same way, to get trapped in a rut of our habitual posture.

The precision of the yoga poses, she said, forces you out of your ruts. It prevents you from falling into the same habits of motion. The restrictions force you out of unthinking repetition and into a new pattern of movement. The strictness of a yoga pose is exactly what helps you build fluidity, because it pushes you to explore something new. The precise specification of a yoga pose is a cage in the short term, but freeing in the long term.

Games are like that, but for action and values. In a game, the rigid rules and scoring system force you into a new mode of valuing, and a new mode of action. Soccer rules say you need to score goals without using your hands, and so suddenly you're plunged into seeing how much you can control a ball with your feet. Rock climbing rules say you have to go up, but without pulling on a rope. So now you are pushed into discovering exactly how much you can do just by refining your balance and controlling the precise angle of your fingers and toes.

Games are yoga for your agency.

CHAPTER 13

The Secret Heart
of Mechanization

Why do we want mechanized values in our real-world systems? What purpose does mechanization serve in our institutions and our public life?

You might think a major benefit of mechanized evaluation is objectivity. And it's true, mechanical procedures are very good at getting us certain kinds of objectivity. But we have to be careful here, because *objectivity* is a very loaded term. It's easy to slip into this simple divide, in which humans exercising intuition and judgment is "subjective" and therefore bad, and following a mechanical procedure for judgment is "objective" and therefore good.

But objectivity is much more complicated than that. There are lots of different kinds of objectivity, and those different kinds often run at cross purposes. Sometimes, by "objectivity," we mean that something is bias-free. But as we've seen, mechanical procedures can be deeply biased toward what's mechanically countable. Sometimes, objectivity means a process is accurate. But mechanical values often fail to capture what we originally cared about.

What explicit bureaucratic procedures are good at, says Theodore Porter, is achieving a very specific thing, which he calls "mechanical objectivity." This means *they can be repeated by anybody to get to the same result.* There is a similar concept in law, says Porter, called "legal objectivity." A legally objective procedure is one that will yield the same result for a given case no matter who applies it. And in the legal context, we are often willing to give up a significant degree of accuracy in order to achieve legal objectivity.

Consider what it is to be an adult. Adulthood involves lots of complex features—emotional maturity, intellectual maturity, and all that. And a lot of the rights we want to grant—the right to vote, the right to decide to drink alcohol—should be pegged to that important but complicated thing called maturity. But maturity is difficult to assess, and different people will come to different conclusions. So we use a clear line: age in years. In the United States, you get to vote when you turn eighteen. Age is just an approximation of maturity. "Eighteen years old" is not a perfect tracker of maturity, but it's a simple and highly accessible substitute.

And this case makes clear why we often want legal objectivity over accuracy. It would be absolutely unworkable to park individual judges at voting booths and let them each make their own assessment about who's mature enough to vote. There is so much danger for biased judgments and corruption here, so we draw a clear, mechanical line. There is no question about whether somebody is over eighteen, and everybody should apply that rule in the same way. Mechanical rules are worth it in this particular case.

But mechanical objectivity isn't always what we want. The philosopher of law Timothy Endicott puts it this way: Laws with vague language—like "the right to vote is granted to people with intellectual maturity"—will be applied by different people in different ways. When we have laws like that, we expose ourselves to one kind of arbitrariness: that of the individual judge. Different people will judge intellectual maturity in different ways, so whether you get to vote depends heavily on the luck of the draw—on who's judging your intellectual maturity. So we often replace those vague laws with laws with precise language, like "the right to vote is granted to people over the age of eighteen." We eliminate the arbitrariness of individual judges. But, says Endicott, precise language introduces a new kind of arbitrariness: that of sharp lines drawn through a world that is naturally full of gradual spectrums and shades of gray. The choice between vague and precise legal language is a choice between two different sorts of arbitrariness.

We can't eliminate arbitrariness; we can only choose between different kinds. So, says Endicott, we should choose our trade-offs with care. Mechanical rules gain consistent repeatability but often trade away deep accuracy. And we will want to trade differently in different contexts. In the legal voting age case, there's not a huge difference between 17 years and 11 months old and 18 years old. But it's worth it to introduce the arbitrariness of sharp lines in order to remove the possibility of biased judgment at the voting booth. Here, mechanical objectivity gives us a huge benefit. But other times we may want a different trade-off. Is my kid old enough to watch *Tremors*, a goofy faux-B-movie horror flick about burrowing mega-worms that eat people? It's PG-13, and my kid is eight, with a love for creepy anime and *Minecraft* faux-horror videos. I could just follow the rule and not let him watch it until he's thirteen—or I could use my discretion. And there's not much upside to sticking dogmatically to a precise rule here. I have a lot of detailed information about this particular movie and this particular kid. Mechanical objectivity has little advantage here. Sticking to it would force us to give up the relevant information about the specific situation that we, in fact, have access to.

My worry is that we are starting to automatically reach for the mechanical rule, abdicating discretionary judgment even when the context calls for it. And this is what we are doing when we let ourselves be value-captured by a mechanical value. We are accepting into our hearts a procedure for evaluating ourselves and the world around us that meets the highest standard of accessibility, at the cost of adaptability and sensitivity. We are choosing consistency of procedure over sensitivity to the particulars.

WHY DO WE WANT MECHANICITY SO MUCH, THOUGH?

Let's first get clearer on what mechanicity is, exactly. Recall Lorraine Daston's notion of a mechanical rule as one that can be used by anybody, without a significant amount of skill. This notion is quite binary: Something is mechanical if it is usable by absolutely anybody, with no skill at all.

But there's a bit more of a complicated spectrum than that. My spouse is a research chemist; she designs new kinds of chemical tests, and once she's finished prototyping, she writes a standard operating procedure (SOP) for lab techs to execute. The SOP is written so that any lab tech can follow it precisely, with the same result. But that's not everybody. The SOP is written specifically so that anybody with a bachelor's degree in chemistry—and a few days of extra internal training—can follow it consistently. The SOP is a set of mechanical rules, but it's not one that absolutely anybody can use. It's a mechanical rule set that's been tuned to a particular group. But if you're in the group and have the requisite technical training, the rules are written so that you can follow them automatically— without judgment or discretion.

So let me offer the following definition of a *mechanical rule*, which is relativized to a particular group.

A mechanical rule is one that can be followed consistently by any member of a specified group.

The size of the specified group varies. Some mechanical rules are designed to be usable by anybody with a fifth-grade-equivalent reading ability. Some demand a more specific technical background, like having a bachelor's degree in chemistry. But a mechanical rule designed for a group could not demand any further special sensitivity or nuance beyond the membership conditions of that group. We must omit any rules that require more specialized understanding to use.

For example, the demands of mechanicity changed how we measure land. In older societies, people often used highly flexible, functional measures of land. In the Domesday Book of 1086, English surveyors measured land using the *hide*. A hide is the amount of land required to sustain an average family.

Notice that a hide doesn't equate to a fixed volume of land. It's a measure not of size, but of fertility and richness. A hide by a river full of fish would be pretty small. A hide in a forest might be larger; one in a grassland even larger; and a hide in a desert would be massive. And notice that the hide isn't even equivalent to some average crop yield. What matters for a hide is the ability to support a family. So if some chunk of land is incredibly fertile most of the time—but every five years it crashes and yields far less than you'd need to survive—it's not a hide.

A hide is a highly functional measure. It tracks a deeply useful piece of information, something that directly matters for human lives. Think about the difference between a king saying, "Give every soldier five acres of land," and "Give every soldier a hide of land." A hide tracks the resources that actually matter to people's real lives.

But hides require a lot of local ecological knowledge to use. So units like the hide tend to disappear as we move away from localized governance toward centralized bureaucracies. In England, the concept of the hide left common usage in the late twelfth century. A centralized bureaucratic government typically wants to use a set of trained land surveyors that can move around the country. This means their methods cannot depend on deep local knowledge of a particular ecosystem. They will want methods that any trained land surveyor will be able to deploy anywhere. So we shifted away from the hide and toward acres and square kilometers. We are making a trade. We are giving up on tracking things that really matter, in exchange for the more accessible technique of drawing straight lines.

WHAT, THEN, DO WE GET OUT OF MECHANIZATION? WHAT DO WE get when we take up Rules on his offer and strictly conform our judgments to mechanical rules? Some of the answers are quite familiar: consistency, accountability, transferability. But underneath those answers, there is a shared foundation. Mechanization makes the world more *fungible*.

To be fungible is to be perfectly replaceable. With fungible objects, there is no value attached to a particular thing. Different instances of the same category will all have the same value.

White sugar and gasoline are highly fungible items. If I borrow a cup of sugar from my neighbor and later give them back a cup of sugar, it doesn't have to be the very same cup of sugar. I don't have to give back exactly the same granules. The value of any cup of refined sugar is pretty much the same as any other.

The most perfectly fungible thing in the world is money. If I borrow twenty dollars from you, I don't have to give back the very same bill. In fact, you can give me a physical twenty-dollar bill, and I can repay you in electronic currency. It doesn't matter.

The least fungible things in the world are our particular human relationships and the physical stuff that relates to them. If you break my precious heirloom — say, the watch my grandfather gave me — you can't just replace it with a different watch, no harm done. And if you steal my spouse, you can't just replace them with a new one.

Much of the efficiency of our world comes from engineered fungibility. Different cups of refined white sugar have the same value to me because they all function exactly the same in my recipes. And that's not just a lucky accident. People — scientists, engineers, corporations — have done serious work to make sugar fungible.

If you've tried unrefined brown sugar from a lot of different places, you'll find there's an enormous variety of tastes and textures. (Try it. Have a brown sugar tasting party.) Some brown sugar tastes intensely vegetal, like grass, with this high crisp, clean note. Other brown sugar is all low notes and infinitely warm richness. I've had raw palm sugars that taste like coconuts and apples, and others that have a wild, electric, raw, flowery, high aroma. Some of these sugars are moist and clumpy, others dry and granular, and others come in hard blocks. Unrefined brown sugars are far less fungible. They have peculiar, specific qualities that you have to work with — and you can't easily replace one kind with another. They can also be quite annoying to use if you've spent your life surrounded by fungible refined white sugar. With refined white sugar, we've worked to remove these various differences and create a universal, interchangeable project. We have created fungibility.

Fungibility often rests on an entire invisible social apparatus, a vast effort of coordination. If I have a quarter-inch nut, I can buy pretty much any quarter-inch bolt and it'll work. But this is constructed magic. It happens because people have put in untold hours making sure every factory that makes quarter-inch bolts manufactures them to a specific set of tolerances. And once they've done all that background work, it makes other parts of life incredibly easy.

But because it is easy everywhere, it tends to recede from our awareness. We forget that the magic of nuts and bolts that fit is the result of a careful and constant effort to keep things in line.

When we create procedures with mechanical rules, *we make workers fungible.* We no longer need to depend on a particular person with a particular long-developed sensitivity. We no longer need to spend years having an expert gradually train their apprentice to be able to do the job. We no longer need to court some small set of specialists. We can look for an easy signal, like having a high school diploma, or a bachelor's degree in the relevant field, and swap out one worker for another with high confidence that they'll do the job the same way, that their outputs will still fit perfectly into the next worker's inputs.

And I mean workers at every level. A mechanical procedure for cooking enables fast-food franchises to swap out entry-level line cooks. But a mechanical metric for corporate success allows us to make CEOs, VPs, and highly paid management consultants into fungible components in an evaluation machine. And making workers fungible isn't just about firing and replacing them. It also means that people from different backgrounds can collect data in precisely the same way. Fungibility is also what enables large-scale data collection. It doesn't matter if you're Korean or Kenyan, raised by corporate type-A go-getters or homeschooled by hippies—you can all count page views and profits the same way.

Worker fungibility also rests on top of a vast, carefully constructed, coordinated social effort. To make sugar fungible, refine it. To make workers fungible, mechanize their procedures. But this, too, is easy to forget about, because mechanization makes things automatic, and automatic things tend to recede into the background.

I met a lady once in a supermarket. She was staring down a shelf full of salsas. There was a tasting table with some samples, and she was chewing her way through them all with resentful ferocity. She turned to me and demanded, "What's all this? What's this salsa verde and New Mexico salsa and all these different kinds? How come these two red salsas taste completely different? And these two are supposed to be medium hot but they're totally different? What the hell? Why do *they* have to make it so complicated?"

There is an underlying worldview implied by her salsa rage. She has assumed that left to its own devices, the world would be regular. Naturally, different people and different companies would have used the same terms to mean the same things. So all the chaos and disorder she was confronting on the salsa-tasting table must have been the result of an intentional conspiracy to disrupt this natural order (presumably one designed to confuse the consumer and make them waste their money).

But in reality, it's the other way around. Left to their own devices, different actors and institutions will naturally tend to use different terms and come up with different procedures. It takes a vast, intentional effort of coordination to bring them into stable order. The reason so many of us expect the world to be simple, stable, and standard is that we have grown up in a world that was carefully made to be that way. We have lived our whole lives in the shadow of a vast conspiracy of order.

WE HAVE NOW MET THE THIRD HORSEMAN OF BUREAUCRACY: Parts. The Horseman of Parts wants pieces that are interchangeable, replaceable. (His full name is Replaceable Parts.) Parts wants to be able to fix the machine. If we lose a screw, Parts wants to be able to buy a new, identical screw. And if we fire a worker, Parts wants to be able to replace them with a new, identical worker. Of course, workers aren't actually identical—each one is a real human being, with their own thoughts and values. But we can make them *functionally* identical, by giving them roles, rules, and procedures. This is why Parts loves Rules. Rules turn people into parts.

This is what Parts asks us to do: Change the world to make workers fungible. To do so, we have created procedures that anybody can execute.

When we mechanize evaluation, we set targets that anybody can count. These new values are accessible, auditable, and utterly comprehensible to all. And when we mechanize our values and targets, we make the job of evaluation fungible. We can swap out one evaluator for another, and they'll still target the same thing and judge success in the same way. We won't need to trust the opaque sensitivities that come from long, nontransferable experience.

You take unruly brown sugar and refine it, removing all the weird differences. The result is the far more fungible white sugar, which functions the same way in different recipes. By suctioning out the variety, you have made standardized procedures work better. In the same way, you can take people and refine them by getting rid of their variable loves and getting them all to care about the same metric. And now they will all function the same way in your institutional machine.

But there is a cost. In order to achieve fungibility, these mechanical measures need to avoid invoking any expert sensitivity or deep and particular experience. The demand for large-scale repeatability gives us the power of vast scale and collective cooperation, at the price of using the specific skills and sensitivities of someone specialized in this particular job, in this particular place.

Parts promises us *interchangeability*. The sacrifice is *specificity*. And when we apply Parts to people, we pay a special version of that price: we give up *individual sensitivity*.

CHAPTER 14

Choice of Difficulty

he Angler is one of my favorite rock climbs in the world. It's
this beautiful line — a perfect forty-five-degree ridge, running
diagonally up an otherwise smooth face of sandstone. It's not
a very hard climb, but it's a Utah classic. It's a technical problem: You
don't need much strength, but you need extremely precise footwork
and body control. The handholds are strange slopy things, like a
ridge made of warped bowling balls. And the footholds are barely
visible: just some tiny soft indentations in the rock. To climb it, you
have to inch over, never letting your hips come too far back. It forces
you into constant intentional, painstaking motion; it requires delicate control of every limb. You become this patient spider-thing,
creeping across the landscape.

The boulder juts out into a river. In the spring, when the river is
high, you can actually end up dangling over the river for the grand
finale. Your face is jammed up against the rock, you can't see a thing,
and all you can hear is the river's roar. Then you throw your hand
over the top, pull over — and suddenly you're standing on top of a

perfect boulder, with the blue-green river rushing all around you. It's a moment of pure climbing ecstasy.

It is also, to outside observers, boring as shit. All the drama is in subtle inner movements — tiny internal shifts in bodily tension, millimeter differences in foot placement. All this is radiantly obvious to the climber themselves. For the climber, it is a gorgeous experience of total absorption. But to the observer, it basically looks like nothing. All you see is the cringing movement of a snail-person inching across the rock face.

I don't climb *The Angler* to impress people. If I wanted to wow nonclimbers, I'd climb something that looked spectacular. If I wanted to impress climbers, I'd climb something harder. I climb *The Angler* because the specific kind of difficulty calls something out of me that I don't get anywhere else — a particular, unforgettable, and distinctive experience of grueling daintiness.

It is a feeling of elegance that is just for me.

NORMALLY, WHEN WE TALK ABOUT ART, WE THINK ABOUT OUR five senses — sight, smell, taste, sound, and touch. These are our outward-facing senses, which tell us about the world. The beauty of the traditional arts usually appeals to those five outward-facing senses. But process art is often inward facing. For physical movement, we have the inner senses — our proprioceptive and kinesthetic senses. The proprioceptive sense is your awareness of where your body is in space — your posture, the relative position of your arms and legs. And your kinesthetic sense refers to your inner sense of your own movement — the power and velocity of your arms. In physical movements, such as yoga, much of the beauty appears to the proprioceptive and kinesthetic senses.

There are all kinds of beauty we can find in our own bodies and minds. One of my favorites is a feeling of being *just right* for a challenge—a sense of harmony between your actions and the obstacles you face. You could call it *practical harmony*. It is the beauty of a special, delicious fit between you and the world.

I have made up my own little classification system for practical harmonies. First, there's the *harmony of the solution*. This is the beauty of a solution that fits the problem exactly. It's the perfect chess move, the right little hip twist that gets you through the crux of a climb, or seeing exactly where that *Tetris* block needs to go. It is the experience of perfect harmony between your actions and the demands of the world. The world is the lock, and you are the key.

The harmony of the solution often appears when things are easy. I climb most gracefully when I'm far below my limit. But that's not the only kind of practical harmony. For many of us, the peak experience of games is not when we come up with perfect solutions to easy problems. It's when we are pushed to our limit. We often lose out on the harmony of the solution here. When I'm climbing at my limit, I'm sloppy, shaking, imperfect. But it feels absolutely amazing. This is a different kind of harmony; let's call it the *harmony of capacity*. This happens when an obstacle takes everything you have. It is a harmony between your maximum capacity and the precise demands of the world. It's not just that your action fits the world; it's that you— your whole self—are just barely enough for the job.

Many of us crave the harmony of capacity. This is one of the reasons why we seek well-matched opponents, or climbs at the edge of our ability. This is why we dial up the difficulty level in our video games. We want the pleasure that only comes when we have to give it our all and just barely scrape by. It is the joy of being exactly what the situation calls for—no more, no less.

In real life, the harmony of capacity is incredibly rare. Most of the time, we do not fit the world so nicely. Sometimes the world is far too hard for us, asking us to throw ourselves at overwhelming problems, like generations-long ethnic conflicts, or a global pandemic, or the wanton destruction of natural ecosystems. Other times, the world is far too easy. It demands that we grind, boringly, at things far below our abilities. Most of the time, either we struggle and fail, or we succeed in boredom. Once in a while we get a hard problem, try with all our might, and just barely solve it—but this is rare magic.

Games are far more malleable than the world. Part of the glory of games is that we can choose the obstacle we want to face. We can dial the difficulty setting up or down, or change opponents, or change games, until we find the level of delicious fit that we want. The harmony of capacity is hard to find in the world, because the world was not made to fit us. But it is easy to find in games—because in games, we make the world. In games, we can manipulate the goals, the obstacles, and the environment, until they suit our capacity—so that we can just soak in the harmony of perfect fit.

When you confront scoring systems in the world, they're often fixed. But games provide you with the possibility of adjusting the scoring system to give you exactly the action you want. The purest form of striving play is when we play for the beauty of the process. It is play for its own sake, for the sheer, gorgeous feel of it. In *aesthetic striving play*, you don't chase victory because the points are actually important. You try to win in order to experience the beauty of ecstatic action.

While I was writing this book, I was also learning to yo-yo. By the way, if you haven't seen what's happened in the high end of modern yo-yo play, you probably have no idea of how absolutely batshit gonzo creative modern yo-yo play has gotten. (If you want a taste of some truly astonishing players, go watch some YouTube videos: Tessa Piccillo's wild slack-string inventiveness in "Kodiak" was what inspired me to learn yo-yo. Also check Jeffrey Pang's "PNWR Yo Yo Contest

2015" documentary, and Charles Haycock's gorgeous stoner weird-ness in "2016 Canada Return Top Classics.")

I was working on a classic yo-yo-trick as I was drafting this chapter—a flipping, delightfully bumpy trick called Candy Rain. It was pretty tough in the beginning, and I almost gave up. Trying the same movement over and over again and missing every time is pretty frustrating. But then you start hitting the trick, once every twenty times. And then something clicks; you start getting it with some regularity. It demands everything; you have to become this cool, elegant, laser-focused being. This is the glorious part.

And then it gets easy. A couple weeks later, I could knock off the trick without thinking about it at all. This is about when it starts looking impressive to the outside world, or at least to your bemused spouse and kids. It turns into a pleasant background fidget, something I can do on autopilot as I think of other things. But as a focused activity, it's a little boring. So I moved on to a harder trick, to start the process all over again.

This is just me. Not everybody is like this, and I'm not saying other people should be. I like a particular spot on the difficulty curve: the moment of epiphany, when things start coming together. So when I have free rein, I pick my challenges to surf my favorite, tastiest spot on the learning curve. But that's just my preference. The world of yo-yo players seems to be full of people like me. There is always some newer, harder trick to learn or invent. Other people like to be elsewhere on the difficulty curve. Some people like eternally repeating a skill they've already mastered. Others can take a level of frustration and failure that I can't handle, and crave games of ungodly difficulty, like *Dark Souls* or winter mountaineering.

This is the incredible part of games: Whatever feeling you want, whatever kind of absorption or intensity you desire, whatever level of difficulty works for you at that moment, you can find it. Games offer you the freedom to sculpt the world, the tasks, and the goal to give you whatever kind of process you want. And they do it because the goals are detached from the world—because you can modify the goals and constraints for your own private joy.

But this is also why devoting yourself to a game can be pretty embarrassing. For a grown-up human being—a parent, a professor, and supposedly an adult—yo-yo is pretty much the most idiotic thing you can do with your time. When I mention my yo-yoing in the company of real adults, I get a lot of barely suppressed eye rolls and condescending chuckles. Yo-yoing is unproductive. It is a profoundly dorky and difficult discipline. Modern high-end yo-yo tricks demand razor-sharp timing and precise control over throw angles. It is an enormous amount of energy to hurl at something utterly useless.

One adult dinner, I found myself trying to hide what I'd been doing in my spare time, until I finally admitted that I'd been learning to yo-yo. But at least, I hurried to say, all this yo-yoing was part of a useful and productive strategy for work. It was a handy little mental break while I was writing; it refreshed my mind and made me more productive. I was trying to justify my yo-yo habit in terms of how it would help my output. But I felt ashamed afterward, because it was a lie. I had betrayed the true spirit of yo-yo. Because the real reason I was doing it was just for the sheer joy of physics made tangible. Yo-yo, for me, is an act of pure play.

YO-YOS HAVE CHANGED DRAMATICALLY IN THE PAST FEW DE-cades. A yo-yo consists of two balanced halves connected by a central axle—the part you wrap the string around. Old-school yo-yos have wooden axles. The axle itself doesn't spin; it is fixed, glued into the rest of the yo-yo. The freedom to spin happens in the slippage between the fixed wooden axle and the string. But there's also a lot of friction. When you throw one of these old-school wooden fixies, the yo-yo will spin for a couple of seconds, then stop.

Over the twentieth century, yo-yos accumulated a huge number of technological innovations, including spinning plastic axles and plastic bodies. Those innovations reached a climax around 2000, when we got what is recognizably the modern yo-yo. The axle is now made from updated, precision-manufactured metal ball bearings, and it spins extraordinarily well. The body is now lathed from aircraft-grade aluminum. The result is a powerful yo-yo that can spin for minutes, with incredible stability and flight control. These improvements enabled the modern vocabulary of intensely complex, high-flying, string-tangling yo-yo tricks.

The first metal yo-yos kept the design language of older plastic yo-yos: round, with most of the weight in the center. But then yo-yo designers started exploring the new possibilities of metal. They produced wildly flared, V-shaped yo-yos with the weight pushed out to the outer rims. Because of the physics of gyroscopes, this flared weight distribution makes yo-yos even more powerful—even longer-spinning and more stable.

It also tends to make them feel less sweet. These new, aggressive yo-yos feel different. Players sometimes describe them as "thunky," "thuddy," and like "bricks on string." They snap back to your hand with a harsh bite. But these hyperaggressive yo-yos absolutely make it easier to land tricks, so they've become dominant in the competition scene.

Some designers still make yo-yos with old-school round shapes—now called "organic" yo-yos—though mostly still with metal and high-end ball bearings. These organic yo-yos are designed to feel sweet on the string. They corner and turn with a pleasing grace and softness. In yo-yoer terms, they feel "floaty." Some designers even tune them to maximize the sweet bell sounds when the string pings against the sides. It is also much harder to land tricks on them. If you're competing, you're going to be using a harsh, modern, aggressive yo-yo. Playing with organic yo-yos requires far more focus to pull off the same tricks with—if, that is, it's even the same trick.

Right now I'm working on a trick called Seismic Slam. This trick involves a big finale in which you have to do a whip multiple times in a row. This is where you form a loop with the yo-yo string, throw it like a lasso, and whip it around the yo-yo in midair. The first time I pulled off the whip sequence, I giggled like a maniac and skipped around the room with pure joy.

With a modern, high-end, aggressive, competition-style yo-yo, I can do the trick pretty easily. Doing the same trick with an organic yo-yo is far harder; those yo-yos are deeply unforgiving of micro-errors. You might think using an organic yo-yo is kind of stupid be-cause it makes it harder to do the same trick. But remember Bernard Suits: The goal of a game is constituted by the constraints you take on. So trying to do the trick with the added constraint of using an or-ganic yo-yo is a *different goal*. Using an organic yo-yo turns it into a different game—a harder one that demands more focus and preci-sion. And I can choose the game that pleases me.

It turns out I have an enormous amount of control over the game of yo-yoing—over which exact game of yo-yoing I want to play. I can fiddle with it, fine-tune it. I can choose the goals and constraints that give me the experience I want.

But sometimes, I might be in a social context that fixes the scor-ing system out of my control. In the yo-yo competition scene, you get points for doing a visibly harder trick, but not for using a more diffi-cult, organic yo-yo. Yo-yo competitions don't judge you on the inner thing—how hard it was to complete your trick. Judges score you on the outward thing—the trick you completed. That's because a tour-nament judge can't look inside your soul and see how difficult it was for you. A judge can, however, easily see that you looped the yo-yo three times around your neck and then landed it behind your back. The demand for public judgment in relatively objective terms drags the entire process away from inner fine-tuning and toward a shared scoring system.

ED HAPONIK IS ONE OF THE GURUS OF THE YO-YO SCENE. HE'D been immersed in the modern competition-style tricks, done on fancy, aggressive, high-end yo-yos, but it all was starting to leave him cold. So he tried something else: He went old-school. He went back to those old, one-piece, carved wooden fixed-axle yo-yos. These are absurdly low-performance by modern standards. They're incredibly narrow and wobbly, and they have almost no spin time. Doing modern tricks with these things is like doing a technical mountain bike ride with one of those Victorian penny-farthing bicycles.

Recently, modern yo-yo trick inventors have discovered a new kind of trick—a stall—that works best on an old-school fixed-axle yo-yo. A stall involves stopping the yo-yo's spin mid-trick by tangling it up on its own string, and then restarting it. And this is where Haponik found a solution to his malaise. The difficulty of working with old-school fixies cultivated, for him, a particular kind of careful, blissed-out mental state. Haponik ended up exploding the vocabulary of stall tricks, and helping birth a new style of yo-yoing—one where you are taking advantage of the specific physics of a fixed-axle yo-yo, stalling and restarting it every few seconds in a delightfully weird stutter.

Haponik is also a martial artist, skateboarder, yoga practitioner, and meditator. Yo-yo, for him, is just one of the many practices that cultivate intense awareness. What draws him to his chosen martial art—the Japanese sword arts—is not self-defense. It is how the sword arts cultivate an experience of constant controlled attention to every movement. And that starts before the swordplay—in how you draw the sword, how you breathe before you draw the sword, and how you walk into the dojo.

A yo-yo does the same thing, he says, except it exchanges the mortal combat part for pure frivolity. "To me," he says, "a yo-yo is a temple that you can stick in your pocket and walk around with."

Right now, I can get up from my laptop, take a break from working on this book, and yo-yo. I can lose myself in that state of meditative attentiveness, of delicate intentional movement to control the yo-yo in sensuous flight. I can choose a sweet floaty yo-yo, an aggressive hyper-stable yo-yo, or a delightfully sensitive wooden fixie. Or I can turn on my computer and fight through complex card-based strategic planning with *Monster Train* and look for clever special-power combos. Or I can break my brain with the alternate-world physics of my favorite puzzle video game, *Baba Is You*, which I know will send me into raging frustration and then give me the glorious sensation of total mind-expanding genius when I finally solve a puzzle.

When the world doesn't force a game and a scoring system on me, I can pick the one that suits me. I can seek whatever thrills, whatever strange form of beauty, whatever meditative state I want. I have a choice of difficulty. And I can flitter between them with ease.

CHAPTER 15

Reflective Control

T o be involved with striving play is to have a particularly personal and purposeful relationship with the goals of the game and its scoring system. A game player's purposes aren't *dictated* by the scoring system. They *use* the scoring system to achieve their purposes. And if a scoring system leads to boring, fruitless activity—the player can tinker with it, modify it, or throw it away and try a different one.

We don't always have that much control. Sometimes the world forces us to play a particular game—a specific sport in high school gym class, or basketball because it's the path to money and status. Sometimes the world presents us with addictive games that we play late into the night until we're exhausted and miserable, because the right buttons have been pressed in our brain. Sometimes our schools and workplaces force gamification on us, to make us more productive, more dialed into the daily grind. The perversity of these forced games is that they fail to take advantage of what's truly special about games: the deep freedom to choose exactly the kind of action that suits us.

Some of the freest game players are the DIY game modders—role-players who hack their own games, board gamers who add house rules, online communities who come up with goofy alternate ways to play beloved video games. Take the world of speedrunning. In one of the early classic speedrunning variants, you played *Super Mario Bros.*, but you ignored the game's standard point system. Instead, you just tried to get to the end of the game as fast as possible. This involved finding and brutally exploiting weird little hiccups in the game system—like spots where you could glitch through the walls and skip past enemies.

Speedrunners ignore the official goal of the game. They've created a new scoring system focused entirely on speed. They're playing a different game—a new one that they've invented by adding their own goals and rules to the given software. This creates a different gaming experience—one in which whole communities work together to find all the unexpected exploits and gaps in the software to abuse the game mechanics in unintended ways. Speedrunning often seems like an exercise not in playing the original game but in creatively and cooperatively breaking it.

These are among the truest heroes of striving play: the game modders, the indie tabletop role-playing-game hackers, the speedrunners. They are taking full control of the games they are playing.

This is the special magic of games. We can try different games and see how they feel. We can hop between them. We can try on different scoring systems and constraint systems and see what we love. We can step into a game, try on that agency, and experience the action on offer. And then we can step back and ask ourselves if we want to play it again or play something different. We can shift difficulty levels, change opponents. We can modify our games, adding constraints, changing the goals. We can explore, we can tinker, we can explode, we can create. That's because games are voluntary indulgences, and unlike the recalcitrant world, we can choose them and sculpt them to give us exactly the experience we desire and cherish.

Let's call this relationship *reflective control*.

HOBBIES AND JOBS ARE SOMETHING LIKE FUZZIER GAMES. THEY usually come vaguely prepackaged with a set of abilities and goals. If you're a hiker, you're supposed to walk through nature and see beautiful new places. If you're gardening, you're supposed to grow plants by planting and weeding and fertilizing. If you're a teacher, you're supposed to educate students with lectures and exercises. If you're a Silicon Valley–type venture capitalist, you're supposed to make a profit by disrupting the status quo.

And I can specify my goals in different ways. If I'm a hiker, it matters if I'm looking for the most beautiful hikes, the chillest ones, or the most grueling. If I'm a teacher, it matters whether I want to encourage my students to be more curious and free or to get the best-paying job. Each of these things will radically shape what I do, as well as the shape and feel of my daily life—and the effects I have on other people. And there's no one correct hobby, no one true goal for everybody. You have to screw around, trying on different activities and then tinkering with the exact goals, until you find something that fits your abilities, your personality, and your particular place in the world.

The same may be true when we zoom out from hobbies and jobs and look at our whole lives and our deep values. There are things you think are important, that guide your decisions and choices in all terrains. Let's call these your values. Your values shape the life you lead. But, says the philosopher Elijah Millgram, there's no single correct set of values that will work well for everybody. That's because, once again, your values need to fit you—they need to fit the particular person you are and the specific circumstance you're in. They need to fit your skills, your personality, the place you live, the communities you live with, and the possibilities the world has left open for you.

And you find out which ones fit, says Millgram, through experiment. You have to actually try living your life by devoting yourself to money, or learning, or travel. And then you get feedback; you find out whether you flourish or wilt. Sometimes you try on a new value and you become happy, engaged, and full of zest. This value fits you. And sometimes you try on a value and you end up bored, miserable, and exhausted. That value doesn't fit. This is a signal that you should adjust your values—which you can do by changing hobbies, changing jobs, or tweaking your goals.

And this is true on a larger scale, too. We have values that fit our particular communities, in their particular contexts. Jane Jacobs, the urban-planning theorist, had a lovely observation about the distinctive values of city folk: People in cities deeply value privacy, because it is so precious in dense urban areas.

People who aren't from cities often value a certain kind of friendliness—making eye contact, having friendly chats with anybody you run into, introducing yourself to strangers. Sometimes, a person will move to a big city, like New York, and at first the people there seem painfully unfriendly. The city people refuse to make eye contact, are hostile toward attempts at chatting, and radiate annoyance at what seem like perfectly normal social overtures. They seem like total assholes. But if newcomers spend more time in the city, that apparently unfriendly behavior will start to make perfect sense. Because a city like New York is too crowded, too teeming with people. In the city—on the bus, on the subway, on the streets—you spend so much of your life surrounded by other human beings that if we valued chatty friendliness, everybody would lose their minds from the constant social intrusion. So people in the big city typically come to place an intense value on *respecting privacy* – on not making eye contact most of the time, on not making conversation most of the time, on leaving people alone, especially if there are any signals that they want to be left alone (earbuds in, head down at their phone).

The point isn't that friendliness or privacy is the better value. It's that there are different ways of life, and different contexts for living, that clearly suit different values. Putting a high value on friendliness usually suits the rural context better, and putting a high value on respecting privacy suits the context of dense cities with crowded subways better. Add to this local variance the huge complex variability of human personalities – the massive differences in what we find frustrating or joyful – and it becomes obvious why we can't have one-size-fits-all values.

So we need to try out values and see if they fit – and if they don't, we can adjust. When we engage in this kind of reflective control, we get values that are tailored to fit our particular personalities and our place in the world.

METRICS DISCOURAGE REFLECTIVE CONTROL.

What is so appealing about metrics and value capture? Making decisions is complicated when we're exposed to the full complexity of life. Let's narrow it down to just one aspect of life – say, parenting. Every day I'm making decisions about what kinds of food my kids should eat, what shows they can watch and games they can play, whether it's OK to let them play in our backyard unattended or let them scramble up that medium-size boulder on their own. There is so much information to consider – all the nutritional science and developmental psychology and economics and physical risk factors. But beyond the science and the facts, there is the even more nauseating tangle of what matters. In most of these decisions, I'm choosing between radically different values. I am trying to balance my kids' physical safety with the value of developing self-trust and independence. I am deciding between the value of a carefree childhood and preparation for a competitive job market.

It's no surprise, then, that we crave relief from all that complexity.

Games offer us one form of relief, an experience of absorption in an alternate, purified world. When I'm climbing, all that matters is my body and the rock. My entire consciousness can pour into that slender universe—the precise angle and texture of a few holds, the exact way my hips are turned and my feet are pointed. And that simplification, that glorious narrowness happens because in a game, we have sharply reduced what matters. In climbing, all that matters is getting to the top of the rock. Everything that doesn't contribute to that one clear goal can just fall away. This cuts the world down to a simpler, more manageable nub. Games give us a moment of value clarity.

In games, simplifying our values is safe, because games are temporary. They don't settle anything permanently for us; we can easily step back and renegotiate the rules and scoring systems if we want. Metrics, on the other hand, attempt to simplify the real world permanently. They promise to reduce everything to a manageable size. They offer us the gamelike pleasures of an utterly clear purpose.

In most games, clarity is completely and happily artificial. The points are made up and detached from the world. They're a temporary goal that we take on for the sake of a fascinating process. But metrics are different. Metrics are institutional systems designed to measure some independent quality. Maybe it's health, or education, or well-being. Metrics make a lasting claim about what is actually important. This is when we have to start worrying about the possibility of error—of a mismatch between the clarity of the score and the density of the real world.

And metrics make a second offer. They don't just promise to simplify our internal decisions. They also promise to simplify the social world—to ease the burden of making ourselves understood. Metrics offer a universal and easily communicable value system. They promise social value clarity.

For many of us, a core experience of life is the pain of being misunderstood. Our weird private whims, the odd bits of beauty we cherish, our habits that make our lives make sense—it is so hard to explain this stuff to other people. It is so hard to explain to people why I have become obsessed with perfecting this one particular Sichuan dish, why this lesser-loved GZA album glows with energy for me. Value capture pops us out of that problem by putting us on a universal value currency.

Metrics make you an offer: If you accept this prefabricated, public value system into your heart, you will become instantly comprehensible. You will gain access to a whole world of ready-made justifications. Your successes will become clear and inarguable. Metrics make values mechanically clear.

And the more public the metric I attune myself to, the more universally comprehensible my actions will be. This might explain why some people will endlessly seek more money, even when they already have far more than they could ever use. This is not just normal selfishness. Some people will wreak havoc on the world while driving themselves into misery—into stressed-out, overworked, friendless exhaustion—all in their pursuit of higher numbers in their bank account. Because money is the ultimate shared scoring system, the system that is maximally legible to the largest chunk of the world. They have been dominated by the clarity of the score.

When you are value-captured by a clear external metric, your reasons become perfectly public. All you have to give up is tailoring your values to fit your own peculiar self, in the light of your own particular experiences. With value capture, you are setting your values using tools that are designed to be rigid, inflexible, and insensitive — precisely so they can be instantly comprehensible at scale.

Metrics discourage reflective control, because their central promise — that we can hop onboard a prefabricated and shared value system — requires that we submit ourselves to an external, rigid system of values.

GAMES ENCOURAGE REFLECTIVE CONTROL. IN AESTHETIC STRIVing play, we take on scoring systems *temporarily*. And the scoring system offers us clear and mechanical standards for success, which make it so much easier to try on. This is part of what makes games so compelling, so absorbing. For a while, we know exactly what we're trying to do, and exactly how well we've done it.

But then the game ends and we step back. We put aside the scoring system and its conception of success. And then we ask ourselves if it was worth it to play the game — if we enjoyed it, if it was fun or satisfying. We evaluate the mechanical scoring system from a standpoint outside mechanical scoring systems.

Games encourage us to take on scoring systems voluntarily, with a fuller understanding of the kind of life they will shape for us. We can adopt them if and when they serve our interests. Games encourage us to choose and tailor our goals to suit our own needs, precisely because they are temporary and disposable.

Consider the yo-yo passions of Tsukasa Takatsu — a minor saint, beloved of a very tiny sect of passionate yo-yo players. Takatsu had gotten bored with the complicated tricks of the modern yo-yo era. He wanted to see how much depth and perfection he could find in simplicity. So he devoted himself to repeaters. A repeater is a very specific kind of yo-yo trick. It begins and ends in the same string formation, so you can do it on an infinite loop. It is an ouroboros of play.

The best repeaters are simple and elegant, but a little bit mystifying. You start your trick—the yo-yo's looping and hopping around, the string's getting more and more tangled—and then suddenly there's a little hop of the yo-yo, a slight twist of the finger, and the string formation resolves. All your tangled knots disappear—and you're right back where you started, on a plain straight string.

Takatsu says the restrictions of the repeater format make it easier for him to find the beauty of trick structure. He finds in them an elegance akin to Japanese haiku poetry. He's spent a decade inventing and filming hundreds of new repeaters, every single one meticulously documented on his YouTube channel. They are always filmed the same way. There is music—sometimes ambient, sometimes jazz, sometimes classical, occasionally punk. He is usually wearing a baseball cap, and he is always in socks. He repeats the trick several times, finishes, looks up briefly at the camera, and walks off to the left. He never speaks.

I have learned some of his tricks, and they are indescribably, incandescently beautiful. This is a strange thing to confess, but one of his repeaters was so gorgeous that when I got it to work for me, I actually cried. It was moving in a way I'd never been moved before. Then I texted my friends about it, and they told me I was a total weirdo.

But the beauty of Takatsu's repeaters is incredibly hard to access for people who don't yo-yo. It's a form of beauty written in an esoteric language of momentum and knots. It is a structural, mathematical beauty, made visible and tactile. Doing his tricks feels like being inside a Möbius strip. Takatsu's tricks remind me of the novelist and engineer Robert Musil's comment that the love for elegant thinking is "a complicated passion for thrift."

Takatsu is a poet of topology, spending untold hours of loving invention and practice on his art. But the wider world will never really notice. He has invented, and filmed, over two hundred repeater tricks; most of these have only a few hundred views each. His aesthetic is profoundly illegible and anti-impressive: He aims at a kind of smooth perfection that makes it look absolutely easy. His tricks are a special gift for those few yo-yoers who recognize the beauty of a haiku written into string.

Takatsu could walk this path because he didn't want to compete and yo-yo was mostly disconnected from his livelihood. And I can ignore the competition scene, be moved by his tricks, and devote myself to learning them, because nothing ties me to any particular vision of success. Nothing hinges on whether I chase repeaters or hard competition tricks, or whether I succeed or fail at any of those things. Because yo-yo, in the end, is stupid. So I can reconceive what counts as success there as I please.

Games matter because games don't matter.

SO WHAT MAKES SCORING SYSTEMS OFTEN SO DELIGHTFUL AND exploratory in games and often so soul-deadening in metrics?

Games give us a safe way to use mechanical scoring systems. These scoring systems can't directly target those weird deep, subtle inner joys and experiences, but they can indirectly *encourage* those things. Remember the difference between a goal and a purpose. In games, there is a local goal, which we directly target in the moment. And there is a larger purpose, which is the real reason we play. I climb to relax and clear my head and feel the bliss of sensitive, elegant movement. But I don't pursue those in the moment. In the moment, I just try to climb the damn rock.

In games, mechanical evaluation procedures are confined to the in-game goals. Our larger purposes need not be mechanical. We can in fact nudge, steer, and modify the mechanical scoring system to satisfy our weirdest, most inchoate desires. I can decide that the pursuit of harder, faster yo-yo tricks isn't giving me pleasure, and switch to the goal of learning Takatsu's elegant repeaters. I can shift the experience point system in my tabletop role-playing game to make it generate more sadistic hilarity.

But that requires taking control and being willing to customize the mechanical scoring system. We become something like a game designer for our own lives, trying games and modding them to fit our purposes. We can use the mechanical scoring system as a tool to approach something subtler, more sensitive, more intimate. We can also do this in fuzzier practices, far away from mechanical scoring systems. We can get involved in a hobby or a job, following someone else's lead for a while and learning to see its subtle value. And then we can start screwing with it, changing the way we do it—which methods we use, what our goals are—to tailor it to us.

But that fine-tuning requires a certain degree of freedom—the ability to change the scoring system. Games make that easy. But you might ask: Why can't we just do that with any scoring system? Can't we simply decide to be more playful with metrics? Why can't we treat our public ranking systems more like games?

The answer is that metrics aren't just passive things that we can freely use in any way we wish. Metrics push back. They resist our attempts to bend them to suit our interests. And then they reach out and transform the world, in a way that makes playfulness and reflective control incredibly hard.

Why? This is where we're going next.

PART 4

STANDARDIZED

VALUES

CHAPTER 16

Values Hidden in the Machine

I n part three, we studied the similarity at the heart of games and metrics: the scoring system. It started to look like what really mattered was our internal attitude toward them: whether or not we took reflective control. And the basic nature of games — temporary and bounded in space and time — encourages us to flit into and out of them, which invites reflective control. But the nature of metrics discourages reflective control, because metrics are pervasive and present themselves as universal.

At this point, you might be thinking there is an easy solution, in two parts:

First, what really matters is your attitude. So perk up, be strong, exert some willpower, and just force yourself to take reflective control over which metrics you let in.

Second, if games help us take on the right attitude, then we should make our metrics more like games. We should gamify them and encourage playfulness all around. Gamify the workplace, gamify education, and we'll help bring back reflective control.

But these solutions ignore how deep the problem is. We can make metrics look superficially more like games, by adding the window dressing of levels and awards and experience points. But their inner workings—their core functionality—won't change. They will still be bound by clear rules and rigidified to work at scale. They still won't encourage us to skip around, to tailor, to change.

This is why it is so hard for us, as individual people, to simply take reflective control. Because metrics are part of a larger world order—a rigid, inflexible structure that resists our attempts at reflective control. Metrics are the vanguard of a whole invading force, all working to subtly erode our freedom to decide, and standardize how we think and what we care about. And we can't just keep the useful bit of metrics and throw out the restrictive parts. The standardizing pressure of metrics is a crucial part of their function. What metrics do *for* us is bound up, inextricably, with what they do *to* us.

In part four we're looking for the bigger picture. We're looking to see how metrics rewrite the world and make us more willing to accept them into our hearts. We've already met the first three Horsemen: Scale, Rules, and Parts. But these do not give us the full story of how metrics function and why it will be so hard to make them more playful. Notice that games also use Scales, Rules, and Parts in the name of play. Games have clear mechanical rules that make them easy to learn. Those rules make things more interchangeable. It's easier to swap out one player for another in a game, or to switch games. And games can scale up; there are international chess ratings and worldwide *Fortnite* leaderboards. But games do not subject us to the same pressure to standardize our sense of meaning. To understand what makes metrics truly distinctive—and truly threatening—we need to find the fourth and final Horseman, the ruling spirit of the whole thing.

Oh, and the neat division between games and metrics is coming to an end. The paths are converging. Things will be messier from here on out.

METRICS, AND THE LARGE-SCALE INSTITUTIONAL FORCES THEY are entangled with, have changed the basic structure of human life. But it's easy to miss how dramatic these changes have been, because we are immersed in this new world. The changes have gone so deep into our way of life that metrics have made themselves look natural. We have a name for this kind of thing, a new way of doing things that shifts the world so profoundly that we forget how things had ever been otherwise. So let's give them their proper name: Metrics are a world-transforming form of *technology*.

Every major new technology alters the pattern of human life. The printing press, the engine, the computer—each ushers in a revolution, upsetting the balance of power, restructuring daily life, and rewriting our psychology and desires.

A technology is a reproducible innovation. And technologies aren't just physical things. Some technologies are ideas—new ways of arranging the world, new procedures for doing things, like the idea of Arabic numerals, or the technique of arranging people into a factory assembly line.

And we, the users of the technology, don't always have full control over what the technology does to us. The intrinsic nature of a technology can push the world in particular directions; technologies almost have a will of their own. The philosopher's lingo for this is that technologies are *value-laden*. A technology isn't merely a neutral tool; each intrinsically embodies and supports certain values over others. And different technologies support different values.

We do not simply use our tools. Our tools also shape and transform us.

Games and metrics are both powerful technologies, but they embody different values. Games push us toward weird variety. They fill the world with radically different modes of action, each full of its own peculiar beauties and joys. They invite us to tinker with them, to tailor them to our needs. This patchwork world encourages playfulness. It reminds us to take control of the shape of our activities and the values that lie under them.

Metrics push us in the opposite direction. They reduce diversity and variety. They especially drain the world of *diversity of meanings*. They steer the world toward a singular and monolithic set of values. They reduce our exposure to deeply different modes of valuing, which erodes our reflective control. It's hard to make an informed choice when you don't even know when there was a choice to be made in the first place.

Metrics push us to *standardize our values*.

There are many technologies of standardization. Rulers are part of the technology that standardizes length measurements, and clocks are part of the technology that standardizes time. But metrics do something even deeper: They are a technology that standardizes how we measure success. They standardize the process by which we judge each other and ourselves. To fully understand the power of metrics, we need to understand the power of standardization—how it works, why we want it, and how it changes the deep tissue of our social lives. And we need to see how standardization gets wrapped up with another powerful force: the force of *centralized decision-making*. Because standardization doesn't appear from nowhere. It needs a central authority to decide on, stabilize, and enforce those standards.

We need to see how these two forces—standardization and

centralization—get baked into the basic infrastructure of the modern world, into our machines and our institutions. And then they start leaking into everything, including how we find meaning in our lives.

WE'RE ABOUT TO DO A DEEP DIVE INTO THE HEART OF THE modern world, to try to get a glimpse of the hidden forces that shape our lives. Things are about to get pretty abstract, so let's start with something relatively simple. Think about how different communication technologies change the basic nature of information flow.

Before the printing press, news mostly spread by word of mouth. Individuals heard stuff and then repeated it to other individuals. Communication happened through a distributed network of individuals who had the power to change, reinterpret, or comment on the news before passing it on. In the technology of oral communication, anybody could insert themselves into the stream of news. Oral communication disperses communicative power, letting lots of people have access over it, for good or ill. Oral communication is deeply *decentralized*.

Now consider the printing press. It is a technology that *centralized* power over communication. Because it was expensive and relatively rare, the printing press tended to concentrate the power of communication in those wealthy enough to own one—governments, corporations, and wealthy individuals. And a printing press created a clear distinction between the "official" word of the press and everybody else's words—because of the basic look and feel of printed information. Even if I crossed out parts of a newspaper and wrote notes in the margins, my additions would be handwritten. Annotations by ordinary people look like second-class bits of information.

The printing press created an informational hierarchy. It drew

constant attention to the difference between "official" and "unofficial" sources, and then concentrated the power to produce official
news in a very small number of actors—in whoever owned the physical press.

Was this good or terrible? There's no easy answer to that. The
printing press centralized the power of informational authority.
This was a profound change to the structure of the social world,
which enabled all kinds of uses and abuses. Centralized communication makes it easier for good-hearted authorities to control the
spread of medical misinformation and to spread the view of trustworthy scientific experts. Centralized communication also makes it
easy for corrupt authorities to spread mass propaganda.

The history of communication technologies involves massive
swings between centralized and decentralized technologies. The
technology of ham radio, as we found it in the early twentieth century, tended toward decentralization. These radios were small, cheap,
and easy to build. Then the technology of broadcast radio, as it ex-
isted in the 1940s, pushed us back toward moderate centralization;
radio towers are much more expensive than amateur radios. Then
came the technology of broadcast television, which, in the 1960s,
involved limited bandwidth and incredibly expensive transmitters
and production costs, so it tended to concentrate communicative
power in a very small handful of broadcast networks.

And things have changed yet again in a way that defies easy categorization. The technology of the internet—and of social media—
appears, on its surface, to be deeply decentralized. Anybody can get
an account on social media, or start a website, and start pumping out
content. But as the social media scholar Zeynep Tufekci points out,
the appearance of decentralization is partly an illusion. Social media lets almost anybody produce content, but it also passes all those
content producers through a massively centralized focal point: the

search algorithm. Anybody can have a website and post anything they want for a couple of bucks—but if you appear far down on the search algorithm, on the thousandth page of search results, nobody will read you. So the internet and social media does something very funky to communication. It decentralizes content production. But it also forces everybody to access that content through a small number of search algorithms—which represent a massive centralization of attention. Now anybody can speak, but we collectively hear only a handful of them.

SOME MIGHT BALK AT THE CLAIM THAT TECHNOLOGIES RESHAPE the world. Some think that technologies are just neutral tools. This is the *value-neutral* theory of technology. According to this view, technologies may make humans more powerful, but a technology has no values, no politics, no interests of its own. It's just a power magnifier that amplifies the interests and values of its users. This is the "Guns don't kill people, people kill people" view of technology. Technology doesn't reshape society, people do.

But many philosophers and scholars of technology reject this value-neutral theory. The philosopher Langdon Winner argues that every technology has an inherent politics. Each technology pushes society in a particular political direction, and these effects are often independent of the intentions of its inventors or users. Maybe the inventors of the printing press wanted to empower democracy and spread education; maybe they didn't want to concentrate communicative power in the hands of a few authorities. But the technology that they actually invented was a big, expensive, powerful thing. No matter what message they wanted to send with the printing press, there was another effect underneath: a force that tended to centralize the power of official speech and centralize trust.

Winner gives us a particularly fascinating discussion of the politics of factories. We're talking about the technique of mass production by using an assembly line, in which different parts of the line each specialize in a different, specific task. While the factory is far more efficient at producing goods quickly and cheaply, Winner says it also encourages a particular kind of government.

Think about what production was like before factories. Imagine a village of cobblers—artisans who individually make whole shoes, from beginning to end. Artisanal shoe production tends to support a world of highly variable, customized objects. Each shoe producer can make what they want to, changing their styles and sizes as their taste and mood dictates. And buyers can easily have shoes made to their exact specifications and preferences, in the style and color they want, fitted to their particular foot. But artisanal production is also very slow.

Now replace all these individual, whimsical artisans with a factory. Shut down their shops, and then hire them back as workers on the factory line. The changes are enormous. Factories work by breaking up a task into elements and getting workers to specialize. In the case of a shoe factory, instead of making an entire shoe from scratch, one worker punches the holes for the laces, another makes little metal rings to go in the holes, and another worker puts the rings in the holes to form the eyelets.

This form of specialization enables a massive increase in production efficiency. But it also requires coordination. The worker punching the holes and the worker making the rings have to make their parts match. So they need to *standardize* a hole size and a ring size. The more we standardize the procedure, the more efficiently we will produce shoes.

But in order to get these gains in efficiency, we have to prevent workers from following their own creative fancies. Factories, says

Winner, require a central authority to enforce a single set of standards and keep everybody in line with those standards. So factories offer a trade-off: If you manage to have a centralized authority, capable of enforcing standards and conformity with the factory, you get enormous gains in efficiency and productivity. This doesn't necessarily mean you need a tyrannical despot—that centralized authority could be democratic. But you still need the kind of democracy that can settle on one set of standards and then enforce them with the factory workers.

So factories, says Winner, push societies in the direction of centralized authority and control. But they don't do it in quite the same way as the printing press. Factories don't create centralized authority. Rather, they need centralized authority in order to function. So the technology of factories rewards those societies willing to build and maintain a centralized authority with more economic power.

Let me add to Winner's story. I think the technology of the factory also exerts pressure in the kinds of things we tend to care about as a society. They push us to care more about *outcomes* than about *processes*. They encourage a world that prefers precise outcomes to dynamic and shifting and improvisational processes.

Suppose an artisanal cobbler wants to build a shoe in some new and different way. Perhaps they want to indulge their curiosity and try to build a footbed out of cork instead of the traditional leather. This affects nobody except the cobbler and their customers. And if their new cork footbed doesn't end up having the same shape as the old leather one, that artisan can adapt the rest of their shoemaking process to fit. Because the work is dynamic and improvisatory, they can adjust on the fly, and then fill in each next step based on what happened with the previous one.

But that won't work in a factory. An efficient factory depends on standardizing work, because later steps in the process depend on precise results from earlier steps. The factory is fast, but fragile. If the worker who makes the footbeds doesn't make enough, then they screw up all the production down the line. If they experiment with a new form of footbed without coordinating with everybody else ahead of time, then it won't slot into the other pieces that have already been made.

This changes the relative cost of indulging workers' quirks and personal whims. If I were the leader of a loose band of artisanal shoe-makers, I could let them experiment. At worst they would fail at their own project; they wouldn't drag anybody else down with them. But I couldn't do that if I ran a factory. The inner procedures of a factory are tightly interdependent, with very little tolerance for variation. So factory overseers must care deeply about getting precise outcomes. They need to make sure the right number, made exactly according to specifications, is getting made at every point on the line.

Factories can, in fact, innovate, but the decision to do so has to come through some kind of centralized authority. What this looks like is probably a highly creative small group of people in research and development, pushing their designs out to the production line, which will execute their plans—which is very different from a village full of independent artisans. In the factory, creativity is also centralized.

To sum up: Factories get their gains through tightly woven *interoperation*. This requires strict mechanical, standardized rules for creation and deployment—so all the pieces fit. Factories are a technology that offers a clear reward to those communities willing to abandon their quirky, individualized artisanal processes and agree to conform to a standardized set of rules. This brings with it an entire mindset of focusing on precise countable outcomes. Factories are a technology that shifts the world toward centralized authority, rigid controls, and precise countable outcomes. This is the politics of the factory. And if we live in the time of the factory, we might forget that things could be otherwise. But this sort of central standardizing authority is not the only way to arrange the world. It is a very specific and relatively new way of living, ushered in through a specific set of technologies.

Let's take Winner's analysis of the factory for a walk back over to metrics. Because metrics are a way of standardizing evaluation and standardizing values. Games use mechanical values, but there is no pressure to force all those varied scoring systems into one standard. But metrics tend toward standardization.

Metrics are factories for values.

You can think of it this way: Games and metrics both use scoring systems, which are engines of convergence. But the world of games is one of *divergent convergence* of a million different scoring systems shaping different kinds of play, for a million different reasons. The world of metrics, on the other hand, is one of *monolithic convergence*, trying to bring everybody into a singular way of evaluating the world. The crucial feature of metrics, then, is not just their mechanical nature, but that they are deployed in a rigid, large-scale infrastructure of meaning.

Games are little detached worlds. Every game does provide a singular verdict, but there are many different games, with many independent scoring systems. There is no pressure to coordinate the verdicts between games. Games do not need to standardize meaning, but metrics do.

CHAPTER 17

Whose Interest Does
Standardization Serve?

B ut why do we let standardization into our lives in the first place? Why not resist standardized metrics and try to shift the world over to decentralized scoring systems? Why not make the world more like a game—or more like an ecosystem of millions of different games? But the cost for such decentralization is high. We have accepted standardization because it is so powerful, because it grants us greater levels of efficiency, and greater volumes of output, than we have ever seen before. But standardization also enforces a particular set of values on us. It plugs us into a whole way of life—the way of the factory.

Let's start by looking at how standardization works apart from metrics. Standardization is the process whereby we take a part of the world that is naturally variable and make it regular across time and space—across different people and different cultures. Standardization of anything, even the most mundane measurement tools, is a deeply value-laden act; it is an enormous transformation of the world, which serves some interests above others.

For people who grew up in the modern, industrialized world, it's hard to imagine life before standardization. We just casually assume that everybody else in the world has access to a ruler that measures the same inches and centimeters, and a set of measuring implements that measure the same cups and tablespoons.

But things were not always that way. Imagine, for the moment, that you live somewhere in the time before industrialization. You make bread at home for your family. You notice that some days the bread comes out better than others, so you start measuring to keep track of what you're doing differently. You'll probably start measuring in the most natural way—say, with handfuls of flour, or with a particular mug that you happen to have hanging nearby. If you want to teach your child to bake, you might figure out how many of your handfuls is equivalent to their handful, or point them to that specific mug.

In this small-scale world, there's no need for the thing known as the standard cup measure, which is held stable across nations and continents. Left to their own devices, people will make all different sizes of cups. To create an international standard cup measure, we need to make sure that thousands of factories around the world are producing measuring cups of precisely the same size. That effort is worthwhile for a specific purpose: instantly communicating recipes to distant strangers. It enables us to write cookbooks and have anybody else easily re-create the measurements. And it enables us to have fast-food chain restaurants, so that we that can get all kinds of different people in different places to make hamburgers that taste exactly the same.

But standardization is not a pure improvement. It is a deep change to the way the world works that helps some parts of human life and hinders others. Theodore Porter provides a mind-bending example about the coming of standardized time. We modern people are now on *clock time*. I live in Salt Lake City, Utah. The time on my watch is exactly the same as the time of somebody five hundred miles to the east, in Denver, Colorado. And the time on my watch can easily be translated into the time for somebody in New York or London—we have a method for adjusting the hours but leaving the minutes and seconds precisely synchronized around the world. Our time is standardized on a global scale, through a vast social effort of establishing time zones and Greenwich Mean Time.

But things were not always so. In an earlier era, most people used what is called *diurnal* time. In one system of diurnal time, six a.m. is pegged to sunrise, and six p.m. is pegged to sunset. When people hear about diurnal time, they often react with complete disgust. It seems, at first glance, like complete chaos. First of all, the hours would expand and contract. A daylight hour would be much longer in the summer than in the winter. And there would be no easy coordination between different cities. Wendover is only a couple hours' drive west of Salt Lake City, but the sunrise there is already nine minutes later.

But it doesn't take long to see the advantages. First, if you work on a farm, it could make perfect sense for the hours to be longer in the summer and shorter in the winter. There's more to do in the summer, and it's fine to sleep more in the winter. When our work is keyed to diurnal time, that happens naturally. And diurnal time is intrinsically keyed to the light. If you had a standing agreement to start work at seven a.m., under diurnal time your work always starts at the same stage of the day cycle. You would always be starting work in daylight.

Clock time is completely different. I take my kids to school at eight a.m. Under clock time, that means sometimes I'm waking up and getting them out the door in full sunlight, but sometimes that means I'm waking up in total darkness, dragging my recalcitrant body out of bed to rouse my kids.

It's not impossible to coordinate clock time with the sun. If we were in clock time and wanted school to start an hour after the sun rises, we could figure out exactly when that was each day and constantly change the start time for school. But that would take an enormous effort. It runs against what clock time is built to do. Clock time is designed to make some interactions effortless (international Zoom meeting at nine a.m. East Coast time), at the cost of making other interactions very hard (meet an hour past sunrise every day).

Diurnal time and standardized clock time serve deeply different purposes and ways of life. This is why the choice of timing systems is value-laden. Diurnal time is keyed to the natural world; it serves the human animal, which likes to wake with the light and sleep with the dark. It serves the person who needs light to work. But it completely fails at coordinating trains, planes, and Zoom meetings. This is why we see the rise of standardized time around the need for precisely coordinating between faraway cities—when we need to arrange exact train schedules, or to all be on the same call at the same time from different cities. Standardized time breaks the relationship to a specific place and season, to the changing light. It detaches us from the sun and our sun-attuned animal nature. In return, it gives us the ability to easily coordinate between faraway places.

I suspect many of our interests fit nicely with standardized clock time—though not all. The part of me that hates standardized time is the part that has to get up an hour before sunrise to start getting my kids ready for school. The point here isn't that diurnal time is objectively better and standardized clock time objectively terrible. The point is that each system serves a different set of interests—each supports some kinds of life and undercuts others. And when we standardize a system, we make one rigid solution designed for one set of interests and then spread it across the world. Instead of having multiple flexible systems tuned to serve many different interests, we have a single system tuned to serve a single monolith of interests.

Sometimes that might work great for you, when your interests align with the monolith. But it's unlikely to work for everybody, precisely because people's interests vary. Standardized systems work by being rigid across vast scales. This enables frictionless coordination, but with a trade-off: Standardized systems strongly discourage sensitive adaptation to the particular local environment.

SOME OF OUR MOST POWERFUL TECHNOLOGIES ARE TOOLS FOR *attention*. They tell us what to notice, and what to ignore. And when we standardize these tools, we standardize our attention.

Consider maps. Maps are one of these attentional technologies. Jorge Luis Borges, the fantastical Argentinean writer, has a one-paragraph short story about maps called "On Exactitude in Science." In it, he imagines a culture in which the mapmakers are so exacting, so demanding, they require that absolutely no detail be left out of a map. Their map of the world will then turn out to be the exact size of the world. But this perfectly complete map is also perfectly useless. It doesn't do the job of a map. Maps work by highlighting certain details, which they do by deleting other details.

Maps work by leaving out what's irrelevant. Or to be more precise: *Maps work by throwing out whatever the person in control of the map thinks is irrelevant.*

Denis Wood, in *The Power of Maps*, says that every map represents a set of choices about what to record and what to conceal. Those choices come out of the interests of the mapmaker and are then embedded into the map. When ordinary people use the map, those interests leak out into the users—quietly, based on what the map shows them and what it doesn't.

Take a look at a standard map that you might find in an atlas, or one of the standard settings on Google Maps. What you're likely to see are roads and road names; the boundaries between states and countries; major nature features like mountains, rivers, and lakes; and elevation lines for topology. The map clearly highlights a particular set of information. For many of us, as we're driving from spot to spot, it gives exactly the information we need.

But there is so much information that is not usually mapped, though it easily could be. For example, asks Wood, why don't we usually map sound quality? It would take some effort to measure the average decibel level at various points in a city, but it also takes effort to survey precise elevation and the exact curvature of every road. Yet we rarely find such maps. The reason, says Wood, is that most mapmakers—and the institutions behind them—don't care about sound quality.

Every map serves someone's purpose. The standard road map serves the interests of travelers, especially drivers, to get to where they're going. The standard property map serves the interests of those who trade in land or tax its owners. A map that conveys information about sound quality, or public access to natural beauty, would serve the people who wanted to have a pleasant life in a city. Each map serves an interest, which is revealed in what the map chooses to call our attention to and what it chooses to ignore.

Standard maps don't record where the interesting graffiti and street art are, or where people tend to hang out on the street at night, but for people like me, that's incredibly important. Almost every map, on the other hand, contains elevation details. It turns out this is because most of our modern maps are built on top of an original set of maps that were created by army engineers to show the elevation and road details in their own countries, giving them a tactical advantage against invaders. They were made as aids for precise artillery targeting.

Maps may look like merely neutral reportage of neutral facts, but they are not. They are profoundly value-laden. They are social actions, full of meaningful choices. They express a particular perspective about what's valuable and what's not. And the choices inherent in maps end up having a profound effect on everybody who uses them.

Standardization doesn't come from nowhere, and maps don't spring magically into being. In our world, some authority decides what is the standard map. Maps are a technology that centralizes decisions about what we should notice.

CHAPTER 18

Who Cuts Up the World?

M etrics are a technology that standardizes attention. A metric focuses us on pursuing whatever it is the metric is tracking. And somebody decided what to track.

Sometimes, that decision is incredibly obvious. When a university administration creates student success metrics and decides to gather data on student graduation rates and employment rates — but not student happiness or the growth of friendships between students — that is a value decision about what counts as success. Here, it is obvious a particular set of values has been baked into the data set.

But often those decisions are subtler. The interests and values in metrics can hide far beneath the surface. To track them, we have to look at another technology — an incredibly pervasive and powerful one. It shapes what we notice, think about, and care about. It is a technology that lies underneath every metric, and every data-collection effort, that colors every data-based decision. It is one of key places where particular values and political interests leak into data and metrics. It is so foundational that it is almost invisible.

We are about to dive into the true beating heart of the standardized modern world and see how deeply external systems can rewrite the basic structure of our world. But when I tell you where we're going, it will probably seem like the most boring thing in the world. So much of the time, the most important decisions hide under a cloak of dullness— in how, exactly, subprime mortgage-backed securities work, or how we regulate the funding for drug trials. I am terrified that in about two seconds, you're going to put down this book in disgust. But I have become convinced, after beating my head against understanding metrics for years of my life, that this is where the action really is.

We need to talk about classification manuals.

Classification systems are how we standardize our categories. They are how we set, officially, how we will all cut up the world. I cannot overstate how important classification manuals are to this whole story. Classification systems are the engine under the hood of metrics and data. They are the conceptual foundation; they set the basic blocks in which institutions will *think*—and how people inside those institutions will talk, remember, and justify themselves.

Why? In order to have a metric, we need to collect data. And to collect data about something, we need a standardized category for it. Without that standardized category, we can't coordinate our efforts enough to collect any meaningful data. So we use things like the DSM (*Diagnostic and Statistical Manual of Mental Disorders*), which coordinates how psychiatrists, researchers, and insurance companies categorize mental disorders. Having the stable, shared categories of the DSM enables us to consistently collect data about mental disorders, to perform research on that data, and then to make decisions about whether, say, you can be diagnosed with chronic depression and get insurance coverage for your treatment.

Classification systems determine which data we can collect. If there's no category for it, we won't get data on it. And if we don't have data for it, we can't target it with a metric. But classification systems aren't just a neutral reporting of the real world. They are, once again, a designed filtration system that translates the real world into something that fits into a database. And in doing so, they standardize what we notice and what we ignore—what we remember, and what we forget.

Classification systems are tools to standardize meanings. And they don't fall magically from the sky; they are not borne of some institutional version of immaculate conception. Somebody made them, somebody decided what they would focus on. Somebody drew the lines. They are deeply value-laden technologies. The key questions are: Who built these classification systems and decided which meanings to standardize? Whose interests do these classification systems serve?

Classification systems determine how we count together. Because counting, too, is a value-laden act.

Counting might seem as easy as 1-2-3, but it's only that easy *once we know what the objects are.* In other words, counting is easy if you've already settled how you're going to sort the world into *categories.* But by the time you've gotten to the 1-2-3 part, the real action is already over. Because in order to count things, we first need to decide how we're going to cut up the world into the things that we're going to count. Much of the time, we have choices about where to draw the lines.

Suppose I hand you a big pile of stuff and tell you to count the lemons and limes. This might seem easy at first. Here are some perfect lemons and some perfect limes. But now you get to the tougher cases. I just found two halves of a lime in different parts of the pile. Do I count that as one whole lime, or two? Here's a lime that's about one-third rotten. Does that count as a lime, or two-thirds of a lime?

What about this thing, which might be a lime, but is mostly just some moldy peel? Does it count—and if so, do I count it as a whole lime or a partial lime? And oh, here are these hybrid fruits from a tree that got cross-pollinated. Do I count them as lemons or as limes? Do I count them as both? Or do I create some other category, maybe called "hybrids" or "other," and count them separately?

When I'm counting, I need to be able to identify what counts and what doesn't in each category. I need some kind of identification criteria. And even if you just tell me to "count the apples in the orchard," I still need to identify apples from non-apples. I'm still sorting the world into two piles: apples and everything else. I need to know where the edges are.

If we're going to count together, we need to share these edges. And to do that, we need to make sure that different people are *counting in the same way*. Which means we need to make sure people are *cutting up the world in the same way*. Suppose I counted apples including only whole, perfect fruit, and you counted apples including rotten bits, mostly eaten cores, and weird, unidentifiable fruit. We add up our count, but the floppy, unstable counting rules mean the final number has lost a lot of its usefulness. The clearer the shared edges, the more meaningful the number.

Sometimes those shared edges are not up to us. Some edges are given by the natural world. The difference between an electron and a neutron, between hydrogen and carbon, is almost certainly a real difference in the world. These are *natural categories*—categories that exist in the world independent of human choice. With natural categories, there are few to no choices to make about where to draw the lines. The lines are given by the world.

But the more we move into the social world—the world of cultures, emotions, personalities, art, and technologies—the less likely we are to find natural divisions. Instead, we are often faced with a complex spectrum, with no clear lines given by nature. So if we're going to count things, we have to figure out a way to divide up that spectrum. The waters of the world are real and natural, but the difference between the Atlantic Ocean, the Pacific Ocean, and the Mediterranean Sea is an artifact of humanity. We took this vast, complex, undivided thing and we drew a few clear lines in it to make it easier for us to go through the social processes of naming, navigating, and communicating.

A lot of the world is more like the Atlantic Ocean than a proton. Take, for example, race. There is a social process by which we sometimes draw up precise lines for sorting out race. I'm not saying there are no natural or genetic differences between me—a moderately brown-skinned, black-haired dude of largely Vietnamese ancestry—and my longtime gaming buddy Andrew, a blond Minnesotan dude of mostly Swedish ancestry who starts burning after three minutes in the sun. There's a real biological difference between us, just like there's a real physical difference between a point in the middle of the Atlantic and a point in the middle of the Pacific. But those differences exist on a spectrum. In much of the natural world, there's lots of variation, but no clear lines. People decide where to draw the lines.

These are *social categories*—those that human beings make up in some important way. Some social kinds are entirely invented. The categories of being "on welfare" or "a professional skateboarder" are obviously social inventions. Other social categories are a bit subtler, like the Atlantic Ocean. It's easy to think these things are natural and uninvented—after all, that's real water, and you could drown in it. What we've added, as a social act, are the sharp lines that break the world up into simple chunks. The vast waters of the world are natural, but the "Atlantic Ocean" is a social category.

But the answer isn't to stop drawing lines. We often have to draw sharp lines for practical purposes. We need such clear lines to collect data together. And we do it for other reasons: to decide whether you get a certain right, like the right to vote, or the right to profit from a tribal casino. So we draw a line that looks like this: You count as part of the tribe if you have more than one-sixty-fourth of tribal ancestry. The world is fuzzy, but corporations and governments usually act in binaries, so somewhere in between, we need to translate the fuzzy world into easy-to-hold chunks—and we need to do it in unison.

This is what classification manuals do. They standardize how we count by standardizing how we draw lines in the world. They make sure we are counting the same way, so that our counts can add up. They are the foundation for data collection. Without a common classification system there are no measures, no indicators, no metrics, no big data. But like maps, classification systems also represent choices about what to pay attention to and what to ignore.

By the way, saying that something is a social invention doesn't mean we're denying its reality. Money, time, dates, and medical degrees are all social inventions. These things are real. They affect the world; we live and die by them. But we should also remember that we invented them; we brought them into being. And we could still decide to make them differently if we wanted. When we remember that we drew the lines in the first place, it reminds us that we could choose to redraw them to better suit our purposes.

HERE'S A CATEGORY I'VE BEEN THINKING ABOUT A LOT AS A parent: "screen time." There's a bunch of empirical research about the problems of "too much screen time." It's easy to get metrics about screen time, and many people treat reducing screen time as a target for themselves and their kids.

But notice that when we're using this category as a basis for gathering data and setting targets, we're implicitly accepting a set of decisions about what to lump together. The category cares about the time a kid spends on a device, like a tablet. But watch my eight-year-old kid on his tablet. Sometimes he's zoned out watching hypnotic YouTube videos about unpacking toys. Sometimes he's navigating through science videos about how black holes work, or about the history of the world conflict leading up to WWII—while peppering us with dozens of questions. Sometimes he's addicted to some dumb free-to-play clicker game. Sometimes he's using a drawing app to animate a story about his alternate dimensional selves crossing realities to team up. Sometimes he's learning to play chess through TikTok videos and online matches. The category "screen time" lumps all that stuff together. It represents a prior decision to ignore the differences between watching YouTube clickbait and making art. It reflects a presumption that what's important is the delivery method—the device—and that what you're doing on the device matters far less.

But "screen time" is a very convenient category, because it's easy to measure. It has a mechanical edge, because we've drawn a line that can be used and processed with mechanical procedures. If we wanted to sort by the informational richness of YouTube videos or the degree of activity and creativity in playing games on the device, we'd have to constantly be making complex judgments, at every instance of data collection. But our tablets can easily monitor the time they're on. "Screen time" is an easy category to gather vast amounts of data about, even if that data doesn't track what's actually important.

CLASSIFICATION SYSTEMS REPRESENT CHOICES ABOUT WHAT *to pay attention to.* This is the point of Geoffrey Bowker and Susan Leigh Star's extraordinary book, *Sorting Things Out: Classification and Its Consequences.* They look under the hood of one of the most in-

nocuous manuals, the ICD-10 – the International Statistical Classification of Diseases and Related Health Problems, formulated by the
World Health Organization. It provides standardized codes for disease and injury, which are used as the basis for worldwide statistics
about disease, accidents, and mortality.

Every classification system, say Bowker and Star, is a set of decisions about what's important to store in institutional memory. Every
category is a bucket. We remember what's at the edges of the bucket
and forget the differences between what's inside. The US census, for
example, includes racial categories for Asian and Latino. This system *remembers* the difference between Latino and Asian, and *forgets*
the difference between East Asian and South Asian.

Classification systems represent a set of decisions about what information is worth recording. That's part of their basic job, which is
to reduce the complex world into a simpler, lower-resolution set of
chunks. Classification systems simplify the world to make it more
manageable; like maps, they make decisions about what to draw our
attention to, and what to leave out.

You can see the interests in the classification manual written
right into the granularity of the categories. The ICD-10 has far finer
granularity – higher resolution, greater powers of attention – in some
places, and far lower granularity in others. For example, in the ICD-
10, there are a large number of very specific categories for the kinds
of accidents typical in the urban world. There are separate categories
for falls from playground equipment, falls from a bed, falls from a
chair, falls from a wheelchair, falls from a toilet, falls from other furniture, falls from steps, falls from a ladder, and falls from scaffold-
ing. But for the kinds of accidents typical in the natural world, we
only have falls from a cliff, falls from a tree, and "falls, other."

It is utterly obvious that the ICD-10 serves the interests of the
urban over the interests of the rural, or of, say, nomadic people liv-

ing in a forest. The ICD-10 has separate codes for injury by a paint-ball gun and injury by a paper cutter, for god's sake. And this is entirely predictable, say Bowker and Star, because the ICD-10 was primarily written by people from the wealthy, urban, Western world. And our shared categories determine what we can institutionally monitor and target. If the ICD-10 doesn't have a category code for, say, poverty as a cause of death, then that information won't get collected and we won't have ready data on it. And we won't be able to easily target its reduction.

Left to their own devices, people will carve up the world in different ways, based on what they think is important. I have hundreds of categories in my head for restaurants and food markets, but my brain just lumps all the vaguely car-related stores into one big car-stuff category. And I have friends who are the exact reverse. But when we count together, we need to standardize a way of sorting the world. We need rigid categories, or our counts won't add up. We need to share categories. And that means, when we are collecting data, we need to enforce a *single set of interests* and a *single system of attention* across a broad set of people.

This is where we start to worry about the neutrality of data. Because data collection is built on top of a hidden set of social decisions. Data is not neutral, because classification systems are not neutral. If you guide yourself with metrics, you can only target what you have data about. And somebody, somewhere, made the decisions that control what we have data about.

This can lead to a feedback loop, say Bowker and Star. Let's say your medical database is set up to record matters of death and physical illness, but not matters of despair and social isolation. So that database will gather data and quantitative outcomes about death and physical illness but not about mental health and social connections. Now let's say I notice that gap, and I try to speak up about the importance of social isolation and connection. But I won't have any data to back up my claims because the system wasn't set up to record that information in the first place.

The demand to always proceed from the data is not neutral, because it binds us to past value decisions—usually by somebody else—about what data was worth collecting.

WE NOW HAVE A CLEARER UNDERSTANDING OF THE HORSEMAN of Parts, who wants replaceability. Parts wants a world of fungible things and fungible workers. But remember, parts are replaceable because of a whole background system that ensures that every instance of a given part is identical in the right way, and that it will interface properly with the other parts in the machine. Quarter-inch screws are replaceable not just because we've carefully tooled our factories to make screws with identical shapes but also because we've made nuts and screw holes to match those tolerances. And to make those, we need standardized manufacturing tools. Parts's desire for fungibility spreads like a crystal, locking more and more of the world into its pattern.

Classification systems are part of the background system that makes workers fungible. The more mechanical the classification system, the more fungible it makes workers. In particular, they make fungible the work of data collection and interpretation. This is a powerful transformation. From the perspective of a corporation, this means they can fire and hire workers far more easily. But Parts is not just about profit. Parts helps enable much of the data collection that powers science and medicine. Data is valuable because there's a lot of it, gathered by all sorts of people in a consistent manner. Standardized categories enable large-scale data collection. But standardized categories also prevent us from independently tailoring how we divide up the world and deciding what we want to keep track of.

Classification systems shape what we collectively focus on and remember. But if there's not a category for something in the data-collection system, we can't build a metric to target it. Our categories set the limits of what we can collectively care about.

CLASSIFICATION SYSTEMS AND DATA-COLLECTION SYSTEMS ARE incredibly powerful tools. But we should always remember that we made those tools. They are the products of human design and human choice. They are not purely neutral reporters of fact; they were built to serve an interest.

So what interests do classification systems serve? Two answers:

First, any standardized system serves *some* set of interests—the interests of whoever made the standardized system. What those interests are will vary between each system. But for each classification system, somebody drew the lines and decided what was worth remembering and what wasn't. Classification systems enshrine their designers' particular choices into the foundation of institutional memory.

Second, every system of standardization shares the same foundational interests. Standardization serves the interests of those who operate at large scale, who want to be able to coordinate mass groups of people. It aims at the kinds of targets huge groups of people will understand. It doesn't serve the interests of people who want to do something peculiar, distinctive, and small-scale.

The values inside classification systems, and all our other decisions about what data to collect, leak up into metrics. They shape what we can target. Metrics, once we have them, also exert pressure on all of us to use them. They are the clear, common system of meaning. This is no accident; metrics are designed to coordinate at scale. They are a universal language of justification. And you don't get that quick aggregation and convergence of judgment if you depart from the metric. Their power comes from their being shared precisely, which depends on keeping them stable and inflexible at scale.

Metrics set what matters to us collectively. They are technology that standardizes values.

CHAPTER 19

Islands of Meaning

lay is the opposite of standardization. Play occurs on an island—on millions of different islands. Different games have different scoring systems, built for different reasons. When we play games, we disunify.

Johan Huizinga, one of the great scholars of play, said that play occurs in a *magic circle*—a space segregated from the rest of the world. In the magic circle of play, we take on alternate roles, alternate cares. Actions change their meaning.

Here's what it looks like in ordinary life. My spouse and I love each other; we spend our days cooperating on a million little things. We try to support each other, care for each other, protect each other. And then it's nighttime. We've put the kids to bed and we finally have some time to ourselves. And then, with our tiny bit of remaining energy, we do the strangest thing: We spend the rest of the night trying to kill each other. We play a board game.

First, we talk about which board game to play, about which one fits our mood. Our decision process is supportive, cooperative, communal.

And then the game starts, and everything changes. I analyze her every move, search for vulnerabilities. My whole consciousness is tuned to her destruction and ruin—at least of her in-game self. But the whole time, we're also being quite nice to each other outside the game—amusing each other, making each other drinks. There is a remarkable division between our full self and our in-game self.

Games scholar Annika Waern puts it this way: Crossing into and out of the game space involves crossing a *boundary of meaning*, in which we have agreed to reinterpret a prespecified set of actions. The fact that I attack my spouse all-out inside the game in no way undercuts my love for her outside the game.

This is another essential feature of the social technology of games. The meanings of what happens in the game are *quarantined* from the rest of life. They're not perfectly quarantined: If we're playing a game and I try to distract you by revealing your most embarrassing secrets or stomping on your toes with my boots, then I've really wronged you. But for a specific set of actions indicated by the game, their meanings are cut off from the rest of the world; there is a boundary between games and the rest of the world.

This quarantine also allows for one of the moral wonders of gameplay: the power of moral transformation. Games can turn competition into cooperation.

Let's say we're striving players, and our purpose for this game is to have a good time together—and we happen to be the kind of people who like cutthroat investment board games. Our larger goal is collective fun. But during the game, each of us can just go all-out for competition. We can throw ourselves into a purely brutal mindset because games are carefully designed structures that convert aggression into fun.

This doesn't apply to achievement players, however. Achievement players actually care, in a deep and lasting way, about winning the game. Achievement play is a zero-sum activity. If two players are competing and they both truly just want to win, they can't both get what they want. But striving players are different. If two striving players are playing a competitive game, they can both get what they really want. Their interest in winning is just a disposable end; what they really want is an interesting struggle. And in a competitive game, we can't both win, but we can both have an interesting struggle.

This is possible because the attitude of striving play, along with the social practice of magic circles, isolates the gaming environment from the rest of the world. It's possible because the points in the game are detached from the rest of the world—because in striving play, winning doesn't actually matter.

This explains what's wrong with a certain kind of gamer asshole—the kind who exports that attitude of all-out brutality from the game out into the real world. This is the financial wizard who plays the stock market like a game, manipulating the world to max out their score. In real games, striving players have a license to be utterly ruthless. They can use every tool at their disposal to achieve victory. This is safe in real games, because games are little quarantine zones for meaning, where you attack temporary constructs and where all the players have consented to be, for a little while. But if you take that attitude out to the real world—where what you do actually matters and permanently impacts other people's real resources and real lives—then you're just evil.

WE HAVE A BETTER ANSWER NOW TO OUR ORIGINAL QUESTION. Why do games and metrics hit so different when they both have a mechanical scoring system at their core?

Metrics are an *unbounded* scoring system. They reach across the human universe, aiming to speak and coordinate more and more of it, to put it under a single standard of value. They make claims about the value of all work, about the healthiness of all foods, about the productivity of all countries.

Games differ from metrics in two important ways. First, each game is *tightly bounded*. We aren't trapped in a game forever; we're not married to its conception of victory. This is built into how games work. We finish a game, we close up the box. We save our game and turn off the gaming console. And when striving players do so, they also step back from the meanings and values set by the in-game victory conditions. This easy fluidity also encourages a certain reflective distance. It encourages us to ask ourselves, from a perspective outside the scoring system: Was it fun? Was it lovely? Games push us to practice fluidity, stepping in and out of the game's conception of success.

Second, there are *many games*, made for *many purposes*. The mechanical rules and scoring systems of games aren't standardized. They are isolated from one another. There is no reason to integrate them into a world-spanning monolith. Each game is its own island; each offers an alternate universe of meaning.

The technology of metrics is oriented toward coordination, so it tends toward a monolith of scoring. The technology of games is oriented toward a splintering of games and scoring systems—and a splintering of our purposes for making and playing games. Each game can be built differently, to satisfy a different set of players.

Instead of giving us a single, universal, lock-step procedure for how to value things, games encourage us to try on radically different ways of valuing. The ecosystem of games supports genuine reflective choice by exposing us and giving us opportunities to choose between different ways of acting and of living—and the deeply different values underneath.

This splintering, this detachment is also what enables us to tailor games. When we play Dungeons & Dragons, we're free to add our own house rules. Let's say we want a more brutal experience, so we add some home-cooked rules about bleeding to death. Does this make our game harder or easier? Are experience points in our bleeding variant worth more, or less? And if more, how much more? There are no official answers to these questions. If you won second place at the regional skateboarding competition and I set a new speedrunning record for a new variant speedrun of *Super Mario Odyssey*, who did better? We can't really say. The two scoring systems don't interoperate; the points don't translate across.

And more important, *we don't need to* translate the points. Because games aren't beholden to each other. With games, we're under no pressure to stabilize the meanings of points between games or provide a precise mathematical translation system. Games are a space where meanings can wander free.

CHAPTER 20

Centralizing Values

Things are profoundly different in the world of metrics and other institutional data systems. The point of a metric is to permit quick comparison at scale. You want to be able to compare the GPA of different students from different schools. So we need to stabilize how we collect grades and what those grades mean. This enforced standardization creates an essential rigidity at the heart of metrics. You can't house-rule GPA.

This might seem obvious at first. Metrics are external systems, after all. But there is a reason for that, which we need to get clear on. We could try to permit house-ruling metrics. You could let professors create their own, different in-house grading systems, and let governments create in-house rankings systems. We could let a thousand metrics bloom. But that would fail to serve the central functions of metrics: to coordinate at scale, and to be generated by and understandable to an ever-changing set of modular and interchangeable workers following explicit and transparent procedures.

If we diversified our metrics, they would then fail to serve their final and most important function: to *centralize* how we measure values.

IN *SEEING LIKE A STATE*, JAMES SCOTT OFFERS A SWEEPING VISION of how centralization transforms our lives. It is a study of how states systematically reshape the world to make it easier to manage.

A "state," according to Scott, is any large-scale information-processing organization: a government, a large corporation, the integrated global financial market. Crucially, Scott finds the same basic logic and problems in both centralized communist bureaucracies and capitalist free-market economies. Both, for Scott, are states. These work by gathering a vast amount of information from faraway places and then funneling that information into some kind of administrative center—a place where information gets analyzed, summarized, and fed to key decision-makers. They use that summarized information to make decisions, and then push those decisions back out to the edges. Maybe those decision-makers are government administrators looking at production quotas; maybe they are CEOs looking at profits and units shipped. But in both cases, information gets compressed, stripped of context, and summarized for a small set of central authorities—and then simple, universal policies get composed by those authorities and pushed back out to the world.

States, says Scott, can only "see" the parts of the world that they can process through bureaucratic systems. They can only see the parts of the world they can classify, measure, and summarize. That is what is *legible* to the state. The rest of the world—all the stuff that's too mushy and variable and weird to be well tracked by state tools—is *illegible* to the state. States have a hard time tracking and managing the irregular parts of the world. They prefer the parts of the world that fit well into a standardized classification system, that can be turned into data, that can be managed with standardized procedures and fungible workers.

Scott gives us examples aplenty. Older cities were laid out in labyrinthine mazes, highly irregular and often adapted to the local landscape. But such mazes are illegible to the state. Suppose you're a local who knows a particular neighborhood well. Now a government representative—a tax collector, a police officer—is trying to track you down. It's easy for you to run and hide. The highly variable, inconsistent maze of streets gives the advantage to the local. Similarly, when the people of the city are rebelling against the government, the state will need to send in troops, which it gathers from somewhere else. If the city streets are laid out in an irregular labyrinth, then the local rebels have a major advantage. If, on the other hand, the streets are arranged in a regular pattern—like a simple grid—then the locals lose their advantage. There is nothing distinctively local for them to have specialized knowledge of. The state can gather an army of soldiers from all over the place who easily navigate the grid. This is why the French government responded to a massive citizen revolt by rebuilding Paris into a simple hub-and-spoke pattern. It made the city more legible to a military made of soldiers from everywhere.

The same is true, says Scott, of the natural world. A world of incredibly variable biodiversity and deeply specific local ecosystems is hard for the state to control. The state prefers to make all the ecosystems in its purview more similar—so it can be easier for a workforce drawn from all over the world to come in and extract resources from any given chunk. This is why, Scott says, forestry management often involves choices that reduce complexity and biodiversity—like replanting forests with a smaller number of species, or planting trees in regular rows—which make it easier for state-level processes to manage and optimize.

What's legible to the state are the parts of the world that are counted through standardized categories and then aggregated. But these techniques, says Scott, are particularly bad at seeing and coping with local variation. The methodology of centralized thinking and decision-making does well when the world is even, regular, and maximally standardized, and does poorly when the world remains subtle, diverse, and variable. What is illegible to the state are the details that vary between local contexts. They defy summarization in terms of standard categories. So that kind of information is lost to the decision-making center. *The state can see only what the state can process.*

So states do better—they are more powerful, more intrusive, and more capable of managing their world competently—when the world is formatted in ways that are more legible. States function better when the world is more regular. This is Scott's central insight: The state is motivated to *reshape the world to make it more legible.* The state wants to tear down labyrinthine streets and rebuild its cities into neat grids, and replant forests into neat rows. It wants farms that have similar soil and plant similar crops using similar methods. The more the world has been reshaped to fit neatly into mechanical categories, the more of the world the state can see. And the more regular the world is, the easier it is for the state to compose simple standard policies that will work everywhere.

WHEN WE COMBINE SCOTT'S VISION OF STATES WITH WHAT WE'VE learned about mechanical rules, we can catch a glimpse of the heart of this whole business.

States prefer to use *fungible workers.* A state loves to have fungible soldiers, police officers, and tax collectors. And states create the prerequisite background conditions for fungibility. When you put a city on a grid pattern, you eliminate the advantage of specialized local knowledge by *eliminating anything distinctive about a particular local area*. Once everything is evened out and similar, then everybody is on equal footing. This kind of engineered accessibility is an advantage when you're a visitor—a tourist or a tax collector. But it requires us to destroy much of the distinctiveness and variety of local areas.

Scott has shown us how states rebuilt the external, physical world to make it more legible. I'm suggesting that this also applies to our insides. States also want *people's minds* to be more legible. States would prefer it if our thoughts and desires were more regular and easier to summarize. They would prefer that people think in terms of standardized categories instead of their own local intellectual dialects. And states would prefer it if our motivations were standardized—if people valued standardized targets instead of following their own illegible muses. The many people of the world are harder to manage if they have each cultivated their own peculiar sense of meaning—if they each want wildly different kinds of beauty, joy, community, and connection. People will be far more legible to the state if they all just want simple things like longer lifespan, more money, and more page views.

WE CAN NOW NAME THE FOURTH AND FINAL HORSEMAN OF BU-reaucracy: Control.

The Horseman of Control wants to make decisions in an organized way, from a central location. Control wants to coordinate actions across a vast institution, across many contexts. (His full name is Centralized Control.) This means Control wants to compress information and send it to a central location, and then issue decisions and push them out to the world. Control is not necessarily authoritarian or malicious. He simply wants to make sense of the world, and then make decisions in a rational and informed way—and enact those decisions upon the world in a coordinated way.

Control gives us the power of complex large-scale institutions, of many people working together precisely. Control lets us harness the power of vast datasets and vast numbers of people working together. He gives us consistency, stability, and a more predictable world. What Control asks us to give up is the ability to tailor the way we navigate the world to our own context.

Control offers us the power of *coordination*. What he asks us to sacrifice is *autonomy*.

CHAPTER 21

Technologies of Work, Technologies of Play

The ecosystem of games encourages us to take on a very different attitude, a light and fluid one. Let's call it the *playful attitude.*

People have used the word *play* in so many different ways, but there are some common threads. The philosopher María Lugones puts it this way: To be playful is to be willing to enter into rule sets, but to hold them lightly. Playfulness, says Lugones, is the capacity to travel between worlds. By "worlds" here, she means different social worlds: the world of Silicon Valley investors, the world of a poet, the world of professional basketball, the family world. Each of these worlds has its own prepackaged expectations, rules, values, and roles. To be in the Silicon Valley investing world is to care deeply about disrupting the economy for profit. To be in the poetry world is to care about creativity and self-expression. To be in the family world is to care about nurturing and supporting your family. For Lugones, to be playful is to be able to slip between these worlds, to easily adopt different implicit rule sets about how to behave and what's supposed to be important. And it's not just going through the motions. To be deeply playful is to be able to flex your soul a little and actually occupy those worlds from the inside—to get yourself to care a little bit.

Playfulness is one of many different attitudes you can have toward rule sets. It will help to look at some others. For one thing, a person could be a *rules dogmatist.* They are stuck in one particular rule set. The rules dogmatist, as Lugones puts it, holds the rules of their world sacred. They never question them or try on a different point of view. This is the businessperson who can't do anything but seek profit—who can't see the value in anything unless it will earn them money. It is the classical music lover who can't flex their sense of how music is supposed to be enough to see the value of rap or hyperpop. The rules dogmatist doesn't explore, because they believe too deeply in their one true world.

Alternatively, a person could be a *rules skeptic.* They aren't willing to enter into any new worlds. They aren't dogmatists, because they might not be especially attached to any particular social world. They don't hold any rules sacred. But they're stodgy in a different way. They're unwilling to try something new. The skeptic refuses to try on any new rules or goals, even for a little while. You may recognize the rules skeptic in everyday gaming contexts: They won't submerge themselves in a new game. They aren't willing to try out caring for something new.

This skeptical attitude shows up outside games, too. The rules skeptic won't try new hobbies or arts. Crocheting seems dumb to them because you could buy clothes for less money. Home gardening seems like a muddy waste of time for just a few veggies. Hip-hop seems stupid because it's just sampling other people's music and talking, for god's sake, instead of singing. They are particularly skeptical about the weird goals embedded in new hobbies. Why start caring about making your own clothes, growing your own vegetables, climbing rocks? They don't see the point from the outside, so they're unwilling to take that leap of faith and try seeing it from the inside.

A lot of the time, you can only see the real value in an activity by actually doing it for a while—and you can only really do it if you get yourself to care about it, just a little. I could never have imagined that after yo-yoing for a while, I would come to cherish particular tricks for their eloquent construction—for having a lovely resonance between how the yo-yo moved, how my hands flowed, and how the string formations weaved and transformed. But I never would have found that without first caring about getting some basic tricks right, to build enough skill and awareness to start feeling that flow.

The rules skeptic will never try out something new long enough to discover its subtle value. They are also stuck, but in a very different way. They don't explore because they refuse to try out any new worlds.

In between the rules dogmatist and the rules skeptic is the *playful* person. To be playful with the rules is to try them on, but lightly—to slip in and out of worlds. A playful person is willing to try on different rules for a while and see how it goes. But they're not stuck there. A playful person is *exploratory*. And part of that is trying on new goals and values. The playful person, as Lugones puts it, occupies a world *creatively*. They are willing to rewrite the rules if they need to.

ONE OF THE EFFECTS OF THIS CENTRALIZED DECISION-MAKING, says Scott, is that it changes the location of skill and autonomous decision-making. In old-school farming, people mostly used polycropping, which involved tailoring complex interacting sets of plants to suit the environment. This requires an intensive amount of detailed local knowledge of the microclimate. Polycropping is a technology that supports a highly specialized farmer. Under polycropping, each farmer was a valuable, difficult-to-replace expert in a specific ecosystem.

States, says Scott, hate polycropping. Every farmer is making different decisions for different reasons; they are all highly autonomous. That variability is illegible to the state. States prefer monocropping. Monocropping doesn't just mean we plant each field with one crop but that we *change all the fields to be as much alike as possible.* The basic logic of monocropping, says Scott, is to change the physical world to make centralized control easier and more effective. A small number of agriculture scientists test out what works well in a few research greenhouses. They come up with genetically optimized plants and carefully researched procedures—but those procedures work best when deployed in soil that is as close to the research greenhouses as possible. So in monocropping, we change all the different ecosystems to match those research greenhouses. We apply fertilizer and pesticide until all the different soils are as similar as possible, so we can farm them all the same way. Instead of adapting to a variable world, we standardize it.

Under monocropping, says Scott, skill and decision-making get concentrated in the center—in the hands of a small number of agricultural scientists and managers, who spend a lot of creative effort to make relatively easy-to-follow rules and procedures, which everybody else in the system then has to follow mechanically.

And here is the awful core of the whole thing, the insight of Scott's that perpetually haunts me. Once the state has created these centralized, easy-to-follow rules, they have eliminated the need for highly skilled local specialists. The state can now employ almost anybody to follow these rules.

Monocropping *de-skills* workers. It takes a highly autonomous, highly skilled farmer and replaces them with a more mechanical rule-follower. And this makes states less dependent on particular farmers. Now it can hire and fire and replace at will.

Value capture is monocropping for the soul.

Institutional metrics support coordinated action. They are highly accessible, which makes it possible for huge swarms of different people to tightly coordinate around a single clear goal. But to achieve that, the shared goals cannot be formulated in a way that varies sharply from one terrain to another. They cannot be tailored to particular people or particular small communities. The goals cannot be formulated in a way that depends on specific sensitivity and expertise.

And because they are so pervasive, metrics invite value capture rather than free play and reflective control. They invite the unreflective acceptance of prespecified values, as set by some external, central authority. Metrics make it easy to stop engaging in the practice of fine-tuning our values, to lose touch with the feedback of our sensations. They put us out of practice with adapting our goals and our activities to suit us. They are a technology that centralizes decision-making about targets and values—and so encourages us to outsource our values to that central authority.

Metrics are a technology that centralizes the process of meaning-making. So metrics de-skill us for the process of setting our own sense of meaning.

BEING PLAYFUL WITH GAMES ENABLES TWO THINGS. FIRST, YOU get the goods of *exploring* new value worlds. You get to know what different scoring systems are like from the inside—what it's like to live under a radically different value. But it also encourages *exiting* value worlds. Playfulness builds the habit of regularly distancing yourself from the scoring system.

And the essential nature of games encourages us to take up that playful attitude. Games are *accessible*. They have mechanical rules and scoring systems, which makes them easy to step into. They are *tightly bounded*. They end. Their boundaries are a signal to us, a reminder to step back from our psychological immersion in the scoring system. Games are *isolated*. The points in a game are usually disconnected from real stakes. This makes it easier to treat those games as unimportant, so that we can flit between different scoring systems.

Metrics are pervasive; they are baked into our ruling institutions and deeply connected to external power structures—to promotions, power, and status. Metrics discourage playfulness.

Most important, the mechanical scoring systems of games are *independent*. They aren't required to coordinate. They use mechanical rules as a communication device to allow different people to write down different values—but different games can have different rules. This freedom—this decentralization of game authorship, this diversification of game purposes—is what creates a varied ecosystem of explorable values. This is the heart of the technology of games.

The technology of games uses rigidity to communicate new modes of agency—lots of them—but doesn't force us to stick with any particular mode of agency for our entire lives. This allows us to explore a diverse ecosystem of different, isolated games. The technology of games gives us quick access to many radically different visions of the good.

Games are a technology that decentralizes the process of meaning-making.

LET'S GO BACK TO THE FOUR HORSEMEN OF BUREAUCRACY: Rules, Scale, Parts, and Control. They will help us give a tidier answer to the original question: Why do games and metrics hit so different when they both involve mechanical scoring systems?

Games and metrics accept the trade from the Horseman of Rules. Both use mechanical rules; both use scoring systems with highly accessible procedures. This makes it easy for anybody to enter into the scoring system.

Metrics enthusiastically accept the Horseman of Parts. They are all in on the world in which workers and data collectors and judges can be easily swapped with one another. If everybody in the software industry cares most about products shipped, or everybody in the journalism industry cares only about page view counts, then we can easily swap people inside that industry. They don't just act in the same way, they will care about the same thing in their core. Precise value convergence makes workers fungible at the deepest level.

Games, on the other hand, have a complicated and tense relationship with Parts. There is a sense in which mechanical rules help players be sorta fungible. After all, the whole point of mechanical scoring systems is that anybody can pick up a game and learn its goals in a moment. So there is one limited way in which games use the power of Parts: Most are written in clear language, so anybody can enter the game and learn the rules.

But there is another sense in which games are deeply inimical to Parts: We can't swap one game for another, or one player for another, and still all be equally satisfied. Our tastes are not fungible, and the distinctive beauty of different games is not fungible. Our purposes for play have not been made interchangeable in the world of games. Mechanical rules make the entry point to a game accessible, but they do not make players, or games, into interchangeable parts.

And metrics and games have entirely different relationships to Scale and Control. Games will happily use the power of Rules, but bend them to a diversity of purposes, to build wildly different games for different reasons and different players. Games reject the need for meaning to be held stable across different contexts. They reject the need for a central authority to dictate which scoring system to use. The basic structure of games encourages personalized modding: house rules, chess variations, speedrun versions. Games tend to exclude Scale and Control from setting the central purpose of play.

Metrics, on the other hand, are inextricably married to Scale and . Control. Metrics are a technology whose central function is to make evaluations and judgments comprehensible at scale, to make data aggregate. This lets authority figures compress the landscape into a legible form, make decisions, and then push out those decisions to the rest of the world—and justify them in ways that anybody can understand.

Metrics are mechanical scoring systems tuned to work at scale; they are standardized and rigidified to serve the purpose of massive coordination. Games use mechanical scoring systems for local purposes, under local control.

PART 5

WHAT DO WE DO?

CHAPTER 22

There Is Too Much World

S o how do we live, as individuals and members of comfortably small-scale communities, in the face of the vast powers of Rules, Scale, Parts, and Control? How do we retain our quieter sensitivities when we're met with the harsh voice of large-scale, denuanced communication?

Some people think we can solve the problem by *building better metrics* — by changing our metrics to capture what's really valuable and eliminating the Gap. But we can now see why this won't work. Metrics are, by their nature, simplified and decontextualized, in order to be highly accessible. By design, metrics flatten the complexity of value. They use and produce unnuanced nuggets of information made to travel easily between contexts. This is value simplification, and it is incredibly useful for institutional functioning. It helps us coordinate very different people embedded in very different contexts. But there is a cost for this communicative speed. The designed portability of metrics is essentially at odds with the richness of human value.

Maybe you want to get rid of metrics entirely. But that would be incredibly costly, because metrics are such powerful tools, good for coordinating collective action. There will probably always be metrics—and we will probably always want them—as long as we continue to work together in large-scale organized groups.

Maybe you think the price of decontextualization is so high that we should give up on large-scale organizations. That's what James Scott thought. The problem, he said, was the states themselves—the fact that our world is dominated by massive information-processing institutions whose essential style of functioning makes them want to even out the world. So we shouldn't have them. We should break up the system of control, give up on having big governments and big businesses and global markets. We should try to live in small communities and avoid scaling up. This is why Scott was an avowed anarchist (though the kind who was also a tenured professor at Yale).

Perhaps this solution is satisfying to you, but it isn't to me. For one thing, I wouldn't be alive without large-scale states. I have a number of chronic medical problems that would have killed me. I need modern medicine and the system of large-scale data collection that makes it work. Standardization may crush souls, but it also saves lives.

For another thing, I suspect that small-scale communal life will be unstable in the long run because of the power of scale. Massive, tightly coordinated institutions are so efficient at producing some kinds of goods—like weapons—that those groups willing to use the Four Horsemen's methods will tend to gain more power. The very existence of ideas and technologies like mass production and factories shifts the balance of power in the world. Small-scale communities can't make nukes, tanks, or even decent assault rifles—or vaccines. The Four Horsemen of Bureaucracy ask a lot, but they give some very powerful gifts in return.

The problem is that we are pulled in two directions. There is a part of us that is well served by intimate, small-scale life, where we can tailor our values to our particular and peculiar selves—where we can be free to play. But there is another part of us that craves the powers of scale—that benefits from all the efficiencies and scientific magic enabled by the Four Horsemen.

Maybe the solution, then, is to try to have it both ways. The Four Horsemen aren't all bad. They offer us potent trade-offs between different ways of life. Maybe the best we can hope for is to manage those trade-offs carefully—to take the trades only when they're really worth it. We want to use the Four Horsemen with care. We don't want them to take over and reshape our values in their image.

So maybe what we need is to separate the scales. We should permit the Four Horsemen into the parts of our lives that profit enormously from the power of scale, but reserve other domains for smaller-scale living. We do something very much like that in governance. Many large nations are built using the principle of *federalism*: You make national laws for the things that only a large-scale nation can handle, but for the rest, you try to leave it to state and local governments to decide for their own particular contexts—to tailor, experiment, and customize independently.

What we need is *value federalism*. We need a few large-scale proxies so we can work together when we need to—like reducing CO_2 emissions and poverty. But for a lot of the rest—for the values that rule our own choice of art, fitness, hobbies, education, and career— we should mostly leave it to individuals and small-scale communities to formulate independently. And cultivating those smaller-scale values will also give us a perspective outside the metrics, which will help us to see when the metrics have gone too far astray.

One thing we know from the actual history of people and metrics is that we rarely stick to value federalism. The big clear metrics tend to swamp more intimate values. So to build a lasting value federalism, we will need to understand exactly why metrics tend to dominate our hearts and our bureaucracies—and how we might resist.

TO START, LET'S TAKE A BIG STEP BACK TO GET A PHILOSO-pher's view from a million miles in the air. There is a central source for the problems and tensions and pressures we've talked about in this book: There is too much world.

The world is incredibly complicated. There is simply too much of it for a single human being to cope with. If we tried to deal with it all ourselves—if we flung ourselves raw and alone at the hugeness of the world—we would be utterly overwhelmed. So we have developed strategies for coping with the world. We simplify, we build tools, and we cooperate.

One of our most powerful strategies for managing the chaotic world is categorization. We mostly don't think about each particular pine tree. We mostly learn things about pine trees in general. We take something we learn about a few pine trees and then apply it to all pine trees. This is how science works. It is, in fact, how most human thinking works. We are lumpers by nature. I don't have to start from scratch with every new dog I meet because I know stuff about dogs. They like to play fetch and get belly scratches, unless they're growl-ing, which means back away. What I'm doing here is porting over in-formation from other dogs I've met and making some assumptions that generally work out. Lumping things together turns down the resolution of the world. It makes the world easier to handle by delet-ing details. We just hope that we're deleting the right ones.

To cooperate in information gathering, we need to *categorize to-gether*. This is why we use classification systems, which are a tool to ensure that we are cutting up the world in a similar way. If we do so, then we can multiply the time-saving power of categorization by the time-saving power of cooperation. A few of us can learn a few things about a few particular pine trees, and now, hopefully, everybody knows those things about pine trees. Collective categorization is an extraordinarily efficient device when it works. It lets individuals mostly skip looking at particular parts of the world, which works really well—again, as long as we're not skipping anything important.

Another way we cooperate is by *specializing*. The philosopher Elijah Millgram puts it this way: The essential feature of the modern world is that science is so complicated that nobody can understand it all by themselves. We need to break up the world into pieces and each specialize in a different piece. But this creates the basic problem of the modern world: The specialists don't understand each other. Our specialties—chemistry, computer science, environmental science, music, engineering, economics, history, philosophy—are each so complex and arcane that no single human can understand all the sciences, or even a tenth of them. So we end up having to trust each other—trust our lives to doctors and aeronautical engineers—without being able to understand everything for ourselves. And this puts us in a peculiar position. There is no single person who completely understands how to build a car or a nuclear power plant. There is nobody who fully understands how a particular dose of antibiotic works. The knowledge is scattered across so many statisticians, physicists, computer modelers, engineers, materials scientists, biochemists, cellular biologists, virologists, industrial process engineers, and on and on. Every modern thought is a fragile chain that crosses a thousand arcane islands, each moderately opaque to the next. And this creates a tension. We have a general simple language that we can talk with each other in, but it doesn't catch all the details that matter. It's just a useful, simplifying bridge. And then we have specialist languages full of jargon and detail and subtlety that catch so much more—but they do not travel well outside their little specialist niches.

We also build tools to help us deal with the overcomplicated world. We invent technologies. There is too much math to do, so we invent calculators and spreadsheets. The world is too large to remember everything we know, so we write things down in notebooks, we collect scientific principles in articles and reference books, we store things in databases. We build these technologies to augment our limited capacities and offload much of the mental strain.

Remember, I said that the problem of value capture is that we're outsourcing. But this was also an oversimplification. Because outsourcing by itself isn't always bad. We're constantly outsourcing to cope with the oversize world. We're outsourcing our memory to notebooks and document files. We're outsourcing our math to calculators and spreadsheets. We're outsourcing our medical knowledge to doctors, our car knowledge to mechanics. And each of the people and things we're outsourcing to is in turn outsourcing to other people and things. Our trust is fractal and expands, rootlike, into incomprehensibly diverse sources. It turns out it's not just that we're too small to know everything about the world, so we have to outsource. It's that we're too small to even keep track of everything we're outsourcing to.

I have been railing against value capture by external metrics and rankings, but here's an honest truth: I use rankings all the time. When I wanted to buy a new refrigerator, I just looked up the rankings online, did a tiny bit of checking to see if the thing met my needs, and bought one of the top-ranked ones. Because I don't have time to investigate everything deeply, and I sure as hell am not going to waste my valuable time learning about the intricacies of refrigerators. I just want to buy a decent one and then get on with the rest of my life.

So I outsourced that decision, because refrigerators aren't that important to me, and because my needs for refrigeration are pretty normal. And every piece of technology has value decisions embedded into its basic design. When I buy a computer, I have outsourced all sorts of value decisions—about the relative value of durability versus cost, about ease versus security. Every time I take a vitamin, I am outsourcing both scientific knowledge about natural facts and value decisions about which health benefits are most important. Our technological systems are dripping with values, stuffed full of other people's complex decisions, and when we start using any technology, we're always outsourcing some of our values.

We have to outsource because we just don't have enough time to think about everything. But we also don't want to outsource willy-nilly. We don't want to outsource away our whole souls. We want to outsource less important decisions to make more room for the really important decisions. And we want to outsource to the right resources; we want to trust the right people and the right technologies.

We'll never get it all perfect. That's the essential and inescapable danger of outsourcing. Because when we outsource, we are deciding not to look too closely at some chunk of the world. Maybe there is deep mystery and wonder in fridge design, and maybe I could have embraced a new part of my humanity if I'd spent time there. But I made a quick, underinformed decision to outsource that part of my life. And the danger is that I might outsource what I thought was a minor matter, but it turns out to be massively important. I might never know how complex and important it really is, because the whole point of outsourcing is to let me skip out on thinking about it.

The philosopher Annette Baier said that the essence of trust was making yourself vulnerable by putting some part of yourself into somebody else's power. That is what we are always doing when we trust somebody else. When I trust a doctor, I cannot verify for myself that their advice is sound, because I simply don't have the time and energy to learn enough medicine to do so. I am making myself vulnerable to their competence and their goodness. And the same is true every time I trust a review about a car or a fridge. And we are inevitably going to screw some of it up. Trust is fraught, imperfect, dangerous—and impossible to avoid. So we need to manage it carefully.

Just how do we manage our outsourcing and our trust? Let's start with the basics. We do well when we manage our outsourcing to suit our purposes. We outsource badly when we choose resources that run counter to our purposes. And we outsource disastrously when we let some external entity rewrite our core values to suit their distant purposes.

We want to use our tools; we don't want our tools to use us. We want to retain reflective control. So why isn't the answer just that simple? Go ye forth into the world and exert reflective control. It's just like with recipes: Use them to explore, but don't let them dictate what you want. Follow recipes to learn, but then let yourself be free. Problem solved.

But metrics make it hard to exert reflective control. They can seduce us into abandoning the truly important decisions. We've seen how they reshape the world and flatten it. In part five, I want to go back inside our psychologies and look at how we experience this reshaped, metrified world—to really see how incredibly seductive it is. We will study how the world of metrics sucks us into unreflective acceptance of other values, how it makes reflective control difficult—and what we can do about it.

The big goal of part five is to think about how we live with the Four Horsemen without giving in to them. To figure this out, we'll need to answer some questions.

First, why is it so hard to check metrics at the door? Why do they tend to invade everything, and then conceal the fact that they've invaded?

Second, where do metrics work well, and where should we try to limit their use?

And third, how do we limit metrics? How do we keep them from redefining everything in the insensitive language of the Four Horsemen? How do we retain space for our own odd, variant, inchoate values? And how do we build social institutions and technologies that will help us keep metrics on a leash?

Our guiding light will be games—because games exemplify how we can use scoring systems for our own weird purposes. They give us a hint to how we can build a world that constantly reminds us to exercise reflective control.

CHAPTER 23

Objectivity Laundering

M etrics hit us on two fronts. First, they discourage reflection
and exploration by creating a *facade of objectivity*. Reflective control involves making a choice, but metrics disguise
and rewrite the situation so that we don't realize there was a space
for choice. Metrics try to speak with the voice of scientific authority;
they make it seem like there is no room for dissent. Second, metrics
offer us the pleasures of *seductive clarity*. They make things look so
simple that we won't think there is anything else to investigate. They
present themselves as the bottom line—as the final word, as a finished thought. These are the two masks of metrics, which conceal
our freedom to choose: the mask of fake objectivity and the mask of
seductive clarity.

LET'S START WITH THE MASK OF FAKE OBJECTIVITY.
Theodore Porter, the historian of quantification, wanted to understand why bureaucrats and politicians seem to obsessively and

unthinkingly reach for quantitative justification. Administrators often seem to prefer metrics to any other form of justification, even when those metrics are clearly flawed or incomplete. This is because, says Porter, metrics gave the appearance of objectivity—which lets their users avoid taking responsibility. Metrics let administrators avoid visibly inserting themselves into the stream of decision-making so that instead, they can point to the metric and say, "It's not me, it's just the numbers."

But this objectivity is only a facade. Such metrics often contain value judgments hidden at the core. We take a subjective choice and then hide it under tons of precise math. It's like money laundering, where we take dirty money and then pass it through enough clean transactions to mask the dirt.

Let's call this *objectivity laundering*. We take a complex matter, like well-being, education, or success. Somebody—often, a very distant somebody—makes a value-laden decision about what that means, about what counts as well-being or success. Then we process it. What comes out the other end looks objective and free of any taint of human values. It seems to speak with the voice of God—or at least the voice of science.

This is the first way that metrics worm their way into our hearts: by presenting themselves as simple matters of fact. They try to convince us that we never had a choice about the matter in the first place. The more universal and objective that metric looks, the more we are tempted to treat it as a given.

I'm worried that in many of our cases, we're playing the role of the responsibility-avoiding bureaucrat in our own lives. We're hiding from the complexity of our value decisions by following an apparently objective metric. But really, we are deferring to the values hidden within that metric. The existentialist philosophers had a term for this: acting in *bad faith*. What they meant was that we humans have the freedom to choose, but sometimes we try to avoid that freedom. We deceive ourselves into thinking that we have no choice in the matter, that we are acting in the only way possible. We are pretending to be mechanical objects. Jean-Paul Sartre thought we often did this by following the scripts attached to our roles and social identities—letting ourselves think that we had no choice because we are a parent, or a police officer, or an American, and that's simply what we had to do.

Value capture is the new bad faith.

THERE ARE DIFFERENT STRATEGIES FOR OBJECTIVITY LAUNDERING. The first is *burying the values*. This happens when we take a value-laden decision and bury it under a mountain of objective mechanical processing, so that we lose sight of the original value-laden choice.

Historian Mary Poovey gives a fantastic example of burying the values, from early in the history of quantification culture. She was interested in understanding the history of something she called "the modern fact" in Western civilization. Before the modern era, she says, we had a very different idea of what made a good fact. We trusted a fact if it came from a trustworthy person—somebody honest, reliable, and competent. Good facts came from good people.

But somewhere on the road to our contemporary world, things changed. We started using a new conception of a fact, a new standard for trustworthiness. A fact was good because it came from *nobody in particular.* It was trustworthy if it came not from a good person, but via a mechanical process. Facts were trustworthy if nothing human had tainted them. They came either from a literal machine or from people who were following clear mechanical rules, which made them into the functional equivalent.

This is the idea behind the modern practice of science and data collection. But, says Poovey, the idea of the inhuman modern fact actually shows up a little bit before the birth of the sciences—in the sixteenth-century invention of double-entry bookkeeping.

Double-entry bookkeeping is a methodology, a precise set of clear and mechanical rules for processing the numbers in your accounting books and double-checking your calculations. Since the rules are mechanical, anybody can do the math, and anybody else can check over the accounting process. Accounting, says Poovey, is the first place where we see moral virtue and human competence displaced from the center of our ideal of human knowledge and replaced with trust in a mechanical system. The precision and transparency of the system is what lends credibility to the bookkeeping procedure. Accounting, it turns out, is the birthplace of our modern conception of objectivity—in which human virtue is replaced with mechanical precision. (And Poovey finds direct evidence that the early innovators of science knew of, admired, and actively imitated the methods of double-entry bookkeeping.)

But that mechanical objectivity is incomplete, says Poovey. There is, hidden at the very root, an entirely nonmechanical, non-inspectable procedure: how we set the starting values. Let's say you're a merchant with an inventory. When you start using this system of double-entry bookkeeping, you need to enter a value into your books for each item in your inventory. Once you've entered those values, the wholly mechanical system takes over. But there are no mechanical rules for the initial valuation. That can come from anywhere—intuition, experience, guesswork, bias, fabrication. But despite that raw, uncontrolled core element, we trust the books because the rest of it is so clear. The subjectivity of the initial input is concealed by the mechanical objectivity of the ensuing processing.

This kind of objectivity laundering remains very common. Economic cost-benefit analyses usually depend on some obscured but crucial value decisions inserted quietly into the calculations. Here's an example from Porter: The National Park Service often uses cost-benefit analysis to justify investments in infrastructure. It's relatively easy to calculate, in a fairly objective manner, the projected profits for local businesses from increased tourist traffic. But the National Park Service also has to calculate the *value of visiting the park* for the tourists themselves—to attach an economic value to enjoying nature. So they set one. One 1948 cost-benefit analysis set the "recreational value" of each tourist visit at 12.5 cents per visitor day. Recreation is a key value of the national parks, but there is no objective basis for this value—it is a human decision about the value of experiencing natural beauty. But the end result is a cost-benefit analysis that looks objective, because we've piled a lot of accounting on top of that recreational value.

There is another obscure-sounding but utterly crucial example of burying the value, and it's pervasive throughout all cost-benefit calculations: the *discount rate*. Whenever we are doing a cost-benefit analysis of present costs versus future gains, even if every other number is entirely objective, there is inevitably one crucial number that is not. The discount rate is how much we discount the value of *future goods* compared with *present goods*. Let's say we need to invest a thousand dollars today in a chocolate factory, and we will get a return of eleven hundred dollars next year. Should we do it? Is it worth losing control of that amount of money now to get that slight profit later? The answer is not an objective matter, because it depends on how we set the discount rate—how we decide to value future goods compared with present goods. If we set the discount rate at 0 percent, then we're saying we think a future potential dollar is precisely as valuable as a dollar in the hand right now. In that case, we should certainly invest in the chocolate factory. If we set the discount rate low—at 5 percent per year, say, then we should also still do it. But if we set the discount rate high—let's say 20 percent per year—then we should not make that investment. By that discount rate, $1,100 in next-year dollars is worth only $880 in present-year dollars. Most economists think setting a discount rate of 0 percent is ludicrous, because it licenses almost any investment with even marginal gains—since marginal future gains, multiplied over the massive time-span of the whole future, will outweigh almost any present cost. We need some kind of discount rate, but there is no consensus on what the right discount rate actually is.

Every cost-benefit analysis must set some discount rate, but there is no objectively correct rate. It is a value decision about how much future goods are worth compared with present goods—a decision about the relative value of the future. But it is hidden, so the cost-benefit analysis appears cleansed of subjectivity—an immaculate conception of pure math.

ON TO THE SECOND KIND OF OBJECTIVITY LAUNDERING; LET'S call it the *objectivity bait and switch*. This is when we take a complex, multidimensional quality, often with a lot of freedom of choice, and substitute a simpler quality that is genuinely more objective. If you are convinced that the simpler measure captures everything important, then the whole process will seem entirely objective. But the value decision is hidden almost out of sight—in the initial decision of which simple quality to sub in.

It can be easy to miss the bait and switch, so let's start with a clear case. I was once talking about this stuff in one of my big lecture introductory classes, and a student from the back row—a dude who definitely worked out—raised his hand and said, "But what if we're just measuring something that's already totally objective? Like if you want to get fit and healthy, weight loss is objectively measurable." And the obvious reply is: "When did we start thinking that health meant weight loss?" And when I said that, the class kind of rippled with nervous shock and laughter. What some of them said after was: It was so obvious once somebody pointed it out to them, but they were shocked that they'd needed it pointed out. Because, obviously, health isn't weight loss, but it's easy, somehow, to get sucked into thinking that way.

The crucial point here is that the value-laden decision isn't hiding in the way we measure weight. Weight really is just a simple, objective measurement. The value-laden decision is one step back, in the decision to use weight as a stand-in for health in the first place.

OK, now for a much more complicated example. Let's look at a hundred-point rating scale that dominates the modern wine world. Wine scorers have tried to make the process as objective as possible. This means a few things. For one, professional wine tasters usually spit out the wine — to avoid getting drunk, so that they can render an objective judgment. For another thing, professional wine tasters, when officially scoring a wine, have it *without food*. This is because having wine with food would create too much variability in the judging process. A wine that might be incredible with a roast chicken might be only decent with fried chicken, and might disappear next to a peppery steak. So, to create a more stable, objective judgment, the official wine-judging process excludes food.

But for many people, much of the joy of wine is how it reacts with food. Wine can change and shift with every sip, reacting dynamically to different bites. And there are different relationships it can have with food; it can be a sharp contrast or a resonant match. But this level of variability would create incredible difficulties for an official scoring process. How could you score a "best" wine if one is incredibly good with tomato sauces but kind of listless with anything else, and then rank it against a wine that is moderately good with every food? So we create an artificially stabilized context; we cut out the variability. We score wine without food. But if we follow that wine-scoring system, we have implicitly adopted a value choice: that objective scoring is more important than the relationship between wine and food.

And that value choice feeds back into the wine itself. The wine-scoring system is transforming the winemaking world, pushing it toward "fruit bombs"—wines with big, bombastic flavors. And since high scores mean better sales, many winemakers have started making more and more fruit bombs. But those wines, though they perform better in the sterile, controlled environment of the wine-scoring process, usually don't react in interesting ways to food. If you grow up in the era of these new fruit bombs, though, you might never know that wine could react so powerfully and variably to food. The wine-scoring system has written itself into reality by transforming the wine-growing industry, blotting out dynamic wines and filling the world with stable and unreactive ones.

OK, now for the most complicated example. Let's get back to the concept of "healthy." We already saw one mistake—substituting weight loss for health. This is a common mistake, but relatively easy to see. But health is also subject to more sophisticated forms of the objectivity bait and switch.

The philosopher Elizabeth Barnes suggests that our metrics and measures for health often end up obscuring our free choice under the veil of science. People act as if there is a single objective quality—health—and a single objective measure for it. If that were true, then health would be something we could measure scientifically—and then establish a singular and objective list of best practices. But this is a mistake, she says—a misunderstanding of what health is. There will, according to Barnes, never be a single clear metric for health, nor will there be a one-size-fits-all set of best practices for all people to pursue health. This is because health is not a static thing, stable across all people. It is a concept that contains, hidden within it, some freedom to choose. What health is depends on a complex set of decisions about what we value about our bodies and capabilities. And different people will make those decisions in different ways.

First, a quick primer from the philosophy of language. Some words have a stable meaning. The meanings of the words *apple* and *four* will usually stay the same in different contexts. But other words have a meaning that varies with context, like *tall*. Am I tall? That depends. Am I tall for a human being? I'm a bit taller than the average human. Am I tall for a professional basketball player? Absolutely not. Such terms change meaning depending on a comparison class. Terms like *fit* and *healthy* can also work like this. Am I fit? That depends. Compared with the average academic philosopher, I'm fit as hell. Compared with the average rock climber, I'm a weak slob.

The meaning of *health* has a very special form of contextual variability, says Barnes. The meaning changes from person to person depending on each person's *interests*. I ask my doctor: Is my knee healthy? Does my current exercise routine support a healthy knee? But there is no single objective answer to that question because the meaning of *health* fluctuates, depending on my interests and goals. There are limits to that flux: No matter your interests, being run over by a bulldozer is unhealthy for your knees. But within those limits, the exact meaning of "health" depends on your particular interests.

Suppose Samantha is an Olympic sprinter. She is interested in whether she will be able to stand up to the rigors of competition and have a chance at a gold medal two years from now. If she has to trade off some late-life functionality and pain for short-term success, she'll do it. Health for her involves short-term high-end athletic functionality. I, on the other hand, am a casual rock climber. I climb to relax, for mental health, and because I love the beauty of the movement. And I run mostly as cross-training, to balance out the abuse that climbing puts on certain joints. I am most interested in whether my knees can keep me climbing well into my sixties, which will include regular ten-foot falls onto a gymnastic pad. If I have to accept some pain in order to continue climbing as long as possible, I will, and I am willing to sacrifice short-term optimal performance for long-term functionality. Health for me involves balancing longevity with moderate athletic functionality, while accepting some degree of pain. Or you might be interested in how long you can continue to walk pain-free, as late in life as possible. Health for you involves long-term functionality, but weighting pain reduction over athletic performance.

The notion of health is essentially fuzzy, says Barnes. It's an approximation—the vague center of gravity of a cluster of different people's interests. There are a lot of things that the sprinter, the climber, and the walker will have in common, and there are some broad generalities that will generally promote knee health. Losing all your knee ligaments is bad news for pretty much any human, whatever their interests, and drinking water is generally a good support for any human functioning. So the rough approximation is good enough for some uses. But that kind of universal prescription doesn't work in every case. This is why there are no true best practices for health—because the right thing to do depends on each person's different interests. The notion of health is messy, says Barnes, because human interests are messy.

But if we take a simple, genuinely objective measure and use it as our meaning of *health*, we can hide from the need to make choices.

And we have some very promising candidates for the bait and switch. There are some qualities that are affiliated with many conceptions of health that are easy to measure mechanically, such as longer lifespan and lower heart attack rate. They are excellent candidates for standardized measurement. And certainly they are decent as rough approximations for our shared interests. But they are incomplete.

Let's say we set the meaning of *health* in terms of some measurable qualities: longer lifespan and lower incidence of measurable disease and injury. Even this is a value decision; it sets certain interests above others. It sets an interest in increasing the number of years and ignores the interest in the quality of those years. It sets an interest in avoiding disease over an interest in developing complex physical skills. It will tell me to run on a treadmill instead of going trail running on difficult terrain, because trail running is riskier and increases the chances of significant injury—and this particular notion of health values avoiding injury over the development of complex motor skills.

I'm not arguing that we can't measure anything objectively or that science doesn't work. Some kinds of things can be measured precisely, because their nature doesn't vary with interests. We can measure, with perfect objectivity and no information loss, inches, pounds, and calories. But concepts like "health" are fundamentally unlike "calories." A calorie is independent of your values and interests. Health is dynamic and variable, because it is essentially entangled with your interests. To be healthy is to have your body and mind functioning as you wish. This involves a choice about which aspects of your functioning you care more and less about. But we can launder the concept of "health" and make it look entirely objective. And if we accept that laundered "health," we will be letting somebody else make value decisions about how we should take care of our own bodies and minds.

—

THINKING ABOUT REAL AND FAKE OBJECTIVITY ALSO HELPS US to answer one of our big questions: When should we trust metrics, and when shouldn't we? When should we be worried about large-scale data collection, and when should we be fine with it?

Very early in the *Nicomachean Ethics*, Aristotle warns that we should not demand too much precision when it's inappropriate. Some areas, like engineering and science, allow for great precision. But you can't expect the same degree of precision in politics and ethics. It is, says Aristotle, the mark of the educated person to seek the appropriate amount of precision for each subject. And you can't expect precision in politics and ethics, because what we should do in these depends significantly on human autonomy and choice.

To sum it up for the data and policy wonks in the audience, large-scale data collection efforts will likely be most useful when they target those qualities that:

1. are highly *invariant* and *stable* between contexts

2. have accessible, mechanical methods for being counted

3. do not involve a value decision

One of the reasons large-scale data collection works so well for figuring out antibiotics is that antibiotics work in a relatively context-invariant way. They are effective on most human bodies, regardless of the place, psychology, or culture of the person. And the positive results of antibiotics are easier to measure, because we can measure the disappearance of bacteria mechanically.

Large-scale data collection efforts will more likely miss the mark for qualities that:

1. are highly *variant* between contexts and dynamic

2. require a nonmechanical exercise of skill, sensitivity, or expertise in order to be counted

3. involve a value decision

Metrics will not capture the goodness of wine because many important qualities are highly dynamic and variant between different dynamic contexts. They will not capture health because health involves a value decision at its core. We can get rough approximations that are helpful for large-scale population work, but we should not take them to be complete or decisive for individuals.

CHAPTER 24

The Seductions of Clarity

The second mask of metrics is *clarity*. Clarity hits us on two fronts at once: first, in our scientific, logical mind, with an orderly, seemingly complete picture of the world. Metrics do this by presenting a seductively clear picture of what's important. They present a precise judgment of success—a neat arrangement of the values of the world, made simple and orderly. Simultaneously, the mask of clarity also hits us in the pleasure center, showering us with the pleasure of getting it, of understanding.

Clarity is a feeling of things falling into place. It is the feeling we get when we understand things—when what seemed confusing and chaotic suddenly snaps into focus and we see the underlying order. Clarity is the feeling of things *making sense*. The psychologist Alison Gopnik once characterized the feeling of getting a good explanation as a kind of intellectual orgasm. There's a satisfying aha feeling, a sense of completeness, when your mind suddenly sees how things work. We take pleasure in clarity—which is useful, because it drives us to try to understand the world.

But the *feeling* of clarity is distinct from real understanding. And so it can be faked. And this is particularly dangerous, because fake clarity can create the illusion that our investigations are done, that everything is settled and well understood, and that we can move on.

So how do you fake clarity? How do you create the illusion of understanding? First, consider the real thing. Philosophers of science and of education tell us that *understanding* is a distinctive phenomenon. It's not just knowing a lot of things. You can know a bunch of trivia, but if it's all just disconnected bits and pieces—a jumble of true facts—then you don't really understand. Understanding is holistic; it is having a working picture of the whole—how the parts fit and how they interact.

In scientific explanation, real understanding involves having a *mental model* of some scientific phenomenon that allows you to make predictions, explain new events, and come up with new solutions. You're not stuck with a few rote, memorized procedures. You can adapt to new circumstances, diagnose new problems, and improvise new solutions, because you understand how the parts fit together. And you can communicate your model to other people.

I know, by rote, that if certain lights turn on in my car dashboard, I should add water or oil, or put air in the tires. But I don't understand how a car works beyond those memorized instructions. I can't figure out why the steering on my car sticks when it gets cold, or why this rattling sound shows up when I hit sixty miles per hour. For that, I need a mechanic who actually understands how cars work.

But I do understand a lot about cooking. Like John Thorne says, if all you can do is follow a recipe by rote, you don't really grasp the heart of the dish. To understand a dish is to get the core—the sense of balance that is the heart of the dish. I understand stews. I know the balance that tastes and feels good, and I can improvise different routes to get there. I know if I have a particularly dank and funky bit of sausage, I can up the sweet and sour to balance it out—maybe with a bit of extra tomato, or maybe apple cider vinegar and honey.

That's real understanding. But if we can fake the feeling of understanding, then we will have an extremely powerful weapon. Because understanding is often the *endpoint of inquiry*. If you think you don't understand something, then you have a reason to keep thinking about it—to keep investigating, exploring, learning. Fuzziness and unclarity is a signal to keep tinkering with your model and checking to see if you've got it right. But when you think you understand something, you're done. The feeling of clarity is a signal to stop improving your model and start using it to explain and intervene in the world. So if we can infuse a belief system with an overwhelming feeling of clarity, we might be able to get people to accept it without further scrutiny.

And if you're designing a belief system to get people to just accept it, then you've got a pretty free hand. If you don't care about the truth, you are free to oversimplify your belief system, to optimize it for the *feeling* of clarity. Accurate belief systems have to be loyal to the complexity of the world. But cheap belief systems can ignore complexity and just amp up that delicious feeling of understanding. (I actually stole this analysis from my mother, who used to say, "Of course fast food is more delicious than what I cook for you. It's because fast-food restaurants only care about being delicious. They don't have to balance that with being nutritious." I'm worried about cognitive junk food.)

So if all you cared about was a catchy belief system, you could build a *fake model*—an oversimplified, extremely coherent picture of everything. So when people started using your fake model, they'd see that everything is connected; they'd feel empowered to explain anything and everything with their fake model. And they could communicate their model easily. This is why conspiracy theories are so appealing. A conspiracy theory offers a powerful but simple model of the world. Like games, conspiracy theories present us with a more manageable, intellectually tractable version of the world.

Conspiracy theories are much more satisfying than actual science, because science has a complexity problem. You can't actually cram all of science into one human head. At best, you'll have partial understanding of a few little patches. There will always be unknowns, in which you have to trust other people. An honest understanding of the real world won't give you that all-encompassing knowledge-orgasm you crave, because the world is too awkwardly large.

I don't think most seductive clarities are the intentional result of malicious design (though some are). Often it's accidental. We make simplifications for all sorts of other reasons: to reduce the cognitive load, to make coordination easy, to manage data across scale. But if those simplifications can give us the feeling of clarity, then they can also accidentally seduce us. Most metrics weren't designed by some evil manipulator. They were designed for familiar and sensible reasons: transparency, objectivity, and all that. But because metrics aim at accessibility and easy comprehensibility—because they offer predigested summaries—they create an exaggerated feeling of value coherence. Metrics offer a seductively clear picture of what's important.

Compare two people; let's call them Artist Andy and Metrics Mike. Andy is a rapper. She started out as a kind of conventional rapper of her era—trap beats, deadpan tight flow, ironic lyrics. But lately she's had other impulses. She's been drawn to simpler lyrics—droning repetitions of simple word patterns. She can't explain why, but it's expressing something in her—her feelings of being stuck at a particular point in life. She's also bored of trap beats; she's been experimenting with chopping up bits of tape of her grandparents speaking, fuzzing them out and looping them. There's something beautiful in the pattern of their accents.

She doesn't have a pat justification for any of this. It's just what she finds compelling. She's definitely being guided by something— some subtle glimmerings of beauty, some new form of expressiveness. But if you ask her why her new songs sound the way they do, she'll stumble around for words. She is sincere, but her justifications are fuzzy and scattered.

Mike, on the other hand, has a clear target. He runs a politics website. He's targeting higher page views. He has good motives; he believes in the mission of his publication. But his actions are all oriented toward that simple metric. He knows which topics get more views; there's good data from the analytics. He knows what kind of language people respond to: clear and unequivocal statements of outrage.

Andy's grasp of why she's doing what she's doing looks less clear. The parts don't fit together so neatly. Mike's explanations look exceptionally clear. He has a single, simplified target, and all his actions flow from it—so he can give sweeping, coherent justifications for all his actions.

To an outsider, it looks like Mike has more clarity about his values. He sounds more articulate. He probably feels more decisive about his actions, internally. His actions are wholly understandable, integrated, and communicable. Andy has none of this.

The problem is that Mike gained this sense of clarity by narrowing his values. He's gamed the process of justifying himself. He's strategically selected values for which it's easier to generate precise data and coherent explanations. This is fake clarity, achieved by avoiding the full richness of what's really important.

What Andy has over Mike is a loyalty to the thick, tangled complexity of what's truly meaningful. But that's hard, because what's really valuable is often subtle and hard to express—especially when we're on the track of something new. If we are sincere and respectful of the value density of the world, we will rarely be able to generate quick, coherent, accessible explanations. The engineered coherence of metrics will win in a clarity fight every time.

GOOD SCIENCE DOESN'T FALL INTO THIS TRAP, BECAUSE GOOD science is *responsive to errors*. Science builds models and then tests those models against the world, alert to any signs that they are incomplete. This is what drives science to move beyond the simple and satisfying models that can fit easily in one's head and toward that brutal, brain-breaking complexity. Those simple models couldn't fit all the evidence, so we had to replace them with something much more complicated. As the philosopher of science William Wimsatt puts it, the scientific method is built to be constantly on the lookout for any signals of error and then relentlessly use those errors to improve its models. Science, says Wimsatt, is built around a system of *error metabolism*.

Seductive clarity works by avoiding error metabolism. One clever way to design for seductive clarity, then, is to build a belief system that conceals signs of its own mistakes.

So here is a recipe for a seductive clarity trap:

First, build a belief system that offers a satisfyingly clear, coherent explanation of the world.

Second, make sure the belief system conceals any evidence of its own error.

In conspiracy theories, the error-concealment device is usually an add-on—a separate set of beliefs about those lying, cheating scientists and journalists. Conspiracy theories build echo chambers by getting their believers to dismiss any nonbelievers as untrustworthy. A good echo chamber will block their followers from receiving any evidence of error.

Hyper-simplified value systems are even better; they are almost perfect clarity traps. First, they offer a feeling of beautiful coherence. But second, and more important, hyper-simplified value systems have a built-in error-concealment mechanism—because values control where you look in the first place.

IF YOUR VALUES ARE TOO SIMPLISTIC, HOW WOULD YOU DIS-cover your error? You'd have to spend enough time looking at some other part of the world to discover some subtle value that you've been missing. But your value system *tells you what's important* in the first place. It tells you where to look—what to pay attention to, investigate, and spend time with. So an oversimplified value system can get you to avoid looking for subtle values—by labeling those soul-opening activities as inefficient wastes of time.

Artificially clarified values set up a nasty feedback loop. Once you've redefined success in such clear terms, it's easy to forget about what's been left out, because it no longer seems important. Maybe you start to think all that's important in life is money. Of course, there are all kinds of things that could show you there's more to life than money. You might find richer, fuller views of a meaningful life in art, literature, philosophy, or friendships. Exploring a hobby like knitting could show you how much joy there could be in intricate, meditative movement for its own sake. But here's the problem: If you've already decided that all that's important in life is money, you'll be very unlikely to spend any time on such useless distractions, because they won't look like good paths to money.

Values control what we seek out. And then the other stuff, we dismiss. Dismissing things isn't necessarily bad; it's part of basic human functioning. The world is overstuffed with things, and we need to ration our attention. We are constantly doing attentional triage; our values guide that triage. But the problem is that what's really valuable in the world is often subtle. So we if we triage too hard, we might end up throwing out all the subtle values, without giving them enough of a chance.

Let's call this *value collapse*. This is a feedback loop whereby oversimplifying your values changes how you approach the world, what you notice about it, and what you spend time exploring. So you run into a narrower set of experiences—which in turn reinforces your oversimplified values. Value collapse is the worst possible end result of value capture. The image I have in my head is of a star collapsing from its own gravity and forming a black hole. Once you've gone this far, there's no escape.

DOESN'T THIS HAPPEN WITH ALL VALUES? NOT EXACTLY. WHAT makes metrics particularly good at seductively trapping us is the *precision and clarity of their edges*. Values with precise edges make dismissal easier.

Take regular, fuzzy values—the old-school kind, with no mechanical scoring procedure. Here are some of my fuzzy values: fun, friendship, connection, and cool ideas. For each of these values, there are some things that are obviously in, and some things that are obviously out. A party in the desert with my climbing buddies is definitely fun, and doing my taxes is definitely not. But in between what is obviously important and what is obviously unimportant is a huge gray area—what we could call the exploratory zone of value. We're not sure whether that stuff is valuable, so we might investigate them to find out more.

When I was dating, I valued fun times and intellectual excitement. And I had a pretty clear idea of what was at the center of my dating values: I wanted somebody witty and curious and intellectually playful. I liked verbal sparring partners, people who I could skip ideas off—and who I could get drunk with and then have cheerful, wild arguments about anything and everything. And I knew that there were some sorts of people—serious, career-oriented, and wholly responsible people who were mostly interested in financial security—who I shouldn't spend any time dating.

But I also ended up dating all kinds of people in the fuzzy middle. I dated a quiet artist who looked carefully at the world. Her idea of fun wasn't getting drunk and arguing with strangers at bars; it was going on late-night runs on the beach. This didn't exactly fit my idea of fun, but it didn't obviously not fit, either. It was a bewildering novelty. So I tried it out.

She particularly liked running on the beach on moonless nights, by starlight. This was at first, for me, an exercise in terror and confusion. But I slowly started figuring out the strange delight in it—the weird disorientation that comes from running in near-total darkness, the heightened sensation of sand in between your toes and the sound of the surf. I tripped and flopped on my face a ton of times. But it turns out that eating shit in the sand at night is actually kind of awesome. It turns out that nighttime beach running is ludicrous and thrilling and sensitizing all at the same time.

But when we precisely define the edges of what we value—when we give our values mechanical edges—we eliminate that exploratory zone. Things are either in or they're out, immediately. Mechanical values have been reengineered with obvious edges, which we can apply instantly, without judgment or deliberation. If you value only what's low-calorie, what gets more clicks and follows, or what gets more money, you can throw out most of the world without a second thought. Mechanical values make it easier to dismiss much of the world.

And it's easy to get stuff done when you've learned how to dismiss the majority of the world in an instant. We can eliminate wasted time exploring worthless garbage. We are now much more ruthlessly efficient and successful—or at least we will *look* successful to anybody who shares our narrowed notion of success.

Some people will tell you to always use maximally precise language in every context. This is a mistake. Precise value language would be entirely appropriate if we already knew all there was to know about what was important. But if we don't, then using clear, mechanical values discourages exploration. Precise values embody a closed-minded spirit about what's important in the world.

Sometimes vague language is better because it expresses the truth that things are unclear or unsettled. This is why poets will often use metaphors and contradictory language; it is a meaningful inarticulateness. Vague language is the appropriate vessel for speaking from a position of uncertainty.

If you value what's fun, what's interesting, what's curious, what's creative—those concepts have imprecise edges. Applying these terms always involves dealing with fuzz and unclarity. But you *should* feel uncertain when you're in unknown territory. Fuzzy values are appropriate when you don't yet know everything about what's important. They encourage exploration, because they don't have sharp edges. Fuzzy values build in an open-minded attitude.

CHAPTER 25

The Triumph of
Universal Language

Our social systems seem to reward those who are most willing to think and speak in terms of mechanically clear values and punish those who care about anything else.

Paul Smaldino and Richard McElreath have studied how science evolves in response to social selection pressures. In their paper, "The Natural Selection of Bad Science," they use computer models to show how incentives shape scientists and scientific culture. Here's one of their models: First, assume there is some gap between methodologies that lead to good science and methodologies that get you more publications. Second, assume that better and more prestigious jobs tend to go to people with more publications. And third, assume that young scientists-in-training tend to imitate those scientists with higher-status jobs.

The central assumption of their model—the gap between good science and publication success—captures a painful open secret of modern scientific research. Scientists who pick the least rigorous methodology will tend to publish more papers. Those scientists who go above and beyond—who use a more painstaking, rigorous methodology—get more accurate results, but that level of rigor forces them to work more slowly, and publish fewer papers.

Smaldino and McElreath's models show that given these assumptions, scientific institutions will rapidly devolve. In science, publication is the socially legible signal of success. This incentive system encourages scientists to maximize their publication rates by selecting the minimally rigorous method that will pass peer review. Prestige and power will tend to go to those scientists who are best at gaming the system.

Maybe, you think, we could fix this by ignoring the simplified public signal and giving the social rewards directly to those who do good science. But that's the whole problem: There's no magic radar that picks up on the "best science." Big institutions need to use public signals; they need to use metrics. And what we've learned is that *public signals inevitably come apart from real quality* (the Horseman of Scale, raising his head again).

This suggests a general principle: Organized social systems will tend to give power to those who game the system, rather than those who pursue what's really valuable.

What does it mean to "game" a system? It means you exploit the gap between the signals a system uses to confer rewards and the genuine goods the system was built to promote. I think we call it "gaming" because we can see two different versions of the same activity laid on top of each other. There's this natural version of the thing, in all its messy value fuzziness. And then there's the explicit, mechanized version, expressed in clear rules and a scoring system—the gamified version of the activity. To game the system is to ignore the natural version and go all in on the gamified version.

This suggests a general theory of the long-term effects of endemic systems gaming—a theory of *society-wide value collapse*. This happens when:

1. a system is built to pursue some rich value.

2. the system offers some clear, stable signals for value.

3. there is some gap between those signals and what's actually valuable.

4. some actors optimize for the social signals of value rather than what's actually valuable.

5. those actors are rewarded by the relevant social systems—with status, resources, and power.

The result is that over time, the ones who gain power in the system will be those who are willing to ignore what's actually valuable and focus on the social signals of value.

Not all social systems will collapse in this way. This is just a simple model, built to try to identify the conditions that might lead to social value collapse. But it will be hard to avoid, because the gap between real value and the social signals of value is baked into the institutional way of doing business. This gap arises from the need to decontextualize information, especially about what's valuable, to enable fast information exchange at scale. It is the Four Horsemen at work.

The power of universal communication tools will tend to swamp delicate, intimate, local speech. This is why people who game the metrics tend to win power: because metrics are the engineered universal language of value, which trades away context and sensitivity in exchange for easy comprehensibility. So those who are willing to use the decontextualized universal language will tend to win more power, which they can use to further the reach of the decontextualized universal language.

This is the feedback loop of language and social power.

LANGUAGE, AND OUR CAPACITY TO COMMUNICATE, ARE NOT themselves neutral. They can be tuned to a purpose — and are so tuned by whoever has the power to control language. The power to communicate itself can be unequally distributed. And that power can compound on itself, in a runaway feedback loop. Remember Hobbes: The ultimate power of the tyrant is the power to define the meanings of words, like *good* and *success*.

The power to communicate is a social resource. It can be distributed unequally and unjustly. The philosopher Miranda Fricker puts it this way: When we imagine social injustice, we usually think of the unfair distribution of concrete resources, like wealth or education or jobs. But there is another, subtler kind of injustice that arises from the asymmetrical distribution of the *ability to participate in the conversation*, the ability to contribute to shared knowledge. She calls this *epistemic injustice*.

There are two kinds of epistemic injustice. The first is *testimonial injustice*. This happens when certain groups of people are automatically trusted in excess of their competence, and certain other groups of people are automatically distrusted beneath their competence. Note that we are not talking about any systematic trust or distrust. We should, in fact, be granting more trust to people who are actually competent and reliable; we should trust good-hearted doctors who know the medicine. And we should be distrusting people who are incompetent or malicious. The problem is we often end up trusting people based on irrelevant signals. You are probably all too familiar with the empirical research here: People systematically tend to trust, for no good reason, people from certain genders, races, and classes over others.

But there is another form of testimonial injustice: We systematically over-trust quantitative claims and under-trust qualitative claims. This is by design. Metrics are *manufactured for public comprehensibility*. They are engineered to be understood more easily. But this very process usually makes them less accurate. They are made comprehensible by systematically cutting off their more nuanced aspects. Ironically, the very process that gives metrics their social power is also exactly the process by which they become insensitive. Metrics foster systematic testimonial injustice against anybody who doesn't speak in the language of metrics. They siphon credibility away from anybody still dedicated to subtle values.

There is a second and subtler form of epistemic injustice: what Fricker calls *hermeneutical injustice*. Hermeneutical injustice arises from the unfair distribution of the *resources of comprehensibility*. It's what happens when our language—and our shared store of stories and images and metaphors—has been tuned to make it easier for some people to express their experiences, and harder for others.

We don't always have the right concepts to describe our experience of the world. We have to invent them. Consider, says Fricker, the term *sexual harassment*. Before the 1960s, there was no term that captured the experience, so common to women, of feeling pressured by people in power to submit to sexual advances. Back then, the closest available term was *flirting*, which means something very different. *Flirting* associates unwanted sexual advances with lightness, humor, and mild joyful rule-breaking. It casts the actions in pleasant, acceptable lighting. It suggests that these behaviors are acceptable and ordinary, and that the right response to them is amused acceptance. There was no term that zeroed in on the unfairness, the awful power dynamics, the inescapable pressure.

The term *sexual harassment* had to be invented. It came out of groups of women talking to each other, trying to express this strange, disturbing experience for which they had no adequate words. Women reported that before they had the term, they often felt isolated—they felt crazy to be so upset by a little "flirting." Their emotions felt unwarranted and silly. But when groups of women finally coined the term *sexual harassment* and started using it, many reported that they suddenly felt sane. They no longer felt like their emotional reactions—fear, nausea, intense anxiety—were abnormal or irrational. Their experience became more comprehensible to themselves, and more expressible to others. It became a shared experience—a real experience. And women who had been harassed could now make themselves and their emotional state more easily understood—their anger, their discomfort, their need to leave whole career paths behind.

And the reason why for so long we had *flirting* but not *sexual harassment* should be obvious: For a long time, men had more social power, and *made language that suited their purposes.* Inequities in the social landscape get written into our resources for communication, which feedback to support that social inequity.

Resistance to this, when it happens, will start in the odd corners—in unofficial speech, in slang, rap, poetry, in the newly invented language of small, sidelined communities. Or, as poet-activist Audre Lorde puts it, in "Poetry Is Not a Luxury":

> For women, then, poetry is not a luxury. It is a vital necessity of our existence. It forms the quality of the light within which we predicate our hopes and dreams toward survival and change, first made into language, then into idea, then into more tangible action. Poetry is the way we help give name to the nameless so it can be thought.

Language isn't just this natural thing that fell from the sky, finished and perfect. We are constantly modifying it—adding to it and reshaping it to suit our purposes. We come up with new language, new metaphors, and new stories to describe our experiences—to make our lives make sense to us and to others.

A close friend of mine is autistic. She says that earlier in her life, it was much harder for her to explain why she had trouble eating enough food—a common problem, she says, among autistic people. But the term *anorexia* was part of the standard cultural language, and so it often got applied to her—but it felt wrong. She felt swept up into an alien network of associations and diagnoses: that her problems were of body image, of media intrusion, of body dysmorphia. That accurately described other people's very real problems, but it didn't describe hers. And the ready availability of that language tended to make other people try to help her in the wrong way.

Things got much better, she said, when improved language for the autistic experience made its way into common currency. When people started becoming familiar with the concept of *sensory issues* associated with autism, it became easier for her to describe her experience— to be understood and to get the appropriate kind of help. And it helped her understand her own experience—to recognize in the moment what was going on with her. It helped her zero in on the real problem of being overwhelmed by textures, especially when she was subject to other kinds of sensory overstimulation. When she had trouble eating, what she needed wasn't counseling about accepting her body. She needed access to lower-stimulus environments, and more texturally simple foods. And that was very hard to understand about herself—and communicate—without the right language.

Steven Kapp and Ari Ne'eman tell a similar story about medical language that surrounds autism. They are part of the Autistic Self Advocacy Network—the leading advocacy group for and run by autistic people. Kapp and Ne'eman documented their attempts to intervene in the definition of "autism" as it was being developed for the *Diagnostic and Statistical Manual of Mental Disorders* (*DSM-V*). The *DSM-V* shapes who gets classified as autistic, helps determine who gets insurance, and guides the focus of medical treatment. But, they said, no autistic person had ever been part of the committee that set the definition. The interests of autistic people weren't adequately represented in the authoritative medical language that ruled their lives.

Kapp and Ne'eman were particularly concerned with the fact that the proposed entry for autism included diagnostic criteria about the presence of "fixated interests" and "repetitive motor movements." Those are medicalizing terms, which present these behaviors as problems to be fixed through medical intervention. Most autistic people vastly prefer the terms *special interests* and *stimming*, which legitimize those behaviors. For many autistic people, say Kapp and Ne'eman, special interests are a source of meaning and richness in life, and stimming is a source of daily satisfaction and pleasure. (As my autistic friend puts it: "My intense hobbies are the best part of my life. Why the hell should I try to get rid of them?") According to Kapp and Ne'eman, the proposed definition of autism, and the language it used, represented the interests of non-autistic people—in forcing autistic people to conform to standard norms of social behavior and behave in a way that makes non-autistic people feel more comfortable. That language did not represent the experiences of autistic people, or their interests in their own happiness and well-being.

Language is a kind of technology. It is the product of social action, and it supports some interests over others. The concepts we have can enable one pattern of thinking and association and suppress others. So the unequal distribution of social power elsewhere in the world becomes reflected in our language. Those in power have more ability to invent language to suit their purposes, and spread that language. Those with less power, even when they manage to invent the language to describe their experiences, will have less ability to spread it into the common lexicon. That's hermeneutical injustice: a subtle, but deep and pervasive, kind of social injustice, in which the *social resources of comprehensibility are unevenly distributed.*

Metrics create hermeneutical injustice.

The world is full of semiprivate, intimate languages. There is the special way we speak to our friends, the in-jokes and the references to shared moments. There are the special languages and expressions in our weird little communities—in the punk scene we grew up in, in the world of tabletop role-playing, in the world of rock climbing, in our geeky online gardening group. There are particular languages that develop in addiction support groups, in trauma survivor groups.

But a lot of these terms don't have widespread social uptake, because their comprehensibility is limited to those small worlds. To understand each of these terms, you need to spend a lot of time in that community. But metrics are the ultimate easy-to-understand, cross-contextual, easily digested language. So there is a greater social power available to those who are willing to speak in terms of metrics and to organize their lives to succeed in those terms, because what they do, and why they do it, will be understood widely and instantly.

Metrics aren't just any old language. They're a language of *justification.* They tell us not just neutral data but whether something has *succeeded* or *failed.* When we point out that a particular attendance policy leads to greater student graduation rates, or that one non-profit successfully delivered more mosquito nets per donated dollar than another, we are doing more than merely reporting some stale facts. We are making value judgments. We are saying who did the right thing and who failed and needs to change. Convincing people requires, in part, that they understand your reasons and consider them significant. Metrics are an *engineered language of fast universal justifications*. They help us coordinate our actions because they coordinate what we recognize as success.

So there is a greater social power available to those who are willing to speak strictly in terms of metrics, to confine their justifications and claims to those terms that have been manufactured to be comprehensible across all contexts. They will be more broadly understood. And this creates a form of hermeneutical injustice—because once metrics have gotten general uptake, all those other more private, strange, and intimate forms of understanding are now second-class citizens in the world of justification. Speaking in the meaningful, rich, and nuanced language of a particular community puts you in a weaker position. You are harder to understand; it is harder to rally people to your side.

Just like money, the social resource of *comprehensibility* can build on itself, accumulate, and grow. Language is also subject to the brutal logic of compound interest.

Imagine there are two people. Let's call them the Compromiser and the Captured. The Compromiser has their own subtle values but knows they have to speak in this ultra-public simplified language of metrics to get anything done. They are using metrics in public to be understood, but they keep their real values separate.

The Captured has no such firewall. They have eliminated any private reasoning and think to themselves only in the ultra-public language of justifications. They only care about success in those public terms. They are fully value-captured; it's metrics all the way down.

The Captured will probably be more efficient at succeeding in terms of the metrics. After all, there is no drag in the system, nothing that distracts them from all-out optimization. It is easy to hit one clear target when it's all you are about. It's much harder to hit a target when you're also trying to balance it against a whole host of other cares.

If that assumption is true—that the Captured will tend to succeed over the Compromiser in terms of the metrics—then we will get the following horrifying result: There will be systematically greater social power available to those who are willing to forget about everything that isn't measured in metrics and will instead optimize themselves entirely to fit what the metrics ask for. They won't be wasting energy on distractions like beauty or community, the joys of pure, playful process—or anything else. They will have transformed their deepest values to fit the most public idea of success.

If this is right, then we will have a truly perilous feedback loop: a long-term, all-encompassing social value collapse. The people who were willing to target success entirely in those simplified, metrified terms will start to outcompete those who were not. They will start to accumulate more social power and more resources. And they will be able to amplify their social power by spending those resources to gain further control of the language—and tying even more social power to success in those narrowed terms.

CHAPTER 26

Play for Its Own Sake

P rocess beauty is everywhere. But a lot of the time, we ignore it. It seems less important, less meaningful than object beauty. All the high arts, the really respectable ones, seem to be the ones where a singular genius broadcasts their art out to us lowly masses, and we just soak it up in relative passivity. And what gets mocked as low geek culture—tabletop role-playing, fan fiction, cosplay—are exactly those communities where everybody gets to be creative, and actively participate in the process of making art.

But why is object art so much better? Why is it better for beauty to be in external, separate objects than to reside in us? Why is it better to concentrate the power to make art in a few geniuses? Why do we seem to look down on those lifestyles that disperse the right to creativity across an entire community?

Maybe it's because we've mostly forgotten that processes can be valuable in and of themselves. We have gotten used to attributing value only to the stuff we make, the countable outcomes we achieve—and not the actions we take to create them. We have come to value perfect finished art and mostly given up the opportunity to be soaked in the creative process ourselves. This outcomes obsession may start on the factory line—where we need to make sure that each station outputs enough stuff for the next step. But it has infected outward to everything else. We have started caring about fitness only when it yields a countable improvement in our capacity. We have started caring about art only when it makes a saleable object that we can transfer.

It hasn't always been that way. For Aristotle, the ultimate value in human life lay not in the products of our activity but in the activity itself. Meaning and value in life came in the doing and the making, and not in the stuff that we made. For Aristotle, the final seat of value is in *autotelic activity*. This means activity that's valuable for its own sake. To put it in our lingo: The meaning of life is not in the outcome but the process. (There's a familiar slogan, "The journey is the destination," which seems to be one of the last surviving remnants of this Aristotelean way of thinking.)

Bernard Suits, our philosopher of games, put it this way: Imagine utopia. In this imaginary utopia, all of our practical problems will have been solved—all our medical problems, all our resource scarcity problems, all our psychological problems. So what will we have to do with our time? We will play games, he says, or we will be bored out of our minds. And if games are what we do in utopia, then they must be the meaning of life.

This argument might sound ridiculous at first. But Suits is just putting his own modern spin on an old Aristotelean argument. (Suits himself was an Aristotle scholar and a self-declared Aristotle fanboy.) One way to put the Aristotelean argument, rephrased for modern ears, goes something like this: What is the meaning of your life? OK, you have a nice job, but what's that for? It gives you money. Well, what's that money for? To buy nice cars and have nice watches.

But what's that for? To impress people, to get a better job and even more money. But what is all that for? Et cetera, et cetera, on and on. What ultimately justifies all the hard work we put into making and getting all that stuff?

The stuff we make is certainly useful. It helps us to stay alive — feeds us, eases our pain, shelters us. And it helps us do even more work more efficiently. But still, what's the point of staying alive and working efficiently, if all you're doing is just making more useless stuff? Where does the meaning get into the system?

Aristotle's answer is that at the end of the day, some activity must be valuable for its own sake. Autotelic activity is what injects meaning into the system. And games, for Suits, make autotelic activity vivid. Because why would you take unnecessary constraints that make the outcomes harder to get to? The answer must be that what you value is the process — a particular kind of interesting action — and not just the outcome. The value of games was, for Suits, a microcosm of the meaning of life.

Not every game is autotelic. Sometimes, Suits said, we simply use games as tools to get something else. The Olympic athlete who only cares about the glory, the boxer who just needs to win a big prize match to support their family — these people are involved with games, but what they are doing is *work*. They're using games as a tool to get some other outcome. But there is another way to interact with games, for the sake of the process itself. This, says Suits, is *play*.

Suits had a particular definition of play. To play, he said, is to take some resource that is normally instrumentally useful and divert it to autotelic activity. For instance, you're playing when you take your ability to do math, which would be useful for accounting and engineering, and use it to have fun solving sudoku puzzles. You're playing when you take your ability to fight, which is useful in war and self-defense, and then start entering Brazilian jiujitsu tournaments for the pure thrill of it. To play, according to Suits, is to take a resource that is normally useful for practical work and just do it for its own sake.

You might be tempted to say that play is wasting useful resources just for fun. Except for Suits, it isn't really a waste. Play only seems like a waste of time if you're stuck in the outcomes mindset, in which doing something is worthwhile only if it yields some valuable product. For Suits, the real waste would be spending your whole life accumulating potentially useful resources and never actually using them to do anything meaningful. You work so that you have the time to play.

But we forget this. We forget about the value of the process and get stuck on the value of the outcomes, because outcomes are easy to track. That's what an outcome is: some countable physical product or measurable increase in our powers, whose worth can be described in publicly accessible terms. But if Aristotle is right, then what's really valuable is something far subtler: rich, interesting, complicated, dense action. And the inner value of action is often extremely hard to capture in publicly accessible terms.

OK, oversimplification time. Let's divide the world into processes and outcomes. Processes are the activity of doing something, and outcomes are what we get out of it at the end. Suppose Aristotle and Suits are right, and what makes our lives good and fulfilling is rich, meaningful activity. The meaning of life is in the process and not the outcome. Meaning lies in doing: in thinking interesting thoughts, having interesting conversations, playing fascinating games. Meaning lies in the process of making things, in moving your body in thrilling and elegant ways, in loving people.

Of course, we also need outcomes. Outcomes are very useful. Some of our activities end up making stuff: shelter, transportation, nutrition, and medicine, all of which we need to survive. But the true value of those things is in the wonderful activities they help us get to, the lovely processes they support. Outcomes are valuable only as means to our true ends: having lovely conversations, thinking interesting thoughts, moving in thrilling, beautiful ways. Outcomes are good only if they eventually cash out in meaningful action. Otherwise, they are empty—just tools bereft of purpose.

This will be especially true if what makes something really meaningful is deeply personal—and if what's meaningful to you is deeply dependent on the particular weirdness of your personality, culture, and circumstances in life. But the physical stuff we make and the measurable increases in our capacities are easy to track. It's hard to measure the joy and wonder of a good trail run, but it's easy to measure your increased lung capacity, improved running speed, and reduced body weight.

The more the world converges on the metric and eliminates any stuff that doesn't hit the metric, the easier it will be for us to collectively forget that there was any other point to doing anything, except to hit that metric.

What we need are reminders from outside the convergence.

One of the major criticisms of large-scale modern agriculture is that monocultures are very fragile. If the majority of our farms are growing one variety of corn using one farming method, then we become incredibly vulnerable. One deadly corn virus or beetle infestation and we lose our food supply. This is part of the reason why biodiversity is important. We need old-growth forests, untamed jungles, and fetid swamps because they are preserves for life outside the farming monoculture.

Our world is dominated by a value monoculture. And not just any value monoculture, but one dominated by measurable outcomes. So to save ourselves, we need some kind of wild preserve—some haven for meaning diversity. We need places in life where a sense of meaningfulness and value runs wild.

And we can't just see it from afar. What's valuable is often subtle. We need to be soaked in it for a long while, to catch on. To be reminded of what's important outside the monoculture, we would need regular exposure. And if we have forgotten how to think of value and importance beyond measurable outcomes—if we have forgotten the value of processes and action—then we will need frequent, lasting, intense encounters with these wild values.

But we can't be trusted to stumble into them randomly or build them on our own. Valuable activities are often very specific and hard to find on your own. We need recipes and instructions. We need structured tools to ease our passage out of the world of standardized outcomes and into the world of beautiful processes. And we need lots of them, wildly different ones, to explore. We need a diversity of pre-packaged value starter kits, to help us find our way back into varied, beautiful action. But we should also expect those value starter kits to look stupid, inane, and useless from the perspective of the outcomes mindset—precisely because they drag us away from a lifestyle laser-focused on efficient outcomes.

And for those of us who have been raised and nurtured in the metrified world of outcomes and measures, who are used to orienting ourselves toward a clear external measure of success, it would be useful if those starter kits resembled the metrified world of outcomes. It would be useful if they had, at their heart, something familiar—some kind of clear ranking or scoring system—so that we who were raised in the metrified world could feel comfortable and secure. We need metrics methadone. But we would want those starter kits to eventually draw our gaze past those rankings and toward beautiful processes.

It's goddamn games.

CHAPTER 27

Art Is a Game

Games give us a hint about the shape of what we're after, but they aren't magic. They are a seed—a starting point, from which to grope our way forward in the face of the Four Horsemen.

If metrics conceal the possibility of choice, then the response is *exposure*: to encounter a greater variety of activities and values in the world.

If metrics push us to quickly dismiss new values alternatives, then the response is *openness*: the attitude of paying attention and taking seriously new alternatives.

If metrics push us to settle our minds, then the response is to *explore*: to continually seek out new ideas, new experiences, and new kinds of meaningfulness in the world.

These are the actions and psychological tendencies that help us to resist intrusion by the Four Horsemen. But it's hard. The price of holding on to such attitudes—and the weirder values they push you toward—is rendering yourself incomprehensible to the wider world.

And there are so many forces pulling in the opposite direction. Sheer willpower is rarely enough. We need practices that will help us to resist the large-scale swamping, to keep it small and particular when it's necessary. We need habits of tailoring.

And those habits already exist. They have names like art, play, beauty, games, irony, and comedy. We need established mindsets—package deals that support these resistant tendencies, which help us to get exposure, openness, and exploration. And I think, hovering at the edges of our entire discussion, we have already seen two such packaged mindsets, built to resist the Four Horsemen.

We've already talked about the first one: the *spirit of playfulness*. Playfulness, as philosopher María Lugones put it, is the capacity to step lightly between rule sets, to cross easily between social worlds. Playfulness is a package of attitudes perfect for opposing the Four Horsemen. It is the spirit of exploring the world in an open-minded way, trying on different forms of life.

The world is constantly beating the playfulness out of us, and the sheer spirit isn't enough. We need practices—rituals, structured activities, and communities to support them—that push us toward playfulness. Lugones herself frowned on the more orderly, strict rule sets of formalized games, precisely because they were too close to those other rigid, dogmatic forms of life. She was more interested in the fluidness and unstructuredness of pure, creative, lighthearted play.

But if I'm right, then there is something profoundly useful and deep about formalized games, when approached with the right attitude. They let us *play around with rigidity*—to try on explicit rule sets and mechanical scoring systems and then step back from them. Games might even act as a kind of spiritual vaccine, an inoculation against the harsher institutional scoring systems that they resemble. Vaccines work by introducing your body to a safer imitation of the real thing, so your body will learn to deal with it. Games might do the same for your soul. Games let you practice fluidity with rigid rule systems—slipping into and out of them. And they enable this best when they have no teeth, when there is no real-world punishment for getting bored with and then abandoning a game.

Games are toy governments, but for fun.

BUT IT DOESN'T HAVE TO BE THAT WAY. YOU CAN ALSO USE ME-chanical local goals to steer toward equally mechanical larger purposes. You can play games as part of your devotion to some larger, rigid scoring system. You could run marathons only to lose weight; you could play logic games only to improve your SAT scores. What matters isn't just that we're playing a game, but the quality of light that guides our game-playing.

And the form of game-playing that seems most resistant to value capture and value collapse is aesthetic striving play. In aesthetic striving play, we control our mechanical scoring system in light of some larger, nonmechanical purpose, like my playing around with my goals in fishing to find which one will give me the most meditative trance. Or trying out different role-playing games and house-rule variations until we find the one that sparks the most raucous creative fizz. In aesthetic striving play, the local goal is explicit and mechanical, but the larger purpose is fuzzy and dynamic.

Aesthetic striving play is particularly powerful, because it connects the spirit of playfulness with another resistant mindset: *the spirit of art*. There's an old thought from Kant on the philosophy of art: We approach art with a different attitude and a different frame of mind. Jerome Stolnitz puts it this way: In art, we view the world impractically.

In ordinary life, we approach the world with a practical frame of mind. We want particular things; we approach the world with preconceived goals. When I'm car shopping, I focus on size and safety, fuel efficiency and price. But I barely notice how the car looks—how sporty or cool it is—or how it feels. For me, a car is just a means to get me to other things that I want or need: work, grocery shopping, camping trips. Everything else gets filtered out.

Most of the time we approach the world with a practical attitude. Our preset interests narrow our attention. But when we approach the world aesthetically, says Stolnitz, we open up. We approach without any particular goals or interests. So for a moment, our vision becomes unfiltered. We see things as they fully are, for their own sake. And this makes it far more likely that we will be surprised by the world. This is where we are most likely to notice things that are far outside the normal filtered world of our own practical needs. We let the world take the lead and teach us what's valuable in it—what's beautiful in ways we hadn't known could be beautiful.

We can adopt this aesthetic attitude toward official art, but it's not just confined to the museum. You can take up the aesthetic attitude toward nature, toward cozy neighborhood parks, toward ordinary household tools—toward literally anything. For Stolnitz, the aesthetic attitude was for open seeing; you could take that attitude toward everything, everywhere.

You might have had an experience like this: There's some object you use daily. Maybe it's a coffee thermos. It does its job well; it's a good tool. But one day you're holding it and you notice something else: It's a particularly lovely shade of deep red. And the texture is nice and nubbly; it feels like a tiny fine-grained riverbed. So you sit there and stroke your coffee thermos like a lunatic and just enjoy the feel of it. The thermos is, in its own quiet way, beautiful.

You might have had this weird shift in vision with people, too. It's easy to get into a networking mindset. You go into a room full of people with one thought in your head: What can these people do for me?

You sort them based on how they can serve your interests. Powerful people, people with the right connections or corporate position— they matter. People who can't do anything for you: worthless. Ignore them. This is a kind of narrowed practical attitude.

But we can shift out of it. We can approach people without that filter and be open to what delights each new person might have to offer. Maybe this person has a weird obsession with gathering and replanting wild ferns in their backyard. That's cool; you didn't even know that was a thing. Maybe that person has some incredible stories to tell about completely falling to pieces after a bad breakup and then pulling themselves together when they got obsessed with fixing their city's terrible zoning laws. Maybe this weird-looking guy with food in his beard has spent years working on a very thorough and heartfelt theory about why Nicolas Cage is the greatest artistic genius of our era. You'll find out, if you let them take the lead.

Value collapse is the ultimate version of narrowed vision, which arises from defining your goal with hyper-precision. The aesthetic attitude is the opposite: It opens you up, because it is approaching the world without clear goals in mind. The aesthetic attitude is an antidote to value collapse.

IN THE MODERN WORLD, WE ARE CONSTANTLY DEPLOYING A kind of summary, quickened vision—an abstracted vision that classifies things as quickly as it can, slots them into our larger beliefs about how things like that work, and then stops looking. Call it *category vision*. When we look at the world, we don't look at every detail. Say you're in the grocery store shopping for pasta. You're constantly categorizing and deleting. You categorize some of those things as people and you step around them politely. You categorize some of those things as crackers and bread; those don't matter today, so you move on. This thing I'm holding in my hand is spaghetti, which is all I need to know, so I'll buy it. Categories are a way to quickly sort the world, dismiss most of it, and process the rest.

But there's also a downside: Category vision is efficient because it harnesses the power of categories to let us *skip looking at the details of the world*. And that basic technique works particularly well where the world is flat, regular, and stable. But it will be far less useful where local variances and individual peculiarities are important. And it is definitely not the right mindset if what we want is to be absorbed in the glory of looking and feeling, for ourselves, all the wondrous details of the world.

The philosopher John Dewey put it this way: There is a difference between *recognition* and *perception*. When we recognize something, we put it in a category, and we stop there. If all I need is a pencil, once I see that this thing is a pencil, I stop looking at it and start using it. But perception keeps going; it keeps searching, seeing, finding. It's inefficient, but delightful.

IF WE WERE TRYING TO BE EFFICIENT ABOUT GETTING THE RIGHT beliefs about art, we shouldn't go to the museum by ourselves, or listen to music by ourselves. We shouldn't decide for ourselves. If our goal is just efficiency, then we should treat art like science. There is a faster way to get the right beliefs about art: Find art experts and trust them. But we avoid it. And there is a fast way to get good art: Don't bother trying to learn to make it yourself, just copy some master. But we avoid that, too. A lot of the time, we try to make new art ourselves, even when there is already more great art than we could look at in ten lifetimes. I still sit at home and play guitar with my spouse, and sing for our friends — even though there are a thousand better recordings of better singers and musicians just a button-tap away.

This all might start to sound a little familiar. What is art but doing things the hard way? Instead of taking the most efficient path, we take on artificial constraints. We insist on doing things for ourselves, for the sake of having a particular process of struggling. We avoid shortcuts so we can be plunged into the process of looking, interpreting, and feeling for ourselves. And we've set up the rules to avoid being able to terminate arguments by deferring to some external authority. This would be strange if it were a science. But it's not strange at all in a game, because the point of many games is to get us buried in endless delightful struggles, with the world and with each other.

Art is a game. And like a lot of games, it's been designed to let us exercise those parts of us that have begun to wither in the modern world. It's a reminder of what life is like when it is deeply disorganized and we're free to revel in that disorder. Art is a game that we built to give us relief from the ruthless efficiencies of the Four Horsemen. It is a game whose rules lead to endless tasty disagreements about strange, subtle objects. And it wouldn't make any sense if you thought the point of the game was just to finish the conversation as quickly as possible and get the right answer. But the game does make sense if the point is to be buried in the act of seeing, looking, thinking, and feeling for its own sake—and if we want to be buried in the joy of endless disagreements with our friends about what we are seeing and feeling for ourselves.

This all might help to explain, by the way, the violently different responses people have had to algorithmic and AI art. I'm talking about those generative tools that do the art-making work for you. Why are some people so excited by their convenience and others utterly repulsed? If you thought that the point of art was to generate, as efficiently as possible, enormous piles of pleasant-looking pictures about any topic you chose, then algorithmic art might sound like a good deal. If the point of art is to maximize productivity—to make lots of art quickly and cheaply—then algorithmic art is a good shortcut.

But if you thought that the point of art was the exercise of human creativity, then algorithmic art is a disaster. If the point of art is to be engaged in the *activity* of making it and appreciating it—if the point of art is to be buried in the process, to be doing it yourself, using your own emotions and invention and sensitivity to fine-tune every detail—then algorithmic art is *cheating*. And not cheating in some boring, legalistic sense but cheating in the cosmic sense. By using algorithmic art-generation tools, we are cheating ourselves out of one of the most precious activities we have left. As Bernard Suits puts it, cheaters don't actually understand the point of playing games. They don't understand that the constraints are there to shape a beautiful activity of doing it yourself. Art is a site of human activity and agency. It is a place where we are set free to indulge in the sensuous, powerful act of creation. If the value is in the doing, then using algorithmic tools to make all the art for you misses the whole point. It makes as much sense as using a robot to run a marathon for you, or do your yo-yo tricks for you—or play charades with your friends for you.

THE SPIRIT OF PLAYFULNESS AND THE SPIRIT OF ART ARE DEEPLY aligned. Art, games, and play are all places where we are de-locked from the demands of the world—and freed from the demands of the scientific and bureaucratic ways of dealing with the world. Art, games, play: These are the places where we're free to find meaning where we want it—where we get to *practice* finding meaning where we want it.

It's hard to predict what will feel rich and fulfilling and what will feel empty. I spent years beating myself up over computer games like *Civilization*—resource-maximization games in which you endlessly fine-tune and tweak little systems to be slightly more efficient and wring a tiny bit more money from your virtual world. You might think the problem is that those games are repetitive. But one of my favorite video games ever, *Super Hexagon*, is hyper-repetitive. You play a simple little ship orbiting the center of the screen, and the rest of the world is a maze that is endlessly shrinking toward you. Your only controls are the left and right buttons, which rotate your ship around the center. And then you have to navigate this pulsating, spinning maze. And there's always too much to deal with. The game keeps accelerating; you can't keep track of everything with your conscious mind. So you have to let go — to let your peripheral vision and your peripheral mind monitor the incoming parts of the maze, and then let yourself instinctively respond faster than thought. It's hypnotic, arresting — and endlessly delicious.

Why does *Civilization* make me miserable and *Super Hexagon* make me happy? I don't know. I honestly have no fucking idea.

But I don't owe it to anybody to explain myself. I don't owe it to anybody to make my joy clear. I don't owe it to anybody to coordinate, to make sense, in the zone of play. I can just accept the unexpected surprise attack of meaning when it finds me.

When I bind my yo-yo just right, it'll roll itself up on the string. I can feel it the whole way. I can actually throw a big curve into the string and the yo-yo will roll itself up along that arcing pathway. I can feel the gyroscopic power as it traces the string toward my hand. And the fact that I can control how the yo-yo rolls itself up — that I can *feel* the yo-yo following the string back to my hand — fills me with unutterable joy every time. It is a sensual and direct experience of angular momentum.

And this may not make sense to you. It may not make sense to most people. But that doesn't matter, because it makes sense to me. And when I am not forced to perpetually justify myself to other people in terms they can understand — when I am at play — that's enough.

CHAPTER 28

Infrastructures of Play

A while back, I noticed that I'd had the exact same dish of ratatouille in four completely unrelated places.

Ratatouille is this incredible peasant dish from Provence, France—a summer stew of long-cooked vegetables. It's some mixture of onions, tomatoes, eggplant, and squash, stewed until it becomes this glorious deep blend. In its natural state, ratatouille is incredibly variable. It's a farmhouse dish, originally made to deal with whatever your farm or your garden was spitting out at you in massive abundance. Just by poking around through my sprawling cookbook collection, I've made about ten completely different ratatouilles. I've made recipes that have you long-caramelizing the onions, cooking the eggplant forever, and adding tomato paste to really boost the warm, caramel tastes. This results in an intensely sweet, caramelized vegetable jam. I've made ones where you don't brown anything, but wetly simmer it down until it becomes delicious warm mush. I've made ones where you just barely cook down some tomatoes and zucchini and onions, so they're still separate, with their own bit of crisp textures and distinct juices. Each of these versions of ratatouille has its own style, its own soul, its own reason for being. And the nice thing is once you learn them all, you have also learned a possibility space. You can move around between the extremes. The variety of possible manifestations of the dish creates a space for your own culinary agency.

But then I had the exact same ratatouille in completely disconnected locations. Three times were at different friends' houses, and once at a restaurant. I asked my friends, and it turns out that every single one of them had used the exact same recipe. It was from *The New York Times*, and it was the first recipe that showed up when they googled "ratatouille recipe." And I will admit, it is an extremely good recipe. It reliably produces a very delicious result. But it is also only one out of thousands of different possible versions. It represents one writer's own taste for a particularly rich, jammy, hyper-caramelized version with lots of powerful sweet flavors. Interestingly, I think it was, for the author, the endpoint of a long journey of decision-making and personalized fine-tuning, adjusting that recipe until it met her own personal ideal. But for the rest of us, who meet this recipe as the official statement of the food authority that is *The New York Times*, it's not. It is the record of some faraway person, made static and authoritative.

So here is the first problem: Centralizing technologies like Google Search tend to invisibly decrease the diversity of food. Only a handful of recipes tend to rise to the top. There is a quiet culinary deletion going on right now, as a rich variety of ways of cooking gets displaced by the few recipes that show up high on Google. But once that deletion gets going far enough, it'll be harder to notice. If you've never actually been exposed to the variety of ratatouille recipes, and you've had only one recipe over and over again, you'll think that's all there is, and all there can be. And if you decide to cook that one recipe, you'll be less likely to recognize that there's a decision space. You won't realize you have the room to maneuver, that ratatouille can be good in different ways. You'll think dense and jammy is the only way ratatouille can be good. The possibility of exercising choice is hidden because the world has now been rearranged to decrease your exposure to different possibilities.

This monolithic spirit is more explicitly embodied in a new kind of cookbook: the kind that promises you they've done all the research to find the One Perfect Recipe for everything. It contains the one right way to make muffins, roast chicken, and poached eggs, all as singular recipes that are absolutely guaranteed to work. These cookbooks usually present themselves with an air of scientific rigor. They offer extremely precise measurements and sequences, which give highly replicable results. They've done the research for you. They've tried fifty ways to roast a chicken, and now here is the very best one. But underneath that, of course, is a value decision—an exercise of taste and preferences about how roast chicken should be. But the book speaks in the voice of authority, and urges you to settle on this cookbook and dismiss all the alternatives, because this one is objectively the best.

What's the antidote? I have a book on my shelf that exemplifies the opposite tendency. It is a simple book, called *Julia and Jacques Cooking at Home*. They take you through a lot of basic recipes: how to make a good omelet or sauté some fish. And for every dish, they give you two completely different recipes: Julia Child's and Jacques Pepin's. And next to the recipes are sidebars in which they bicker with each other. They explain why their version of the recipe is the way it is, what decision they made to get which effects—and why the other person's recipe misses the mark. The book is formatted this way because it is the companion piece to an old PBS TV show. It is the record of an argument—a rowdy conversation between friends.

And the effect on me, as I learned to cook from this book, was to undermine the sense that there is a single, correct way to cook. Instead, it revealed every cooking act as a set of decisions through a network of legitimate but different alternatives. You want your scrambled eggs to be fluffier? Use higher heat and faster motion. You want them to be like sweet pudding? Turn the heat down low, add more butter, and stir it for a long, slow time. And once you learn those two endpoints of cooking scrambled eggs, you will know how to improvise in between. The book uses mechanical recipes to communicate — but by pairing different recipes and introducing dissent, it frames them differently. It undermines the monolithic authority of the classic cookbook, offering a landscape of variation, of different choices you can make, guided by different tastes. It is an unsettled cookbook. The paired recipes appear not as the Right and Official way to do things, but as points on a wide spectrum. The book uses mechanical recipes to create space for your culinary agency.

THE FORCES OF RULES, SCALE, PARTS, AND CONTROL ARE BAKED into the infrastructure of the world. They are built into how institutions hand out incentives and promotions; how we are measured and evaluated in school and work and fitness; how corporations, governments, and media outlets think and communicate and organize. That's a lot to fight with just spunk and fortitude. The problem is that our technologies and our infrastructure hang around and constantly press on us, conditioning and shaping how we interact and think. So we need to build supports for art and play into the structure of the world — into our technologies, institutions, and communities. Fight fire with fire, and fight infrastructure with infrastructure.

We need infrastructures of art and infrastructures of play.

So how do you structure the world to create the space for play, and to encourage it? What kind of technologies would you use?

The danger here is that if we aren't careful, we'll try to send a message of play via a technology that undermines play. Remember Langdon Winner and his analysis of the printing press. Maybe the inventors of the printing press wanted to spread democratic control and empower the people; maybe its users wanted to advance anarchy and decentralization. But none of that matters as much as the basic material nature of the printing press itself: It is a big, expensive piece of machinery. Its basic material nature pushes the world toward centralized authority and control, no matter what you try to use it to say.

I've seen a particularly ironic mirror of this in some of my fellow philosophy professors. I have known other professors who will teach classes about the problems of power, domination, and centralization. They will rail against authoritarianism. They will rage gloriously about how institutions rob people of their freedom to choose. At the very same time, in the very same classes, these professors will implement rigid and punishing grading scales, with tests written to enforce one very specific mode of thinking. When it comes to the systems they build, it turns out that they are entirely willing to use grading as an incentive to push around students' attention and cares. And I suspect the authoritarian structure of their classes might end up undermining the antiauthoritarian message of their lectures.

So we have to be very suspicious of how, exactly, we implement our message of play.

THE TOOLS OF THE FOUR HORSEMEN DO NOT LEAD INEVITABLY to doom. You can find, in certain places, people carefully using some of those tools but not being dominated by them.

While I was writing this book, my five-year-old was hospitalized when a particular nasty cold virus went into his lungs. He couldn't breathe right and starting flopping over; we rushed him to the hospital. It turned out he'd inherited my asthma. He, too, will spend a lifetime dependent on modern medicine for survival.

At the hospital, once they figured out that it was asthma-related, they started him on something called an "albuterol protocol." Albuterol is the asthma rescue drug that I've spent my life using. They gave him a truly massive dose and repeated it every four hours, gradually tapering it. The tapering was controlled by an objective scale with fairly mechanical checkpoints, like how much he was gasping, how wheezy he sounded, his blood-oxygen level, and how much his belly was protruding with each breath. There was a scoring system that added up the checkpoints and told the doctors and nurses when to reduce his dose.

We had a great medical team, and they seemed to know exactly the powers and limits of the albuterol protocol. They didn't treat it as sacred text. Many of them told me they had to mostly abide by the "objective" point system, but they put air quotes around *objective*. They would say things like "He looks better than the point system says right now," or "He's on the edge of the next step in the point system, but he still looks pretty bad to me, so I'm not going to taper yet."

But they also mostly stuck to the protocol, and I could see why. Over three days and nights at the hospital, mostly during the weekend shift, we went through about seven different nurses and three managing doctors. And if they'd each used their own individual gut, my kid would have gotten pretty inconsistent care. The albuterol protocol enables a consistent plan of action across a changing staff, who often couldn't talk with each other at length. That's exactly what mechanical rules and edges are for: consistency between ever-changing people. Mechanical rules cobble together a unified plan of action out of an ever-shifting mass of humanity. And that's very important sometimes. But it was also important that every nurse and doctor knew that the protocol was only a coordinating device. They didn't blindly follow it. They knew it didn't pick up everything, but they also knew if they strayed too far from it, their decisions would start to conflict with each other's. So they used it as a moderately strict anchor, which they would depart from when things just didn't feel right.

Part of why it worked, though, is that the team was pretty small. This was coordination across ten people, not ten thousand. When they departed from the protocol, they could add a note to my son's chart, or explain to each other what was happening at the shift change. And I could tell that the team trusted each other and trusted each other's decisions to depart from the protocol. Without those tight relationships, I doubt this could scale up. But still, it's one example of how we might use but not be ruled by the Four Horsemen.

Standardization doesn't always kill creativity. I've gotten deep enough into yo-yos that I've started modding mine—changing the bearings and axles and other little pieces out. It works because many of the parts are standardized. I can swap out different axles and rubber friction rings and weight rings to make it play and feel different, because most of the key parts have been standardized to certain measurements, and there are a bunch of little one-man companies and DIY modders who have made alternate parts that I can swap around. With yo-yo modding, the *parts* are fungible, but the *purposes* are left open.

Toys and games are also examples of how we can flirt with the Four Horsemen without giving in to them. Games and toys often selectively use mechanical rules, interchangeable modules, and interchangeable players to enable play. They let us judo the powers of the Four Horsemen and use them to serve our purposes.

—

PART OF WHAT MAKES GAMES WORK SO WELL IS PRECISELY THEIR detachment from worldly outcomes, the lack of a demand for interoperability. How do we take these lessons from games and apply them to a highly scaled, interconnected, and efficient world?

It's incredibly hard, and I don't have a great answer here. I've been fighting for a decade with the one scoring system that is moderately under my control: the grading system in my classes. I've been experimenting off and on with various schemes of alternative grading and ungrading.

The ungrading movement has been preaching the gospel against grading for years. Grades typically track easily testable qualities, like memorization, and rarely track more important qualities, like curiosity, reflectiveness, originality, and openness. Grades seem to kill curiosity and a love of learning and replace it with a dead hyperfocus on tests. So, says the ungrading movement, stop grading. Give the students work and give them detailed feedback, but don't give them summarizing letter grades at the end. If you're in an environment that requires you to grade them, give them a guaranteed A on the first day, which will remove the incentive of grades. And, so the theory goes, they'll learn better.

I have tried ungrading with profoundly mixed results. I believe in the ideal, and I want to believe in the theory. And when students are already highly self-motivated and independent, it can work great. The most success I've had with ungrading is in the philosophy of games class I teach to game design students. It turns out that most game design students don't care about grades. They're in it out of their deep love of games, and they will pay attention to anything they think will help them make better games. But ungrading has been a disaster in my introductory classes. The moment the students figure out that the class is ungraded, the vast majority just stop coming. I'd hoped ungrading would give them the freedom to find their own love of the material. But they never actually explored the material long enough to fall in love with it, because they stopped coming after the first day.

The reasons are pretty obvious. My students have told me directly that without the grading incentive, they won't come. Some have even told me that they found my class fascinating and exciting, but they can't justify spending the time on coming to class if they're already guaranteed an A, because their grade in their engineering class still hangs in the balance. So they are forced to reallocate their time to where it will move the needle. Some of them said they wished my class was graded, so they could justify coming. So, grudgingly, I have given up on ungrading in many of my classes.

But we can see the larger reason why. My grading system does not exist in isolation. A college class is not a game. It does not exist in a magic circle; its scores are not disconnected from the rest of the world. Class grades lead directly to aggregate grade averages, which lead directly to scholarship and job opportunities. And what matters to most of my students, at least for the very next stage, is not what they learned, but what grade they got—because that is how the world will evaluate them. The scoring system in my class is part of a larger scoring system, a world-spanning one, that is out of my control. And if I try to detach myself from this large-scale scoring system, I render my class irrelevant to the powers of the large-scale system.

I've done what I can—little moves, like offering students their choice of the most interesting question from a long list on exams, or offering them the chance to pitch wildly different alternate final projects. It restores a little bit of room for exploration. But it isn't much, and I haven't figured out anything better to do. The sweep and power of the large-scale scoring system mostly beats out my little efforts.

THE SINGLE BEST TECHNOLOGICAL IMPLEMENTATION OF RANK-ings and metrics I have ever seen is, surprisingly, on a board game review site. The site is, to my eye, carefully designed to support reflective control and independent values. Or maybe it's not so surprising that the best use of rankings comes from a board game review site. The community of board games is full of people who, deep in their hearts, know that rankings and scoring systems are there to be used, modified, and abused for their own enjoyment.

During the early 2000s, I spent a lot of time on a website called Boardgamegeek.com. It was made by and for board game lovers, and quickly became the hub of a sprawling community. The site is full of data and rankings and metrics—but is structured to put the process firmly under user control.

Any user can post a review of any board game; you can give it a rating on a 1-to-10 quality scale and write a qualitative review. And every board game does get a single numerical score based on all its reviews. The site will also list all the games in its database ordered by their score. But my sense is that most serious users of the site don't put much stock in that large-scale ranking. It quickly becomes obvious that the central ranking draws from every kind of user— from the hardcore wargamers to lifestyle *Magic: The Gathering* players to silly party gamers to newbies who have only played a couple of games in their lives. The large-scale rankings turn out to be pretty useless, and they are easy to ignore. But that is because the site makes them easy to ignore, by defanging their authority through design.

What I, and most of the serious users, pay attention to is the massive, sprawling database of reviews and rankings that cut in every direction. First of all, the site lets anybody make their own ranked lists—called GeekLists. There are so many different ranked lists, for things like "Top 20 Games by Reiner Knizia," "Top 15 Silly Party Games," and "Best Simulations of the Civil War." Hundreds of thousands of lists, by tens of thousands of users, that let you see a massive plurality of tastes. The site bombards you with highly accessible ranking alternatives, made by different people, guided by their different sensibilities.

You can also, whenever you find another user who likes similar stuff or has interesting takes, drill into their profile and reviews. Everybody's profile page has a list of their top ten games of all time, and the top ten games they're playing right now. Another click and you can drill into their individual rankings of games—usually accompanied by a lengthy text review. And you can designate people whose tastes you share as your GeekBuddies, and then get the site to generate averages based on only your GeekBuddies' rankings—and get yourself a tailored aggregated ranking, generated by whose taste you trust. So you can quickly slice and dice the data to create your own, personalized ranking—and you can easily change how you're slicing and dicing.

And, crucially, if you click on a game's overall score, you're immediately taken behind the scenes. The site gives you instant access to all the individual numerical ratings that went into that score, always paired with their qualitative reviews. And it becomes incredibly obvious how different people's reasons are. One reviewer will explain how they gave the game a 10 because the game is perfect to play with their twelve-year-old son, who is super-anxious about losing but loves crazy special powers. Another reviewer will explain that the game is a fantastic goad for creativity if your playing group is full of jokester storytellers—but if you focus on playing the mechanics to win, it's super boring. Yet another reviewer will explain that this game is their absolute favorite, but also very fragile, and perfect only if everybody is really into it and tries hard. But if the circumstances are right, the game will give you this experience of pure brutality, a knife-fight-in-a-phone-booth of aggressively restructuring each other's incentives. The qualitative reviews make it obvious how different people's tastes are. It makes prominent the chaos of context.

This is the opposite of objectivity laundering. It is, you might say, subjectivity remindering. BoardGameGeek makes clear the superficiality of the overall scores, by making it incredibly easy to plunge past them. It makes all the weird nuanced qualitative stuff prominent and accessible.

I think the most important thing to say is that even though it presents a number, BoardGameGeek doesn't actually have a scoring system at all—not in the sense we've been talking about. It doesn't declare an official, singular verdict, nor does it urge everybody to converge. The user interface undercuts all that. It gives you different ways to sort the space, different ways to find and generate radically different rankings. It gives you informational access to an incredible diversity of games and an even more incredible diversity of tastes and opinions of all those games. It presents a single average rating for a game—and then presents a thousand alternatives. It makes dissent and difference of opinion easy, and then records that dissent and makes it easy to find. It is a database of argument.

BoardGameGeek is a technology tuned toward reflective control. It is an infrastructure of art and an infrastructure of play. It—and the community and way of life that surround it—encourages movement between different realms, plunging into new experiences and backing off. It encourages stepping back and evaluating games from an outside angle.

I spent a lot of time wrestling with myself, by the way, about whether to put BoardGameGeek at such a prominent place at the end of this book. It seems like such a silly, stupid example. It's a board game review site, for god's sake. But that silliness is, perhaps, the point. Because what is BoardGameGeek? Why was it made? Whose interests does it serve?

The technologies of metrics we've seen serve the interests of the Four Horsemen. They are made for efficiency, often to extract money, and almost always to optimize. They are there to summarize, to interconnect, to organize people into cohesive acting wholes. They are usually made by distant people, for distant purposes. But Board-GameGeek is a community-made technology, designed by and for board game aficionados, to help them find more games to appreciate. It is not tied to any certification or to any need to generate a single score. It was made to facilitate a love of games—and love does not have to converge.

CHAPTER 29

Some Endings

I wrote two endings to this book. One is cynical and sad, and mostly a cry of despair. The other isn't exactly cheerful, but it does have a certain measure of hope—and some ideas for progress. I couldn't really decide how to end the book, because I'm really of two minds about all this stuff myself.

So, in the spirit of games, you get to choose. There is Ending A: The Cynical Sad One. And there is Ending B: The One with a Little Measure of Hope. They are ordered that way not out of my preference, but because it was the order in which I wrote them.

So do what you want. It's Choose Your Own Adventure time. Pick one ending and tear out the other one, unread. Read both and let them bang around in your head for a while. Or read them, then cut and paste the bits you like and add some more. Write yourself a better ending. Or stop right here, stand up, say, "Fuck you, you dumbass philosopher," and go play some games instead.

Up to you.

ENDING A: The Cynical Sad One

This has all been complicated and exhausting, so let me try to put it all as fable.

Once upon a time, we were a bunch of different people who wanted different things, but we thought we could help each other, so we decided to work together.

We needed to make a language to work together—to describe what we were trying to do, and how we were going to do it. But private pleasures, intimate connections between peculiar people, and the strange joys in the process—these were hard to point to and name. They were hard to make language for.

What's easy to make language for, though, is all the basic stuff in the world. And we all need some basic stuff: food, clothes, tools. And we tend to need pretty similar kinds of stuff in our quests to fulfill our own idiosyncratic desires. This stuff was just some tools—useful to get what we really wanted. But those tools were easier to put labels on. It's easy to point to a chair or a sandwich and give it a name, and much harder to point to the strange beauty of feeling yourself in a moment of balance. So we ended up with more language to describe the basic stuff and less language to talk about the strange, rich, but private pleasures. We had less language to talk about what we really cared about.

But it's easier to think about the stuff we have language for. Especially when we tend to forget things, and need to write things down to remember them.

So we started talking more about how much we cared about the basic stuff, and less about the weird loves that had originally inspired us. And because talking with other people is very motivating, we mostly started thinking and caring about just the basic stuff. So we ended up working really hard to make more piles of that stuff, and forgot what it was all supposed to be for in the first place.

We did, though, sometimes notice there were still these vestiges lying around: odd bits of junk leftover from what we used to care about. We didn't have good words for them, and had mostly forgotten about what they were for, anyway.

So we gathered up all that weird, incomprehensible junk, and we shoved it into one big garbage bucket.

And the name we gave that garbage bucket was "play."

ENDING B: The One with a Little Measure of Hope

What's meaningful is impossible to capture in metrics, but easy to find in games. And this is because metrics are designed from the top down and enforce a centralized view of the world. They presume a kind of sameness to life. And games, at their best, offer the possibility of a splintered, decentralized, hyper-tailored form of life. The meaning of life, whatever the hell that is, defies centralized approaches. It arises from a complex interaction between our personalities, our context, our histories, and the peculiar details of our lives.

By the way, if at the end of this book you expected me to pull back the curtain and tell you, clearly and precisely, what the meaning of life was, then prepare to be totally disappointed. Because giving a simple, singular answer at this point—a one-size-fits-all answer—would be the ultimate hypocrisy. What I've offered instead is a diagnosis of how we came to expect, in the first place, that there could be a simple, clear answer that worked for everybody.

Meaning eludes mechanical approaches. Maybe it's because the meaning of life is something you have to figure out for yourself. Or maybe meaningfulness is real—but whatever real thing it is, it's bound up with all the messy fine grain of your particular life and circumstances. It's made out of the peculiar bricks of your own place in the world, your own personality, and the strange meaning wrung from the details of your life. Whatever it is, the world-spanning, context-crossing view from on high of institutional metrics will inevitably miss all that fine grain. The distant metrics-makers cannot offer tailored values. And if anything should be tailored to you, it's your values.

Games—and art, and all the other sorts of play—allow you to take a bottom-up, sideways-scuttling approach to meaning, because games afford a deep degree of freedom. They let you experiment with rules, let you try on different scoring systems, modify them, flit between them, until you find an activity that's meaningful to you. Games let you take advantage of the cognitive ease of clear rules. But the smallness of games frees you, keeps you from being trapped by any one particular rule set. Because in games, you can have far greater control over which rules and which scoring systems you let in. You can navigate by feel and decide for yourself which games you want to play.

And maybe playing games can also be a reminder of a truth that doesn't have to be confined to games. Maybe sometimes, when we are lucky enough to get some control over our lives, we can try to steer ourselves in the direction of whatever activities grant us our preferred sense of meaning. We can exchange precise goals with each other, but then we can keep on fine-tuning those goals in pursuit of our own weird, illegible purposes.

ACKNOWLEDGMENTS

I'd like to thank Melissa Hughs, for an endless pile of love, support, encouragement, useful criticism, and the deepest kind of intellectual playfulness—without which this book would absolutely not exist.

Thanks to my agent, Eric Henney, who had faith in the weirdness of the project and helped hash out how a book could possibly be about both games and metrics.

Thanks to the entire Penguin team, most especially my editor, Virginia Smith, who helped the book become less like an academic droning, and more like a human confessing.

Thanks to Oxford University Press and my editor there, Peter Ohlin, for taking the chance on me and supporting me as I wrote my utterly bizarre first book, *Games: Agency as Art*—from which the current book draws deeply.

Thanks to my friends and colleagues and beta readers, who have heard me thrash out these ideas for over a decade. There is no way I could keep track of everybody who has helped me think through the ideas in this book over a decade of philosophy conferences and conversations, but I can thank at least some of you—and apologies to everybody I left out. Thanks to: David Agraz, Olivia Bailey, Elizabeth Barnes, Kara Barnette, Christopher Bartel, John Basl, Thomas Bretz, Sarah Buss, Eliya Cohen, Anthony Cross, Adrian Currie, Steve Downes, John Dyck, Anne Eaton, David Ebrey, Carolina Flores, Rachel Elizabeth Fraser, Stacie Friend, Kristina Gehrman, Jonathan Gingerich, Keren Gorodeisky, Andrew Grace, Sherwood Hachtman, Emma Heflin, Sukaina Hirji, Tom Hurka, Aaron James, Alex King, Brian Kogelmann, Joel Lehman, Dom Lopes, Aaron Meskin, Shelby Moser, Ethan Nowak, Samantha Matherne, Shannon Mussett, Stephanie Patridge, Michael Ridge, Nick Riggle, Regina Rini, Hollis Robbins, Derek Ross, Ezgi Sertler, James Shelley, Matt Strohl, Nick Schwieterman, Jim Tabery, Katherine Thomson-Jones, Peggy Yin, Christopher Yorke, Natalia Washington, Jose Zagal, Elliot Zans, and the whole gang at Western Rivers Flyfishing. Special thanks to Maegan Fairchild, Joyce Havstad, Tim Sundell, and Olufemi Taiwo, coauthors and collaborators—this book draws directly on our co-projects.

And special thanks to my philosophy parents. My philosophy mentors: Elijah Millgram and Elisabeth Camp, who kept me from quitting the profession in despair, and who believed in the games project when it was still a baby. To Calvin Normore, who first put Suits's *The Grasshopper* in my hands. And to my graduate school adviser, Barbara Herman, who may not have realized it, but set my whole life on a new course when she casually, in the middle of a graduate seminar, said: "Of course there's a difference between a goal and a purpose. When you're playing cards with your friends, your goal is to win, but your purpose is to have fun."

NOTES

PART 1 OPENING MOVES

CHAPTER 1: IS THIS THE GAME YOU REALLY WANT TO BE PLAYING?

8 **good and evil:** Thomas Hobbes, *The Elements of Law, Natural and Politic*, 2nd ed. (Cass, 1969), 174; Arash Via Abizadeh, "Hobbes on the Causes of War: A Disagreement Theory," *American Political Science Review* 105, no. 2 (2011): 298–315, doi: 10.1017/S0003055411000098.

8 **Call it *value capture*:** C. Thi Nguyen, "Value Capture," *Journal of Ethics & Social Philosophy* 27, no. 3 (2024): 469–504, doi: 10.26556/jesp.v27i3.3048.

11 **kind of communication:** C. Thi Nguyen, "How Twitter Gamifies Communication," in *Applied Epistemology*, ed. Jennifer Lackey (Oxford University Press, 2021), 410–36.

11 **game design process:** Dave Chalkey, "Reiner Knizia: 'Creation of a Successful Game,'" *Critical-Hits* (blog), July 3, 2008, https://critical-hits.com/blog/2008/07/03/reiner-knizia-creation-of-a-successful-game/.

CHAPTER 2: STRIVING PLAY

29 **not the *purpose*:** This theme that catching fish is not the true point of fly-fishing winds throughout John Gierach's work. It is particularly clear in *Sex, Death, and Fly-Fishing* (Simon & Schuster, 2003), 55–71; *Standing in a River Waving a Stick* (Simon & Schuster, 1999), 13–21, 155–67; and *At the Grave of the Unknown Fisherman* (Simon & Schuster, 2003). The distinction between a "goal" and a "purpose," as I use it, I learned from Barbara Herman, my graduate school mentor, during a graduate seminar. I believe that Gierach also used the distinction between a "goal" and a "purpose" somewhere in his many books, but have been unable to locate that moment. So perhaps he did, or perhaps I merged these two people in my memory.

30 **different motivational states:** Much of the analysis of games that follows draws from my first book, Games: *Agency as Art* (Oxford University Press, 2020). Though I have removed some of the technical language for accessibility, I take the substance of my discussion here to improve on the older book in a number of ways. This is a result of many wonderful conversations during the intervening years, but also from my own process of thinking about games against the larger context

of metrics and other social scoring systems. Where the present book differs from the earlier book, please take this new presentation to be my updated view.

CHAPTER 3: VALUE CAPTURE

44 **regulators have been captured:** Ira Glass, host, *This American Life*, podcast, episode 536, "The Secret Recordings of Carmen Segarra," WBEZ Chicago, September 26, 2014, https://www.thisamericanlife.org/536/transcript.

44 **anthropologists, and historians:** We will encounter, later in this book, many of the key figures: Mary Poovey, Theodore Porter, Wendy Espeland, Michael Sauder, Sally Engle Merry, and James C. Scott. Much of this work occurs in an interdisciplinary field called science and technology studies, which has its roots in such figures as Bruno Latour, Ian Hacking, and Alain Desrosières.

45 **richest empirical studies:** Wendy Nelson Espeland and Michael Sauder, *Engines of Anxiety* (Russell Sage Foundation, 2016).

46 **average GPA and LSAT:** This was true as of 2016, when Espeland and Sauder published their study. Since then, some of the details have changed about how *U.S. News & World Report* ranks universities, but the monolithic song remains the same.

48 **outsource my attention:** The classic discussions are in Andy Clark, *Supersizing the Mind: Embodiment, Action, and Cognitive Extension* (Oxford University Press, 2008); and Andy Clark and David Chalmers, "The Extended Mind," *Analysis* 58, no. 1 (1998): 7–19, http://www.jstor.org/stable/3328150. For my own discussion of how trust in technology constitutes mental outsourcing, see C. Thi Nguyen, "Trust as an Unquestioning Attitude," *Oxford Studies in Epistemology* 7 (2022): 214–44.

CHAPTER 4: SCORING SYSTEMS CREATE CONVERGENCE

56 **how high you can get:** This point seems commonly accepted among many skateboarders, but rarely documented. Some of the clearest complaints emerged when skateboarding became an Olympic sport. As skateboarder John Cardiel puts it: "To me, skateboarding is all about individuality and originality. It has nothing to do with highest, furthest, longest. Skating being an Olympic sport contradicts everything that I believe skateboarding to be." thrashermagazine.com/articles /skateboarding-in-the-olympics/. Something similar happens in yo-yo competitions. Early yo-yo competitions focused on scoring the number of "string hits," which lead competitiors to move away from stylish, flowing tricks and toward a "locked-in" style optimized for speed. Competition rules would later shift to try to award points for difficulty and originality, to combat the speed-optimizing trend. youtube.com/watch?v=omcLfyApifU.

58 **is a dead thing:** The theme of live dishes and dead recipes is threaded throughout Thorne's astonishing body of food writing. Some places where the theme rises to the fore are in John Thorne, *Outlaw Cook* (North Point Press, 1992), 19–65, 311–25; and John Thorne, *Serious Pig* (North Point Press, 1996), 278–316.

59 **toss them with:** Arthur Schwartz, *Naples at Table: Cooking in Campania* (HarperCollins, 1998), 139–40.

PART 2: WHAT SCORES DO

CHAPTER 5: THE ART OF AGENCY

66 **Bernard Suits's book:** Bernard Suits, *The Grasshopper: Games, Life and Utopia* (Broadview Press, 2014).

CHAPTER 6: TRANSPARENCY IS SURVEILLANCE

75 **is a terrible metric:** Joseph Stinn, "Donors Need to Stop Pressuring Nonprofits to Pinch Pennies," *Conversation*, November 25, 2019, https://theconversation .com/donors-need-to-stop-pressuring-nonprofits-to-pinch-pennies-126656; Kelsey Piper, "One of the Most Frequently Used Criteria for Judging a Charity Is Also the Worst," *Vox*, November 27, 2018, https://www.vox.com/future-perfect/2018/11 /26/18103372/overhead-charities-effectiveness-donations-giving-tuesday.

78 **Merry was an:** Merry's entire discussion was deeply influential on this book. Sally Engle Merry, *The Seductions of Quantification: Measuring Human Rights, Gender Violence, and Sex* (University of Chicago Press, 2016). The discussion of sex-trafficking measures is on pp. 112–60.

79 **O'Neill studied trust:** Onora O'Neill, *Autonomy and Trust in Bioethics* (Cambridge University Press, 2002). O'Neill's brief comments on trust and transparency are the primary inspiration for the discussion of this chapter. See Onora O'Neill, *A Question of Trust: The BBC Reith Lectures in 2002* (Cambridge University Press, 2002), 73. An extended version of my discussion of transparency and O'Neill is in C. Thi Nguyen, "Transparency Is Surveillance," *Philosophy and Phenomenological Research* 105, no. 2 (2022): 331–61.

81 **evidence of corruption:** Jennifer C. Lena, *Entitled: Discriminating Tastes and the Expansion of the Arts* (Princeton University Press, 2019).

83 **Decades of empirical:** Patricia G. Devine, "Stereotypes and Prejudice: Their Automatic and Controlled Components," *Journal of Personality and Social Psychology* 56, no. 1 (1989): 5–18; Tessa E. S. Charlesworth and Mahzarin R. Banaji, "Patterns of Implicit and Explicit Attitudes: I. Long-Term Change and Stability from 2007 to 2016," *Psychological Science* 30, no. 2 (2019): 174–92.

83 **Becoming an expert:** I'm relying only on minimal, generally accepted views about intuition and skill from this literature. The classic philosophical discussion of skill is in Hubert L. Dreyfus and Stuart E. Dreyfus, *Mind over Machine* (Free Press, 1986). For a useful criticism of the Dreyfusian approach, pointing out that they fail to account for the possibility of expert bias, see E. M. Selinger and R. P. Crease, "Dreyfus on Expertise: The Limits of Phenomenological Analysis," *Continental Philosophy Review* 35, no. 3 (2002): 245–79. For a modernized version of Dreyfus and Dreyfus's insights, which combines a survey of cognitive science with philosophical work on skill, see Ellen Fridland and Matt Stichter, "It Just Feels Right: An Account of Expert Intuition," *Synthese* 199, no. 1–2 (2021): 1327–46, https:// doi.org/10.1007/s11229-020-02796-9. The key work from psychology and cognitive science is Daniel Kahnemann's work on fast, intuitive System 1 thinking and slow, deliberative System 2 thinking: Daniel Kahneman, *Thinking, Fast and Slow* (Farrar, Straus and Giroux, 2011).

85 **That richer sense:** Talbot Brewer, *The Retrieval of Ethics* (Oxford University Press, 2009).

CHAPTER 7: THE BEAUTY OF THE PROCESS

91 **resisted letting photography:** Peter C. Bunnell, "Pictorial Photography," *Record of the Art Museum, Princeton University* 51, no. 2 (1992): 11–5.

91 **He embraced the fact:** "Henri Cartier-Bresson: There Are No Maybes," *New York Times*, June 21, 2013, https://archive.nytimes.com/lens.blogs.nytimes.com/2013 /06/21/cartier-bresson-there-are-no-maybes/.

94 **it smells amazing:** Michael Ruhlman, *Ruhlman's How to Braise: Foolproof Techniques and Recipes for the Home Cook* (Little, Brown and Company, 2015), 5.

97 **every piece of art:** John Dewey, *Art as Experience* (Perigee, 2005).

CHAPTER 8: THE LIMITS OF DATA

103 **His 1995 book:** Theodore Porter, *Trust in Numbers: The Pursuit of Objectivity in Science and Public Life* (Princeton University Press, 1995), 9–86.

CHAPTER 9: THE SCORE SHAPES THE STRUGGLE

116 **D&D's critics put:** Some of the most influential criticism of D&D came from a set of essays by Ron Edwards on the Forge, a discussion forum for indie tabletop role-playing designers. Ron Edwards, "GNS and Other Matters of Role-Playing Theory," Forge, October 14, 2001, http://www.indie-rpgs.com/articles/1/; Ron Edwards, "A Hard Look at Dungeons and Dragons," Forge, June 4, 2003, http://www.indie -rpgs.com/articles/20/; Ron Edwards, "Fantasy Heartbreakers," Forge, April 1, 2002, http://www.indie-rpgs.com/articles/9/.

117 **get XP for hitting:** Some of my favorite designs from this indie role-playing game world are Apocalypse World, Blades in the Dark, Masks, The Quiet Year, and Fate.

PART 3: WHY USE MECHANICAL SCORING?

CHAPTER 10: SCORING SYSTEMS CHANGE THE SUBJECT

123 **Then you move:** Donna Farhi, *Yoga Mind, Body & Spirit: A Return to Wholeness* (Henry Holt, 2000).

CHAPTER 11: MECHANICAL VALUES

133 **The older conceptions:** Lorraine Daston, *Rules: A Short History of What We Live By* (Princeton University Press, 2022).

CHAPTER 12: FLEXIBILITY THROUGH RESTRICTION

150 **change the reasons:** Carol Rovane, *The Bounds of Agency: An Essay in Revisionary Metaphysics* (Princeton University Press, 1997); Carol Rovane, "What Is an Agent?" *Synthese* 140, no. 1–2 (2004): 181–98.

154 **games kill play:** Miguel Sicart, *Play Matters* (MIT Press, 2014), 3, 86–91.

CHAPTER 13: THE SECRET HEART OF MECHANIZATION

162 **achieve legal objectivity:** There is a long tradition in the philosophy of law concerned with legal objectivity. H. L. A. Hart famously suggests that explicit legal standards prevent the use of discretion and adaptability to changing conditions in specific applications of law. H. L. A. Hart, *The Concept of Law*, 2nd ed. (Oxford University Press, 1994), 126. For a modern discussion, see Diana Raffman, "Vagueness in Law: Placing the Blame Where It's Due," in *Vagueness and Law*, ed. Geert Keil and Ralf Poscher (Oxford University Press, 2016), 49–64.

163 **choice between vague:** Timothy Endicott, "The Value of Vagueness," in *Philosophical Foundations of Language in the Law*, ed. Andrei Marmor and Scott Soames (Oxford University Press, 2011).

166 **hide left common:** There is a useful discussion of land measures and grain measures in Theodore Porter, *Trust in Numbers: The Pursuit of Objectivity in Science and Public Life* (Princeton University Press, 1995), 24–5, drawing from Witold Kula, *Measures and Men*, trans. Richard Szreter (Princeton University Press, 1986).

CHAPTER 14: CHOICE OF DIFFICULTY

174 **Also check Jeffrey:** More amazing videos: "Kim Moon Jun / Empathy / Physix." Doctor Popular's "Weave," and A-RT's "Diptych." For a completely different style of yo-yo, in which the yo-yo is tied not to your hand but to a free-swinging counterweight, watch "Ryosuke Kawamura Presents: Shingo Terada" and 5AGOAT's "5a Angel."

180 **"a yo-yo is":** Ross Levine, host, *Kill Your Yo-yo*, podcast, episode 24, "Ed Haponik: Enter the Yoyo Dojo," Hollywood Modern Yoyos, September 26, 2022, https://open.spotify.com/show/4cMMVQwDBVzdOHlDEPtHVd.

CHAPTER 15: REFLECTIVE CONTROL

184 **tweaking your goals:** Elijah Millgram, *Practical Induction* (Harvard University Press, 1997); Elijah Millgram, "On Being Bored Out of Your Mind," *Proceedings of the Aristotelian Society* 104, no. 1 (2004): 165–86.

184 **People in cities:** Jane Jacobs, *The Death and Life of Great American Cities* (Random House, 1992), 58–9.

189 **an elegance akin:** Doctor Popular, *An Interview with Tsukasa Takatsu*, Patreon, September 21, 2021, https://www.patreon.com/posts/56349530.

190 **"a complicated passion for":** Robert Musil, "The Mathematical Man," in *Precision and Soul: Essays and Addresses*, ed. Pike Burton and David S. Luft (University of Chicago Press, 1990), 40.

PART 4: STANDARDIZED VALUES

CHAPTER 16: VALUES HIDDEN IN THE MACHINE

200 **far down on:** Zeynep Tufekci, "It's the (Democracy-Poisoning) Golden Age of Free Speech," *Wired*, January 16, 2018, https://www.wired.com/story/free-speech-issue-tech-turmoil-new-censorship/.

201 **Langdon Winner argues:** Langdon Winner, "Do Artifacts Have Politics?" *Daedalus* 109, no. 1 (1980): 121–36.

CHAPTER 17: WHOSE INTEREST DOES STANDARDIZATION SERVE?

210 **easily coordinate between:** This discussion of standardization is guided by Theodore Porter's discussion of standardized time in his *Trust in Numbers: The Pursuit of Objectivity in Science and Public Life* (Princeton University Press, 1995), 21–9.

211 **every map represents:** Denis Wood, *The Power of Maps* (Guildford Press, 1992).

213 **made as aids:** William Rankin, *After the Map: Cartography, Navigation, and the Transformation of Territory in the Twentieth Century* (University of Chicago Press, 2016), 119–62. Rankin draws on Yves Lacoste, *La géographie, ça sert, d'abord, à faire la guerre* (F. Maspero, 1976).

CHAPTER 18: WHO CUTS UP THE WORLD?

221 *Sorting Things Out*: Bowker and Star's work is one of the key influences on this book and one of the most important works in understanding politics of data. Geoffrey C. Bowker and Susan Leigh Star, *Sorting Things Out: Classification and Its Consequences* (MIT Press, 1999).

CHAPTER 19: ISLANDS OF MEANING

227 **the magic circle:** Johan Huizinga, "Nature and Significance of Play as a Cultural Phenomenon," in *Homo Ludens: A Study of the Play-Element in Culture* (Beacon Press, 1955).

228 **scholar Annika Waern:** Annika Waern, "Framing Games," Proceedings of DiGRA Nordic 2012 Conference.

CHAPTER 20: CENTRALIZING VALUES

234 **systematically reshape the world:** James C. Scott, *Seeing Like a State* (Yale University Press, 1998). Let me draw particular attention to the general introduction of legibility on pp. 9–84, and the overtly Aristotelean discussion of the specificity of practical skill versus the generalizing tendency of the state on pp. 309–41.

CHAPTER 21: TECHNOLOGIES OF WORK, TECHNOLOGIES OF PLAY

239 **capacity to travel:** María Lugones, "Playfulness, 'World'-Travelling, and Loving Perception," *Hypatia* 2, no. 2 (1987): 3–19.

PART 5: WHAT DO WE DO?

CHAPTER 22: THERE IS TOO MUCH WORLD

253 **Every modern thought:** Elijah Millgram, *The Great Endarkenment: Philosophy for an Age of Hyperspecialization* (Oxford University Press, 2015), 1–53.

255 **essence of trust:** Annette Baier, "Trust and Antitrust," *Ethics* 96, no. 2 (1986): 231–60.

CHAPTER 23: OBJECTIVITY LAUNDERING

260 **The more universal:** The idea that standardization leads to the appearance of something being a natural fact comes from Geoffrey C. Bowker and Susan Leigh Star, *Sorting Things Out: Classification and Its Consequences* (MIT Press, 1999). It is discussed directly on pp. 53–106 and is a recurring theme throughout their work.

261 **Historian Mary Poovey:** Mary Poovey, *A History of the Modern Fact: Problems of Knowledge in the Sciences of Wealth and Society* (University of Chicago Press, 1998), 8–13, 29–91.

263 **cost-benefit analysis set:** Theodore Porter, *Trust in Numbers: The Pursuit of Objectivity in Science and Public Life* (Princeton University Press, 1995), 181.

264 **no consensus on:** For the early history of discount rates, see William Deringer, *Calculated Values: Finance, Politics, and the Quantitative Age* (Harvard University Press, 2018), 202–10. See also William Deringer, "Compound Interest Corrected:

The Imaginative Mathematics of the Financial Future in Early Modern England," *Osiris* 33 (2018), 109–29.

265 **wine-judging process:** This section builds on Alice Feiring's account of how the Parker wine-scoring system re-centered the wine world on big, non-dynamic wines. Alice Feiring, *The Battle for Wine and Love: Or How I Saved the World from Parkerization* (Harvest, 2009).

267 **different people will make:** Elizabeth Barnes, *Health Problems: Philosophical Puzzles About the Nature of Health* (Oxford University Press, 2023), 224–50.

267 **average rock climber:** This paragraph's category-relative analysis of health also draws from Elselijn Kingma, "What Is It to Be Healthy?" *Analysis* 67, no. 2 (2007): 128–33; and Jacob Stegenga, *Medical Nihilism* (Oxford University Press, 2018).

CHAPTER 24: THE SEDUCTIONS OF CLARITY

273 **The psychologist Alison:** Alison Gopnik, "Explanation as Orgasm*," *Minds and Machines* 8 (1998): 101–18.

274 **Philosophers of science:** I offer an extended discussion of understanding and faking understanding in C. Thi Nguyen, "The Seductions of Clarity," *Royal Institute of Philosophy Supplements* 89 (2021), 227–55. I draw from previous work on the philosophy of understanding, including Michael Strevens, "No Understanding Without Explanation," *Studies in History and Philosophy of Science Part A* 44, no. 3 (2013): 510–5; Jonathan L. Kvanvig, *The Value of Knowledge and the Pursuit of Understanding* (Cambridge University Press, 2003); Stephen Grimm, "The Value of Understanding," *Philosophy Compass* 7, no. 2 (2012): 103–17; and Catherine Z. Elgin, "Creation as Reconfiguration: Art in the Advancement of Science," *International Studies in the Philosophy of Science* 16, no. 1 (2002): 13–25.

278 **Science, says Wimsatt:** William C. Wimsatt, *Re-engineering Philosophy for Limited Beings: Piecewise Approximations to Reality* (Harvard University Press, 2007), 3–36.

279 **good echo chamber:** For an extended discussion of how echo chambers build systematic distrust, see C. Thi Nguyen, "Echo Chambers and Epistemic Bubbles," *Episteme* 17, no. 2 (2020): 141–61.

282 **vague language is:** Elisabeth Camp, "Metaphor and That Certain 'Je Ne Sais Quoi,'" *Philosophical Studies* 129 (2006): 1–25.

CHAPTER 25: THE TRIUMPH OF UNIVERSAL LANGUAGE

285 **how science evolves:** Paul E. Smaldino and Richard McElreath, "The Natural Selection of Bad Science," *Royal Society Open Science* 3, no. 9 (2016): 160384.

288 **She calls this:** Miranda Fricker, *Epistemic Injustice: Power and the Ethics of Knowing* (Oxford University Press, 2007).

288 **People systematically tend:** Joyce Berg et al., "Trust, Reciprocity, and Social History," *Games and Economic Behavior* 10, no. 1 (1995): 122–42; Nancy R. Buchan et al., "Trust and Gender: An Examination of Behavior and Beliefs in the Investment Game," *Journal of Economic Behavior & Organization* 68, no. 3–4 (2008): 466–76; Damian A. Stanley et al., "Implicit Race Attitudes Predict Trustworthiness Judgments and Economic Trust Decisions," *Proceedings of the National Academy of Sciences* 108, no. 19 (2011): 7710–5.

290 **women who had:** Fricker, *Epistemic Injustice*, 147–75.

290 **"For women, then":** Audre Lorde, "Poetry Is Not a Luxury," *Chrysalis* 3 (1977).

292 **interests of autistic:** Steven K. Kapp and Ari Ne'eman, "Lobbying Autism's Diagnostic Revision in the DSM-5," in *Autistic Community and the Neurodiversity Movement*, ed. Steven K. Kapp (Palgrave Macmillan, 2020), 167–94, https://doi .org/10.1007/978-981-13-8437-0_13.

CHAPTER 26: PLAY FOR ITS OWN SAKE

300 **To play, according to:** Bernard Suits, "Words on Play," *Journal of the Philosophy of Sport* 4, no. 1 (1977), 117–31.

CHAPTER 27: ART IS A GAME

306 **We let the world:** Jerome Stolnitz was writing in the midtwentieth century. The contemporary philosopher Bence Nanay has shown that modern cognitive science confirms Stolnitz's observations. Psychological research shows: When we approach the world with a practical attitude, we narrow our vision and attention to a small number of features—the ones relevant to our particular interests. When we approach the world with an aesthetic attitude, our attention meanders, looking at everything, trying to find unexpected connections. Bence Nanay, *Aesthetics as Philosophy of Perception* (Oxford University Press, 2016).

INDEX

2 04